# THE SOCIAL CAGE

ALEXANDRA MARYANSKI

JONATHAN H. TURNER

# THE SOCIAL CAGE

*Human Nature and the*

*Evolution of Society*

STANFORD UNIVERSITY PRESS

STANFORD, CALIFORNIA

Stanford University Press
Stanford, California
© 1992 by the Board of Trustees of the
Leland Stanford Junior University

Printed in the United States of America

CIP data appear at the end of the book

*To our good friend and colleague*

RANDALL COLLINS

# PREFACE

We have thought about the ideas in these pages for many years, and, to be frank, we have been reluctant to write them down. To talk about "human nature" would seem passé these days, were it not for the fact that sociobiology and its new offshoots in behavioral ecology and coevolution have forced sociologists to reconsider the biological basis of human organization. To view the long-term historical transformations of human societies as "evolution" also goes against current ways of talking about sociocultural change within sociology.

Yet, in our view, sociologists have become comfortable in certain assumptions that they make about humans and the properties of industrial society. Our goal is to challenge some of these assumptions. The thrust of this effort revolves around a reanalysis of human nature as it evolved over millions of years of primate history and a reassessment of societal evolution in light of the primate legacy that humans possess. We use the metaphor of the "social cage" because societal evolution after hunting and gathering has involved a process of caging humans in ways that infringe on their nature as primates. Of course, discussions of sociocultural constraint are hardly new to sociologists, but we add the twist that industrial and post-industrial societies are far more compatible with human nature than most sociologists realize or concede. For we will argue that humans are not collectivists, nor are they particularly social at a biological level. The problems of modern societies as portrayed by both classic theorists and recent "post-modernists"—alienation, impersonality, egoism, fragmentation, de-centering, noncommunalism, anomie, isolation, and so on—may not be so incompatible with humans' primate nature. And in fact, modern societies represent the first major transformation (since hunting and gathering societies) that has allowed humans to partially escape highly restrictive sociocultural cages and to realize some of their needs as hominoids. Again, this line of argument goes against many current conceptions about the power of politico-economic constructions to invade and colonize the "lifeworld" and interpersonal domains of humans. Moreover, our thesis goes against the chic pessimism and relativism of post-modernists, because it asserts that the lack of center, structure, and integration is highly compatible with human nature.

For us, it was fun to write these lines of argument down and to develop their details, even if some people will be displeased. Our goal is to provide an alternative approach to sociobiology and its newer variants, all of which invoke some unnecessary and unsubstantiated assumptions.

A host of individuals and institutions have contributed to the development of this book. Much of this contribution resides in moral support for our venture into the areas of biology, culture, and society—obviously a venture that must overcome many obstacles. The ideas for the book were originally formulated by A. R. Maryanski at the Irvine and Riverside campuses of the University of California in the late 1970's. They were developed further by both authors' yearlong stay at The Netherlands Institute for Advanced Study and Clare Hall at Cambridge University. The Academic Senate and Dean of the College of Humanities and Social Sciences at the University of California at Riverside, Brian Coppenhaver, provided critical funds for research and manuscript preparation. The following persons have been especially supportive and helpful in giving advice and stimulating our thinking, not just on this work but on the entire line of inquiry: Lee Freese, Randall Collins, Ramon Rhine, Vernon Reynolds, Bruce Mayhew, Robert Hinde, Walter Goldschmidt, Lin and Sue Freeman, Greg Pollock, Sandra Thompson, Kim Romney, Douglas White, Michael Burton, Peter Molnár, Tom Pettigrew, Barry and Beverly Wellman, Anita Iannucci, Linda Stearns, Masako Ishii-Kuntz, Hugh and Marie Turner, Aki Nigawa, and Malcolm Dow. Others provided an atmosphere in the late 1970's for planting the seeds that grew into this book: Alan Beals, Alan Fix, Gene Anderson, Sylvia Broadbent, and Martin Orans. Our thanks also to Barbara Mnookin and Julia Johnson Zafferano for their splendid editorial assistance in preparing the manuscript. Finally, we wish to thank Clara Dean for typing the manuscript. We very much appreciate her attention to detail and her tireless energy in seeing the book to completion.

A. M.

J. H. T.

# CONTENTS

1 / Humans Are Animals     1

2 / The Origins of Human Social Structure     6

3 / The Origins of Human Culture     33

4 / The First Human Society: Hunters and Gatherers     69

5 / The Cage of Kinship: Horticultural Societies     91

6 / The Cage of Power: Agrarian Societies     113

7 / Breaking Out of the Social Cage: Industrial Societies     139

8 / The Overly Social Conception of Humans and Society     163

Bibliography     173

Index     207

# TABLES AND FIGURES

TABLES

1  Social Network Ties in Reproductive Units Among
   Nonhuman Hominoidea                                    18
2  Social Network Ties in Reproductive Units Among a Few
   Well-Studied Cercopithecoidea                          26
3  The Organizing Dimensions of Hunting and Gathering
   Societies                                              86
4  The Organizing Dimensions of Horticultural Societies   96
5  The Organizing Dimensions of Agrarian Societies        120
6  The Organizing Dimensions of Industrial Societies      148

FIGURES

1   A Simplified Primate Taxonomy                          8
2   A Cladogram of Hominoids                               16
3   The Evolution of the Mammalian Brain Over the Limbic
    System and the Reptilian Brain                         37
4   Some Key Areas of the Human Brain                      39
5   The Evolution of Culturally Based Patterns of Social
    Organization                                           74
6   The Dynamics of Political Centralization               116
7   The Decline in the Rate of Technological Innovation in
    Excessively Centralized and Militarized States         118
8   The Process of State Breakdown                          130
9   Factors Determining the Success or Failure of an Empire 132
10  The Dynamics of Industrialization                       142

# THE SOCIAL CAGE

# 1 /　　　HUMANS ARE ANIMALS

Human culture and organization are the creations of an animal, a large-brained and evolved hominoid.[1] The sociocultural accomplishments of this animal are circumscribed by an evolutionary history, forcing the conclusion that an analysis of human organization cannot ignore biology. But having said this, how do we approach the biology of human social patterns? The initial answer to this question in sociology involved positing lists of "human instincts." A cursory review of early sociological works, for example, would reveal assertions that humans have "drives," "needs," "impulses," or "instincts" for such behaviors as affiliation, group membership, domination, prestige, fighting, and so on. Although these early hypotheses soon fell into disrepute, new versions of "instinct sociology"—if we can invent a label—appeared. Konrad Lorenz (1960) was probably the most influential in his assertion that, unlike the forms of ritualized violence developed by other mammals, human aggression is maladaptive because there are no accompanying instinctual rituals or other biological mechanisms for regulating and channeling such aggression. Soon, other scholars joined in speculating on the nature of human aggression. In *The Territorial Imperative*, Robert Ardrey (1966) portrayed a "Killing Instinct"; Desmond Morris (1967) gave us a "Naked Ape" with various hostile instincts; Lionel Tiger and Robin Fox (1971) postulated "The Imperial Animal"; and Pierre van den Berghe (1973, 1974, 1975) saw humans as aggressive, territorial, and hierarchical.

For social scientists like van den Berghe, Tiger and Fox, and Morris, evolutionary processes have worked to produce "bioprogrammers" that, in broad terms, direct and circumscribe the patterns of social organiza-

---

[1] The superfamily to which humans and apes belong is Hominoidea (hominoids).

tion developed by humans. True, culture and society are more than mere reflections of these bioprogrammers; systems of symbols and social structures reveal their own dynamics and emergent properties. But these dynamics and properties are not wholly divorced from human biology. This basic insight is still crucial to understanding human organization, although we will argue that it has been overdrawn and based on a misinterpretation of primate and human evolution (see Chapters 2–4).

Just as this "instinct approach" reemerged in the social sciences, biologists were in the process of creating a new discipline: "sociobiology."[2] From the perspective of sociobiology, human bodies, systems of cultural symbols, and patterns of social organization are "survivor machines" (Dawkins 1976) to facilitate the real units of natural selection and evolution: the genes. These genes are viewed as selfish and trying to maximize their "fitness," or survival in the gene pool. The phenotypes of organisms thus constitute only temporary vessels for housing genotypes, enabling them to survive and reproduce (Williams 1966). Similarly, social structures and culture are but more elaborate vessels or survivor machines for ensuring that genes can maximize their fitness. Patterns of kinship and altruism (Hamilton 1963, 1971), then, as well as reciprocal altruism (Trivers 1971), are the products of natural selection as it worked to provide better survivor machines for genes trying to maximize their fitness. Thus, if the basic structural building blocks of human organization are to be explained by the process of genic selection, the social sciences should be a branch of biology. As Edward O. Wilson (1975: 4) confidently proclaimed: "It may not be too much to say that sociology and the other social sciences, as well as the humanities, are the last branches of biology waiting to be included in the Modern Synthesis" (to be provided by sociobiology).

There is an incredible irony here, because the titular founder of sociology—Auguste Comte ([1830] 1896: 4)—confidently proclaimed that "while Biology has hitherto been the guide and preparation for Sociology . . . Sociology will in the future [provide] the ultimate systemization of Biology." Now, some biologists and their allies in psychology (e.g., Daly and Wilson 1984), anthropology and sociology (e.g., Dickemann 1985; van den Berghe 1981, 1986; van den Berghe and Barash 1977; Lopreato 1984), and even philosophy (e.g., Rosenberg 1981) proclaim just the opposite: biology will provide for the ultimate systematization of sociology!

Yet these sweeping assertions have proved to be not only contentious

---

[2] For a review of how this perspective emerged and was adopted by sociologists, see Maryanski and Turner 1991.

but also unacceptable to most social scientists. In particular, sociologists' reaction to human sociobiology has been either hostile or derisive, with sociobiologists being viewed as ignorant and pretentious thinkers who have tried to cannibalize sociology while knowing little about the subtleties and complexities of human organization. Such a reaction is justifiable because sociobiologists often admit that they know little social science. Of course, a few in sociology who *do* know a great deal of social science have championed this biological perspective (e.g., van den Berghe 1981, 1986; Lopreato 1984), but most sociologists remain unaware of the formidable challenge that it poses to how they conceptualize the social world.

As the extremes of early sociobiology were being rejected in the 1970's, new varieties of biological thinking emerged. Many of these represented the repackaging of sociobiological ideas, others were extensions and elaborations, and still others were alternatives to sociobiology. One line of thought represented an effort to address the process of cultural evolution in sociobiological terms (e.g., Alexander 1974, 1987; Lumsden and Wilson 1981, 1985). In these approaches, genic selection is seen as having produced individuals who are programmed to prefer certain cultural traits because they are compatible with genotypes. And, though learning, socialization, and other processes of cultural transmission and adoption cannot be ignored, they are circumscribed because genotypes constrain the preferences of phenotypes, or individuals selecting and adopting cultural traits. Another line of thought has involved analogizing from the forces of biological evolution to cultural change. While the conceptualization of culture varies among theorists, the basic argument emphasizes that the relative frequencies of cultural ideas (Durham 1990, 1991) or cultural traits (Cavalli-Sforza and Feldman 1981) can be traced to the forces of cultural evolution that are roughly analogous to those in biology. For example, cultural units such as "memes" (Dawkins 1976) as well as holomemes and allomemes (Durham 1991) become the units of selection. Moreover, there are sociocultural forces maintaining variations in a kind of cultural meme pool: innovations (the equivalent of mutations in biological evolution), migrations (gene flow), and cultural drift (genetic drift). And cultural selection operates to affect the relative frequency of cultural units in this cultural meme pool. These kinds of approaches emphasize coevolution or dual inheritance (Boyd and Richerson 1976, 1985) because cultural evolution and biological evolution represent distinctive inheritance systems that can operate independently of each other at times, and in concert at other times. Still other lines of theorizing reject both sociobiological assumptions and coevolutionary analogies, arguing instead for a multidimensional model focusing on the interconnections among biological, behavioral, interactional, and macrostructural forces (Baldwin and Baldwin 1981).

All of these approaches, then, focus attention on the biology of human organization. But the question is, Which approach is most useful? In a sense, the verdict is not in for all of the approaches. Our own view at this point is that sociobiology cannot explain the complexities of human organization and culture. We find coevolution approaches more viable and intriguing, but analogies to biological evolution, like the organismic analogies of 100 years ago in sociology, may not hold up. For whatever isomorphisms between cultural and genic evolution may exist, it is not clear that they can explain the complexities of sociocultural evolution. And pleas for multidimensionality are reasonable, and indeed appropriate, but trying to piece all the levels of reality together theoretically may prove difficult. How, then, are we to get a handle on the biology of human evolution without dragging in questionable theoretical assumptions or overburdening ourselves conceptually? We propose a much simpler path than is currently in vogue. Our approach assumes that humans have biologically based predispositions that characterize the species and that emerged over the 60 million years of primate, anthropoid, hominoid, and, finally, hominid evolution. These tendencies facilitate the survival and reproductive success of individual organisms, but whether they always represent a maximization of fitness is, we think, a most arguable assertion.

It is better, we feel, to use the available data and provide a description of how selection processes worked to produce a given behavioral tendency or structure. But if one *begins* with the assumption of maximizing fitness, then mere descriptions of selection processes are usually abandoned in favor of an ad hoc scenario about how biological or cultural fitness was maximized by a given behavior, cultural idea, or structure. We propose in the next chapters to avoid this proclivity to construct ad hoc scenarios to shore up theoretical predilections. Instead, we will assume that humans are animals with certain innate predispositions and that these were the result of a long evolutionary history. Although such behavioral dispositions have been dramatically embellished and elaborated on by sociocultural processes that reveal an emergent and dynamic quality of their own, we do not need to conceptualize these in terms of presumed isomorphisms between cultural and biological evolution. Rather, we will seek to discover our "human nature" by looking at the past—the very distant past of mammalian, primate, and human evolution. We also look at our closest living relatives—modern-day apes, or the gibbon, orangutan, gorilla, and chimpanzee—to see what inferences we might draw from their behavioral and structural proclivities. In so doing, we can perhaps infer some of the basic behavioral and organizational tendencies of humans arising in their primate heritage as it was modified by evolutionary history.

This analysis is not a theory or even a precise description. It represents an effort to bring biological processes back into sociological analysis without the extremes of early instinct theories or contemporary sociobiology. Our assumption is that human evolutionary history is the key to understanding the qualities making up human nature as it interacts with culture and patterns of social organization. Although there can be no definitive answers about the biological basis of human organization, we will offer some reasonable inferences about humans' innate predispositions as they emerged during the history of primate evolution. And, as we will come to see, these inferences will question some of sociology's more cherished assumptions about "human nature" while providing an alternative to present-day approaches within the sociobiology movement.

# 2 / THE ORIGINS OF HUMAN SOCIAL STRUCTURE

Patterns of human organization are produced and reproduced by an animal—a big-brained primate—with an evolutionary history. Our brains and capacity for culture have not completely liberated us from our phyletic ancestry. The heritable characteristics allowing for culture are, like all of our biological characteristics, the result of selection processes operating over 60 million years of primate evolution. Those features that facilitated adaptation and reproductive success were retained in the genotypes of our ancestors; those that hindered survival were selected out. Human sociobiology and many of its variants add to these simple points some (in our view, unnecessary) assumptions: for example, the maximization of fitness and genes as the only unit of selection. Instead, it is only necessary to see the ancestors of humans as adapting to a variety of habitats with selection favoring phylogenetic structures that, at the very least, have circumscribed the organizational patterns of those species on the line of human evolution. Thus, we need not invoke the extreme assumptions of sociobiology to document the biology of human organization.

It is less conceptually burdensome, we believe, to trace the history of primate evolution in various ecological niches, and then to use this history to understand the nature of the first "societies" among hominids, or those primates who were near to or directly on the evolutionary line to humans.[1] And, most important, it is necessary to consider data on the social structures of our closest living relatives—the apes—to help reconstruct the nature of the first hominid society. Hence, a reconstruction of the first hominid society begins with the emergence of the primate order.

[1] The term hominid is a popular form of the word Hominidae, or the family of bipedal primates that includes modern humans as well as their direct and near ancestors (e.g., robust australopithecines).

Primate Classification and Evolution

The primates are an old order of mammals who emerged about 60 million years ago in the Paleocene epoch, from which the earliest archaic primate fossils have been found (Szalay and Delson 1979; Savage and Russell 1983). The first true primates or prosimians (Prosimii) appeared during the Eocene epoch 55 million years ago, when primate diversification dramatically accelerated, creating over 50 prosimian genera that reigned supreme in the trees for millions of years (Conroy 1990). After this "Golden Age," prosimians declined to the point where only about 20 genera exist today, making up about 25 percent of all primate species. Living prosimians are scattered throughout Asia, continental Africa, and Madagascar; and while they are arranged into an eclectic variety of primates—e.g., lemurs, lorises, and galagos—prosimian species are easily recognized by their nocturnal habits, their wide staring eyes, their vapid facial expressions, their moist, doglike nasal patch, their grooming "tooth comb" and "tolet claw," and their locomotion pattern of vertical clinging, leaping, and hopping (for general references, see Doyle and Martin 1979; Charles-Dominique 1977; Napier and Napier 1985; Tattersall et al. 1988).

Early monkey/apelike primates (or generalized Anthropoidea) make their first appearance in the fossil record more than 35 million years ago, during the late Eocene or early Oligocene (Simons 1990; Simons and Rasmussen 1991). Although the details of simian (i.e., monkey and ape) evolution are still to be documented, primitive anthropoid fossils are easily distinguished from those of prosimians by dental characteristics and many cranial features, including a reduced snout, expanded visual cortex, and larger braincase (see Conroy 1990: 142–64). As represented in Figure 1, these and many other differences have led to the recognition of two major primate divisions: the "lower" primates consisting of prosimians, and the "higher" anthropoid primates of monkeys, apes, and humans.[2]

Today the primate order is large, with nearly 190 living species, but most of these are monkeys. Represented by at least 30 genera and nearly 130 species, monkeys account for about 70 percent of all nonhuman primates species. The superfamily of New World monkeys, Ceboidea, is found in southern Mexico and South America. These monkeys are all tree-living and can be identified by their specialized dentition, widely

[2] Tarsiers (Tarsioidea) actually defy classification because they share features with both prosimians and anthropoids; we have taken the liberty of including them within a generalized prosimian radiation on the logic that their earliest relatives date from the Eocene, and that extant tarsiers appear to have changed little since that epoch.

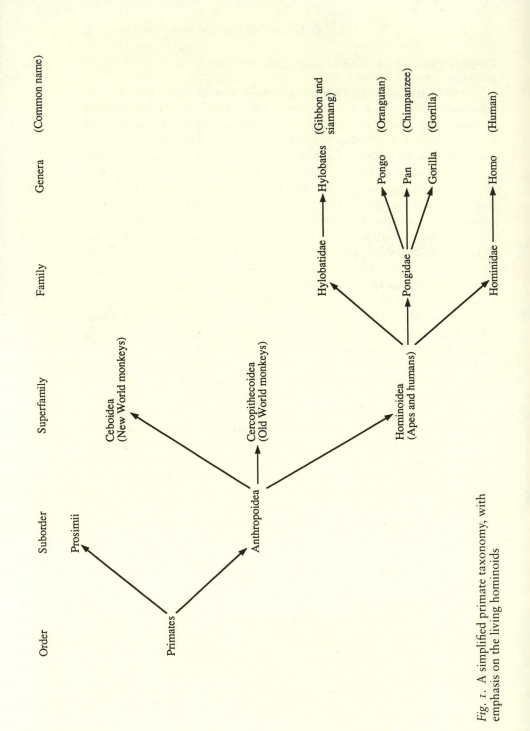

*Fig. 1.* A simplified primate taxonomy, with emphasis on the living hominoids

spaced nostrils that point sideways, and, for some, prehensile tails (for general references, see Moynihan 1976; Hershkovitz 1977; Coimbra-Filho and Mittermeier 1981). The superfamily of Old World monkeys, or Cercopithecoidea, is found in Asia, Europe, and Africa. Old World monkeys are identified by distinctive dentition, close-together nostrils that point downwards, and a tail that is not prehensile. Moreover, though most Old World monkeys are arboreal, some are also terrestrial, moving on the forest floor, alongside woodlands, or in savanna environments (Napier and Napier 1985; Roonwal and Mohnot 1977; Fleagle 1988). Despite such differences, however, New and Old World monkeys have fundamentally similar skeletal structures, and though some monkey species have evolved secondary adaptations in locomotor equipment (like prehensile tails that serve as a fifth limb), most monkeys possess relatively immobile shoulder joints, a narrow rib cage, a small collarbone, and limbs of similar length with a tail for balance. This basic anatomy gives monkeys generalized quadrupedal movement that enables them to move along the tops of tree branches or, for ground-dwellers, to move along with palms and soles flat on the surface (Napier and Napier 1985: 45; A. Jolly 1985: 100; Tattersall et al. 1988: 321–23).

The superfamily Hominoidea contains apes and humans. The ape families, Hylobatidae and Pongidae, are found in Asia and Africa. In terms of both numbers and diversity of species, monkeys are the most successful of living primates, whereas apes are the least successful. Hominoidea constitute only about 5 percent of all primate species, and in absolute numbers (excluding humans), apes continue to decline. The Lesser Apes, the gibbon and siamang gibbon (Hylobates), are found in Southeast Asia, along with one Great Ape, the orangutan (Pongo). The two other Great Apes, the chimpanzee (Pan) and gorilla (Gorilla), are found only in Africa.

A glance at the primate tree in Figure 1 highlights the hominoids, although from an evolutionary view, hominoidea are a failure in their competition with monkeys or even prosimians. Yet, as our closest living relatives, the Great Apes are set apart from other primates because of their humanlike size, their bigger brains, their greater capacity to learn complex tasks, and their more flexible behavioral patterns. In all these respects, apes are closer to humans than to monkeys. Moreover, they are anatomically closer to humans (see illustration). All hominoids lack a tail but evidence an enlarged and more developed collarbone than monkeys, mobile shoulders, a shorter spine, a set of distinct, unequal limbs (in apes front limbs are longer than hind limbs), and a short, deep trunk. Hominoids also have a distinctive skeletal structure consisting of specialized shoulders, wrists, and hands for greater flexibility and mobility (Hunt

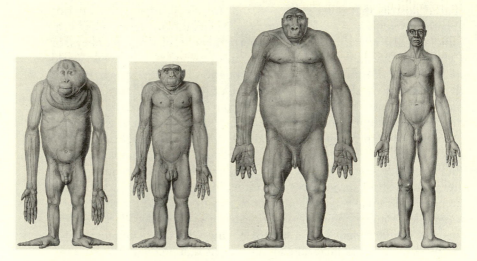

Great Ape males and a human male. *From left to right:* Pongo (orangutan), Pan (chimpanzee), Gorilla (gorilla), and Homo. Each hominoid is set to the same scale in an erect position without body hair and with the lower limbs straightened for comparison. Drawn by Professor Adolph Schultz (1933). Courtesy of E. Schweizerbart'sche Verlagsbuchhandlung.

1991). This increased dexterity enables all hominoids to use their forelimbs alone when hanging from branches. This suspensory hanging adaptation makes possible brachiation (under-the-branch swinging locomotion), allowing apes to propel themselves by their forelimbs alone (Napier 1963; Lewis 1974). But since large Great Apes cannot easily hang suspended underneath branches, only the gibbon uses its forelimbs as a primary means for traveling and while feeding. Although the Great Apes occasionally use the arm-swinging locomotion, they are classified as modified brachiators (Napier and Napier 1985: 45).[3]

The fossil and molecular evidence suggests that gibbons diverged from the Great Apes about 20 to 15 million years ago. Then, about 16 million

[3] Primates show a complex and versatile array of movement patterns, with four basic locomotor categories recognized: vertical clinging and leaping; quadrupedalism; brachiation; and bipedalism (Napier and Napier 1985: 45). Most monkeys share a quadrupedal gait, with various modifications that include leaping and arm-swinging with the use of a prehensile tail (ibid.). Monkey limb proportions often differ between arboreal and terrestrial forms: forelimbs in arboreal forms are usually somewhat shorter than hindlimbs, whereas terrestrial monkeys have limbs of nearly equal length. Gibbons are classified as brachiators, with the orangutan, gorilla, and chimpanzee seen as modified brachiators because the bones, joints, and muscles in the limbs and trunk of all hominoids (including humans) still reflect an arm-hanging, "brachiator" adaptation—that is, propulsion dominated by the front limbs (see Hunt 1991).

to 10 million years ago, the Great Apes divided into Asian and African forms (Pilbeam 1984). Finally, though the speciation of the African apes and humans still lacks fossil representation, early hominid fossils as well as molecular data on living hominoids indicate that gorillas, chimpanzees, and humans shared a last common ancestor between 8 and 5 million years ago (see Tattersall et al. 1988: 248–55; Corruccini and Ciochon 1983; Pilbeam 1984).

Thus the primate order is composed of prosimians, Old and New World monkeys, apes, and humans. Each superfamily is separated by a number of physical, biochemical, and cognitive differences. In the case of living prosimians, most differences are explained by their early primate radiation and retention of some early mammalian traits. Differences between monkeys and apes, however, are not so easily understood. Although the poor fossil record makes it difficult to reconstruct the origin and evolution of anthropoids, early anthropoid fossils are sufficiently plentiful to infer that these monkey/ape forms evolved at about the same time (Simons 1984; Conroy 1990: 136). Only later in the Miocene did monkeys and apes become differentiated. Such differentiation is most evident in the joints, muscles, and limb bones of apes and monkeys, which, in turn, indicate their varying modes of locomotion. Monkey limb bones signal an adaptation dependent on a quadrupedal progression with emphasis on the hind limbs for propulsion, whereas hominoid bone structure denotes an original arboreal adaptation dependent on the propulsion of the body through space with emphasis on the forelimbs. These anatomical differences reflect adaptation to varying niches, but, more important for our purposes, they also signal *differences in patterns of social organization between apes and monkeys.*

## The Organization of Old World Higher Primates

Unlike most mammals, both male and female primates typically remain together throughout the year. For slowly maturing, highly intelligent animals with relatively long lifespans, such permanent social arrangements require the integration of a diversity of age and sex classes—not just the adult males and females, but also younger age groups. For this reason, individuals in primate groupings are usually classified on the basis of characteristic physical and social traits into infants, juveniles, adolescents, and adults. Such variation in age groups, combined with year-round living together and a dependency on socialization processes that result in a large repertoire of learned behaviors, ensure that the social orders of primates are complex and flexible enough to meet environmental demands, although most species exhibit a modal group size and a typical age- and sex-class ratio (see Eisenberg et al. 1972; Southwick and Siddiqi 1974; Clutton-Brock 1974; Clutton-Brock and Harvey 1977; A. Jolly 1985: 115–20). Although the workings of primate societies are not fully understood, the available data suggest that ecological conditions, as well as innate predispositions for particular kinds of social and sexual relations, help restrict and regulate the movements of individuals (Carpenter 1942; Hinde 1979, 1983; Cheney et al. 1986). For example, while the dispersal patterns of species in a given environment are strongly influenced by the nature of the food supply, sleeping sites, and predation pressures, an inherent preference for particular kinds of social bonds seemingly influences the structure of primate groupings, even when individuals must adjust to varying ecological conditions. Moreover, it is now well established that primates form alliances and support networks and socially groom not only for immediate benefits but to establish and maintain particular social relationships that may last a lifetime (Cheney et al. 1986; Hinde 1983).

With few exceptions, primate reproductive units are classified according to the number of breeding males within a unit and the endurance of heterosexual bonds (Wittenberger 1981; Gouzoules 1984). Among Old World monkeys and apes, three generic organizational patterns can be distinguished: a "monogamous" pattern of one male, one female, and their young; a "harem" pattern of one male, several females, and their young; and a "horde" pattern of multiple males, multiple females, and their young (Southwick and Siddiqi 1974; A. Jolly 1985: 125–39). A species having one of these mating practices will also evidence a mechanism for dispersing specific age and sex classes in and out of the social unit in which mating occurs (Pusey and Packer 1987; Greenwood 1980). These migration patterns are not directly caused by the mating system, and it is usually difficult to determine why an individual departs from a group at a particular time. Nevertheless, among all studied Old World monkeys and apes, a mating pattern for a given species is associated with a stable transfer pattern where either males or females, or both, leave their natal group at puberty (Greenwood 1980; Pusey and Packer 1987). In turn, the system of mating and transfer is linked to distinct patterns of tie formation or social attachments within and between age and sex classes. And, as we will come to appreciate, variations in these dispersal or transfer patterns, as they create or break social ties, will provide valuable clues in reconstructing the nature of the first hominid societies.

## Reconstructing the Primordial Hominoid Society

The fossil record offers few clues about the kinds of social structures or networks of patterned social relationships that existed among primates in the distant evolutionary past. Nevertheless, there are strategies for inferring what these early social structures were like. One useful approach is to seek what we can call the Last Common Ancestor (LCA) of the hominoid line. At some point in the distant past, all present-day apes and humans shared an LCA, and if we can uncover the features of the social structure organizing this ancestral population, we can make inferences about the origins of human society. This search for a common *hominoid* ancestor makes use of the rich data now available from long-term field research on humans' closest living hominoid relatives. Like humans, apes are the end products of the hominoid lineage, a superfamily that originated in the Miocene (about 20 million years ago) and that, as noted above, can be conveniently divided into the Lesser Apes, the Great Apes, and humans. Despite the absence of fossilized samples, then, it may still be possible to reconstruct some of our social history, if we are willing to entertain the idea that the combined data on the social relations that make up the social structures of existing hominoids can be used as a kind of "distant mirror" in which images of the original social structure of the LCA of apes and humans are reflected.

Our basic argument is that the adaptive potential of all extant hominoids (that is, apes and humans) was probably limited by genetically based social predispositions that permitted only particular forms of organizational structures to emerge, despite variations in the habitats that hominoids occupy. Our central finding is that, compared with most Old World monkeys, the reconstructed blueprint of the social structure of the LCA of apes and humans reveals the hominoid lineage as predisposed toward low-density networks, low sociality, and strong individualism.[4] This pattern of weak tie formation, low sociality, high mobility, and strong individualism was to pose, we will argue, a difficult problem for hominoid species, especially those on the human line, once they moved from a forest to an open-range habitat.

In the best of circumstances, the use of historical data is the preferred and most direct way to reconstruct past events. But when the historical record is sparse or nonexistent, the comparative method has become a standard tool for reconstructing the past in such fields as textual criticism, historical linguistics, and evolutionary biology (Platnick and Cameron 1977; Andrews and Martin 1987; Jeffers and Lehiste 1979; Maas

[4] Density in network analysis is formally defined as the proportion of social ties occurring relative to the number of possible ties. Although the number of ties is important (e.g., gibbon populations have low-density networks because so few adult individuals actually interact), our usage here is more general and refers to the degree to which primate conspecifics in particular age and sex classes interact and rely on one another for social support and other resources: that is, the strength of ties. (For general references on network analysis, see Freeman 1976; Freeman et al. 1989; Wellman and Berkowitz 1988; see also Maryanski 1987; Granovetter 1973.)

1958). In all these fields, a limited group of entities believed to be the end points or descendants of an evolutionary or developmental process is identified. Then, an evaluation of the historical interrelationships of these descendants is conducted with the idea that the "original" or common ancestor can be reconstructed through the presence of shared features, or what has come to be called "derived characters." Although the implied genealogical relationships are not themselves directly testable, this approach posits two key assumptions: a "relatedness hypothesis," or the assumption that the similarities found in a class of objects are due not to chance but to a historical connection to a common ancestor; and a "regularity hypothesis," or the assumption that the changes from the ancestral to the descendant form will follow systematic and characteristic patterns (see Jeffers and Lehiste 1979: 17ff). Thus, in textual criticism, the comparative method is used to evaluate the interrelationships of alternative forms of the same manuscript and to reconstruct the original text from which all subsequent ones were derived (Platnick and Cameron 1977; Maas 1958). In historical linguistics, this approach is used to evaluate lexical forms showing similarities in form and meaning that have descended from the same original word to reconstruct the parent "speech forms" from which daughter languages were all derived (Jeffers and Lehiste 1979; Hoenigswald 1950, 1960; Gaeng 1971; Hass 1966). And in the biological version of this approach—termed cladistic analysis—the strategy involves evaluating organisms on the basis of a number of shared, distinguishing characteristics. In evolutionary biology, a sister lineage or "the outgroup population" is also identified, with the idea that differences between characteristics of the taxa in this sister lineage and those in the population of interest can be used to help assess the derived or novel characteristics from the common ancestor (Andrews and Martin 1987; Hennig 1966).

Our goal, then, is to identify the shared features of the network linkages or patterned social relations evident in the handful of living non-human hominoids so as to reconstruct the ancestral social structure from which all descendant hominoid forms were derived. The central assumption here is that if all or most of the living apes possess the same social character, then this character was also likely to have been present in their common ancestor. The alternative position is to presume that each character evolved independently, a much less likely possibility. This parent structure can then serve as a basic blueprint for considering the original hominoid social structure that, we suggest, constrained the nature and evolution of *hominid* social patterns.

As we noted earlier, monkeys are overwhelmingly dominant in the primate order, and they are widely distributed in a variety of ecological niches. In contrast, there are only four genera of living apes, which are often seen as "atypical relict forms" (Corruccini and Ciochon 1983: 14) and as "evolutionary failures" (Andrews 1981: 25) since they are quite specialized and very restricted in their distribution (Temerin and Cant 1983; Andrews 1981). Yet when primitive hominoids (as distinguished from generalized Anthropoidea in the Oligocene) first appeared in the fossil record during the early part of the Miocene epoch, they were far more abundant than monkeys and occupied a broader variety of ecological zones (Andrews 1981; Tattersall et al. 1988). While the lack of fossils makes it difficult to determine the time and place for the origin of hominoids, the widely accepted hypothesis is that gibbons, orangutans, chimpanzees, gorillas, and humans form a monophyletic grouping or cladogram strongly suggesting that all hominoids originally evolved from a single common ancestral population (Andrews and Martin 1987; L. Martin 1986). One well-supported ancestral tree is shown in Figure 2 (Tattersall et al. 1988: 136; L. Martin 1986; Andrews and Martin 1987).

Both molecular and fossil data are the basis for constructing this cladogram, and the time of divergence of the major branching points is based on the oldest record of the fossils contained within their respective clades. Following the cladogram, the current consensus is that the gibbon branch diverged first from the ancestral hominoid stem (Cronin 1983; Boaz 1983; Tattersall et al. 1988: 251) between 20 and 15 million years ago. Then, from 16 to 10 million years ago, the Great Apes diverged into Asian and African forms, and the orangutan branched off (Cronin 1983; Boaz 1983; Zihlman and Lowenstein 1983). The last group, the African apes and the ancestors of humans, was late to separate, with the molecular data suggesting that gorillas, chimpanzees, and humans continued to share a common ancestor until between 8 and 5 million years ago (see Corruccini and Ciochon 1983; King and Wilson 1975; Pilbeam 1984; Ciochon and Fleagle 1987). The contemporary remnants of this split of apes and hominids from the common ancestor can, we argue, give us a clue about the nature of the first hominid society. Let us now turn to a brief overview of the social organization and relational ties of present-day hominoids.[5]

[5] To array hominoid and cercopithecoid social ties, we used two simplifying procedures. First, ape and monkey social bonds were assumed to be positive and reciprocal. That is, while negative and asymmetric relations are also characteristic of primates, affective ties were assessed on the basis of mutually reinforcing and friendly interactions between dyads, making the assessment of characteristic relational profiles possible. Second, degrees of attachment were described along a simple scale of tie strength: absent ties; weak ties; moderate ties; strong ties. Individuals who have unknown ties (e.g., father-daughter where paternity cannot be known) or who seldom, if ever, interact have absent ties; those who interact occasionally and in a positive friendly manner have weak ties; those who affiliate closely for

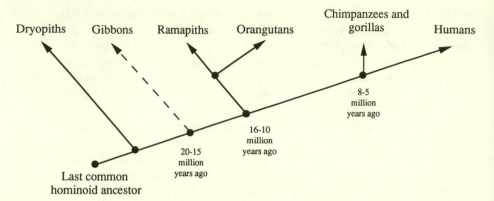

*Fig. 2.* A cladogram of hominoids. A cladogram is a set of relationships and as-sumes that trait patterns are developed as a result of ancestor-descendant re-lationships. In this limited cladogram, Dryopithecus and Ramapithecus, two extinct ape genera known only through the fossil record, are included for illustra-tion. Among living hominoids, the gibbon is believed to have branched off first, although its placement relative to ramapiths and dryopiths is still conjectural (as indicated by the broken line). Orangutans and ramapiths are conjectured to be sister genera by a number of scholars on the basis of morphological characters. And on the basis of both molecular and morphological characters, chimpanzees, gorillas, and humans are considered to have a very close phyletic relationship. Controversy exists, however, on when they diverged from a common ancestor, with four possible outcomes: (1) all three branched off simultaneously; (2) chim-panzees and gorillas continued to share a common ancestor while the human line branched off; (3) chimpanzees and humans continued to share a common an-cestor while the gorilla line branched off; (4) gorillas and humans continued to share a common ancestor while the chimpanzee line branched off (see Sibley et al. 1990). Here we show chimpanzees and gorillas sharing a common ancestor longer, with the human line separate (i.e., outcome #2). This choice is based on both the dating of fossils and the molecular clock, and is the one still favored by most researchers. Recent molecular data, however, point to chimpanzees and hu-mans sharing a common ancestor, with the gorilla line separate (outcome #3; see, for example, Goodman et al. 1990; Hayaska et al. 1988; Sibley et al. 1990). Cladogram redrawn from Ciochon 1987.

## Gibbons (Hylobates)

Gibbons are small apes (weighing on average 20 lbs.) that are widely distributed in the tropical rain forests of southeastern Asia. They are ar-boreal frugivores that live high in the forest canopy, where they exhibit a

---

a time but without emotion or endurance over time (at least for adults) have moderate ties; and those who exhibit extensive physical contact accompanied by observable affect (e.g., reciprocal grooming), mutual support, high rates of interaction, and stable relations over time have strong ties. Scaling tie strength for well-studied primate species was a straightfor-ward procedure since the clear-cut social tendencies that age and sex class conspecifics re-veal have been consistently confirmed by researchers (see Cheney et al. 1986; Hinde 1983).

rare monogamous "family" group structure with a modal size of about four individuals (Leighton 1987; Groves 1984; Ellefson 1974; Gittens 1980; Chivers 1984). Manifesting little or no sexual dimorphism, an adult male and female (and sometimes dependent offspring) fiercely protect a small, stable territory. This conjugated alliance may facilitate the formation of the strong heterosexual pair bond that seemingly comes close to the monogamous ideal of "mating for life" (MacKinnon and MacKinnon 1984: 291). Normally, adult gibbons have few social relations outside the nuclear family, leaving the mated pair socially dependent on each other and on bonds with their immature offspring (Tilson 1981). Established gibbon partners typically interact in a relaxed, tolerant, and well-coordinated manner (Leighton 1987), and mated pairs (depending on the species) engage in such companionable activities as singing morning duets (Leighton 1987; MacKinnon and MacKinnon 1984).

Unlike the vast majority of primates, gibbons are considered "codominant" in most daily group activities, with each sex involved equally in such leadership responsibilities as guiding daily foraging progressions (Leighton 1987; Chivers 1974). Moreover, gibbon fathers also lend a hand in child care by playing with and grooming their offspring (Chivers 1984; Leighton 1987), an adaptive strategy that culminated in the subgenus Symphalangus, or siamang gibbon, where the male shares the burdens of child care with the female. However, as gibbon offspring mature (from five to seven years old), social bonds between parents and offspring weaken; at puberty, both sons and daughters leave their natal group and move to another territory (see Tuttle 1986: 249–55). This one male–one female organizational arrangement, with a strong heterosexual pair bond, paternal care, and offspring transfer at puberty, is a consistent pattern among all six gibbon species (Napier and Napier 1985: 161) and is connected to the social network patterns (as indicated by the nature of "ties" among individuals) outlined in Table 1 (Maryanski 1992).[6]

### Orangutan (Pongo)

Orangutans are large Asian apes (females average about 80 lbs., males about 150 lbs.) comprising a single species that is restricted to the tropical islands of Borneo and Sumatra. Among apes, orangutans are as unique for their solitary habits as gibbons are for their monogamy (Tuttle 1986: 12). The orangutan is an arboreal frugivore that forages in the

---

[6] Although distinct bonding patterns exist for all age and sex conspecifics (e.g., infant-juvenile ties), only the key classes of social ties are shown in Table 1. The nature of the 11 classes of ties for both hominoids and a sample of cercopithecoids is adequate for this comparative analysis of primate social bonds because these relations are the core of any primate social structure. Social structure is defined here in a narrow way to refer only to the network of patterned social relationships for a given genus.

TABLE I

*Social Network Ties in Reproductive Units Among Nonhuman Hominoidea*

| Genus | Adult kinship or voluntary relations | | | Adult-child procreation relations | | | |
| | Male-male | Female-female | Male-female | Mother-daughter | Mother-son | Father-daughter | Father-son |
| --- | --- | --- | --- | --- | --- | --- | --- |
| Gibbon | Absent to weak ties | Absent to weak ties | Strong ties | Strong ties | Strong ties | Strong ties | Strong ties |
| Orangutan | Absent to weak ties | Absent to weak ties | Weak ties | Strong ties | Strong ties | Absent ties | Absent ties |
| Gorilla | Weak ties | Absent to weak ties | Moderate to strong ties, females with dependent children; weak ties, females without dependents | Strong ties | Strong ties | Unknown ties; likely absent | Unknown ties; likely absent |
| Chimpanzee | Weak to moderate ties; voluntary strong ties between siblings | Absent to weak ties | Weak ties | Strong ties | Strong ties | Absent ties | Absent ties |
| Last common hominoidea ancestor | *Absent to weak ties | *Absent to weak ties | *Weak ties | *Strong ties | *Strong ties | *Absent ties | *Absent ties |

NOTE: The strength of an attachment among and within any given mating system is usually determined by qualitative measures such as social grooming, spatial proximity, cooperation, mutual aid, and the formation of alliances. These values are assumed to be positive and symmetrical. The asterisks denote reconstructed forms based on the shared relational features.

tropical forest each day, usually alone or in temporary subgroupings of two or three individuals (Rodman 1973; MacKinnon 1971; Rodman and Mitani 1987). While the particulars of orangutan organization are still unclear, field researchers agree that an orangutan population (or all those animals moving about in a single continuously inhabited block of forest) can be divided into "residents" (those present throughout the year) and

| Adult-adult procreation relations | | | | Gender dispersal from mother at puberty | Organizational type | Residence type for offspring after puberty |
|---|---|---|---|---|---|---|
| Mother-daughter | Mother-son | Father-daughter | Father-son | | | |
| Absent to weak ties | Absent to weak ties | Absent to weak ties | Absent to weak ties | Males and females | Monogamous group | Neolocal, males and females |
| Absent to weak ties | Absent to weak ties | Absent ties | Absent ties | Males and females | Horde group | Neolocal, males and females |
| Absent to weak ties | Absent to weak ties | Unknown ties; most likely absent | Unknown ties; most likely absent | Males and females | Horde/ harem group | Neolocal, males and females |
| Absent to weak ties | Strong ties | Absent ties | Absent ties | Females | Higher-level horde/ community regional population | Neolocal, females; virilocal, males |
| *Absent to weak ties | *Absent to weak ties | *Absent ties | *Absent ties | *Males and females | *Horde group | *Neolocal |

"nonresidents" (those present only part of the year) (Rodman and Mitani 1987; Sugardjito et al. 1987). The adult females are the most stable residents, whereas adult males often wander in and out of a particular ranging area (Rodman and Mitani 1987; Galdikas 1985).

When observed, adult orangutans are withdrawn and usually alone. The most common and stable grouping is that of a mother and her dependent offspring; the most gregarious is that of young adolescents, who join up and form temporary traveling bands, seemingly for purely social reasons (Galdikas 1988; Sugardjito et al. 1987; Rijksen 1975). When adolescents reach maturity, however, they normally shun contact with other conspecifics (Rodman 1973). Though normally solitary, adult males are sociable when engaged in sexual activity, and although mating is relatively promiscuous, adult females seemingly prefer adult males who reside within their ranging area. Sexual liaisons may last for several days, weeks, or even months (Galdikas 1985; Rodman and Mitani 1987), although unlike gibbons, adult male and female orangutans are rarely observed together in the forest (Tuttle 1986: 255; Galdikas 1985). A strong bond exists between a mother and her dependent offspring until the age of seven years, but as juveniles mature they begin to lag behind their mothers and forage at their own pace. Finally, at puberty both males and females depart from the mother to range on their own. Although daughters appear to forage near the ranging area of their mothers, contact between mothers and daughters is infrequent (Galdikas 1988). Sons appear to lead a more nomadic life, often traveling to other forested areas. Among same-sex adults, social interactions are infrequent; adult females normally avoid each other, and adult males typically reveal intolerance for one another (Galdikas 1985; J. Cohen 1975). The solitary lifestyle of this Great Ape is considered unique among higher primates, and its relational patterns are shown in Table 1.

### Gorillas (Gorilla)

These pongids are the largest of the Great Apes (males average 335 lbs., females 185 lbs.). In foraging habits, gorillas are folivores, and unlike the other apes, they travel, feed, and rest mostly on the ground (Watts 1991). Gorillas are found in two widely separated areas, one in West Africa and the other in Central Africa, where they inhabit secondary (i.e., regenerating) or montane rain forest (Tuttle 1986: 18–19; Dixson 1981) and sometimes swamp forests (Fay et al. 1989). In marked contrast to other apes, gorillas reveal two patterns of organization: relatively stable groups, with an average of ten members; and unattached, single adult males (Maryanski 1986; A. Weber and Vedder 1983; Fossey 1976). Although some reproductive groups have up to four adult males, a typical gorilla group is composed of one mature male along with several females and their dependent offspring (Harcourt et al. 1981; Yamagiwa 1983). Four or more gorilla groups and some single males typically share a home range (averaging 15 square miles), with resident groups occasionally meeting up, traveling, and even bedding down together overnight (Fossey 1972; Yamagiwa 1983; Schaller 1962). Normally, each gorilla group is headed by a dominant "silverback male," who is typically the preferred sexual partner for the resident females, although females may elect to mate with other resident males. Within gorilla groups, social relations are fluid and casual. Familiar adult males, though tolerant of each other, are aloof, engaging in few overt social interactions (Fossey 1976, 1983; Harcourt 1977; Schaller 1962). And, despite residence in the same group, sometimes for years, adult females rarely interact, though they are tolerant of each other (Harcourt 1979a, 1979b; Stewart and Harcourt 1987; Yamagiwa 1983). The social ties between a dominant male and adult female vary dramatically, being crucially linked to the status of the male and the maternal responsibilities of the female. A female with dependent offspring is usually found during day-resting periods sitting in close proximity to the leader silverback. A female without dependents (or with sudden loss of her offspring) is typically found on the edge of her group; such peripheral females are likely to abandon a male entirely and migrate to another group or to a lone male. In a gorilla group, all adult members are free to leave any group for any reason. It is conjectured that a mother will form a stable, moderate tie with a leader male only when she is successful in raising her offspring (Harcourt 1977, 1979a, 1979c; Yamagiwa 1983). Perhaps for this reason, leader males are quick to help mothers with their dependent offspring; they often play and groom immatures, and even "baby-sit" for extended periods when a mother is busy with other activities (Harcourt 1979a; Stewart 1981). Subordinate adult males and females interact only occasionally. Although relations between a mother and her young offspring are intimate, both male and female offspring migrate out of their natal group at puberty (Harcourt 1977, 1978, 1979a; Harcourt et al. 1976). For an overview of the social structure of this single species of ape, see Table 1.

## Chimpanzees (Pan troglodytes)

Chimpanzees are large apes (males average 100 lbs., females 85 lbs.) that are distributed throughout the western, eastern, and central forest belts of tropical Africa (C. Jones and Sabater Pi 1971; Tuttle 1986). Common chimpanzees are primarily frugivores and are considered the most versatile of the Great Apes, moving about easily on the ground or in the forest canopy and inhabiting primary and secondary forests, as well as open canopy woodlands and forest fringe habitats. Chimpanzee organization is centered on the creation of brief groupings or parties within a more inclusive regional population of 25–100 members. That is, chimpanzees evidence a "community" form of organization (Goodall 1986) because individuals may move about alone or freely join or leave a variety of temporary clusterings within a clearly defined region, although the regional population itself is relatively stable over time (Goodall-Lawick 1975; Halperin 1979; Nishida and Hiraiwa-Hasegawa 1987). Within a community, mating habits are relatively promiscuous, with an adult female choosing one partner for a consortship (i.e., an exclusive temporary liaison) or sequentially mating with a number of adult males (Tutin 1979; McGinnis 1979; Tuttle 1986; Nishida 1990).

Ties between adult males are normally strong between siblings and weak to moderate with other adult males; males choose on an individual basis what are regarded as "friendship ties" (Nishida and Hiraiwa-Hasegawa 1987; Takahata 1990b). In contrast, ties between adult females are very weak, since most adult females are detached and move about alone or only in the company of their dependent offspring (Wrangham and Smuts 1980; Hayaki 1988; Nishida 1979, 1990). In part, the relatively solitary state of females is due to their migration to another community when they are between seven and ten years old and to the shyness of incoming females toward each other. Male-female bonds are also weak; unless sexually receptive, females spend very little time socializing with adult males (Pusey and Packer 1987; Wrangham and Smuts 1980; Nishida and Hiraiwa-Hasegawa 1987). In contrast, mother-son relations normally remain strong, in part because males are not burdened with dependents and because males do not leave their natal home range. Although mother and adult son do not travel about or feed together on a daily basis, they are observed together frequently in close companionship (Hayaki 1988; Pusey and Packer 1987; Takahata 1990a). Father-offspring ties are, of course, unknown. The kinds of social ties that exist among common chimpanzees are summarized in Table 1.[7]

[7] Two chimpanzee species are recognized: the widespread common chimpanzee (*Pan troglodytes*) of eastern, western, and central Africa discussed in the text, and the pygmy or bonobo chimpanzee (*Pan paniscus*), a small, isolated species that inhabits the Zaire River Basin (F. White 1989). Pygmy chimpanzees are more gracile, weighing less than common chimpanzees, although much overlap exists (Zihlman et al. 1978). Pygmy chimpanzees also evidence the rare "fission-fusion" or "community" organization, with female transfer between communities (Furuichi 1989; Vehara 1988). While social relations among bonobos are still not well understood, available data suggest that mother-son ties are similar to those of the common chimpanzee, and male-male ties are evident but are expressed less among bonobos (Nishida and Hiraiwa-Hasegawa 1987; Furuichi 1989). Bonobos are distinctive, however, in the more affiliative relations between males and females and between females themselves. Takeshi Furuichi (1989) suggests that pygmy chimps evidence two mechanisms that, in part, account for greater tie density: *Pan paniscus* females are sexually receptive much longer than *P. troglodytes* females; and *P. paniscus* females, when in close spatial contact, perform a "genitogenital rubbing" (or GG), where two females make physical contact by rubbing their genitals together rapidly as they ventrally hold each other. Habitat diversity—the existence of large, predictable food patches with little or no competition (in contrast to "small-patch," competitive feeding in common chimps)—is viewed as a primary factor creating denser social networks among bonobos since superabundant food patches

In looking over the organizational profiles of the present-day apes, it is clear that organizational differences exist. First, the apes are adapted to highly diverse and far-flung habitats, with the gibbon and orangutan living in Asia and the chimpanzee and gorilla residing in Africa. Second, the apes utilize many different kinds of space. The gibbon and orangutan are almost wholly arboreal, whereas the chimpanzee is mainly arboreal but partially terrestrial, and the gorilla is mostly terrestrial. Third, the apes have different reproductive strategies. The gibbon is monogamous; the gorilla is usually polygynous (although very loosely so); and the chimpanzee and the orangutan are relatively promiscuous. Fourth, the apes evidence differences in dispersal patterns, but, for all apes, offspring no longer remain in daily face-to-face contact with mothers after puberty. For the gibbon, orangutan, and gorilla, both males and females migrate outside of a mother's ranging area; for the chimpanzee, only the females disperse to another ranging area. This diversity highlights the strong selection pressures that must have been operating since living hominoids shared a last common ancestor.

Still, we should consider why the differences among such closely related genera vary so dramatically and why the social arrangements of the present-day apes are so novel and peculiar relative to primates in general. Without doubt, the contemporary Old World monkeys also underwent selection pressures, but they tend to reveal considerable similarity within families. Overall, most Old World monkeys are organized into discrete groups with reproductive units that follow either a one-male harem plan or the multiple male–multiple female horde organization (A. Jolly 1985: 129; see also Smuts et al. 1987). Moreover, the dispersal patterns of al-

---

are associated with large, mixed groupings of adult males, females, and young (F. White 1989), with much more group stability over time (Furuichi 1989). Field studies on *Pan paniscus* are still recent, and, given the relational inconsistencies between the Zaire study sites (see F. White 1989 and Furuichi 1989 on adult males, for example), we felt it best to exclude the species. Female GG rubbing presented an additional problem, for while this behavior is technically an expression of female sociality, it is, as Furuichi (1989) stresses, a very different type of female cohesion compared with matrifocal monkey females, who continually socially groom and otherwise evidence strong social ties. Indeed, GG female rubbing, unique to bonobo females, is not really seen as a bonding behavior but is considered more a ritualized contact activity to ensure that females will tolerate proximity while feeding near one another (F. White 1989: 162) and to "reduce tension, even in the midst of agonistic interactions" among unrelated females (Furuichi 1989: 186). It seems that prolonged female receptivity (to create male-female ties) and GG rubbing (to create female-female ties of some sort) was selected for in the bonobo habitat. In our view, the bonobo social system illustrates perfectly well how selection for tie-building in hominoids engendered not only novel but, in the case of GG rubbing, rather bizarre cohesive behaviors in an effort to work around the phylogenetic constraint of female dispersal at puberty, a hypothesis to be discussed shortly.

most all monkeys (and even prosimians) follow a male-biased dispersal system, with the females remaining in their natal units usually in company with their female relatives (Pusey and Packer 1987; Greenwood 1980; Andelman 1986). Thus, it is largely through female bonding that group continuity over time is sustained in most Old World monkeys (and in most mammals; see Greenwood 1980). In contrast, for three ape genera, both males and females disperse their natal unit at puberty, leaving the group without intergenerational recruitment. Only in the chimpanzee, where females disperse at puberty, is there a sense of intergenerational continuity, but in this case continuity is through males living within the same regional population.

What, then, can these network patterns, as summarized in Table 1, tell us about the LCA? First, in line with the "relatedness hypothesis," we can assume that any feature common to the gibbon, orangutan, gorilla, and chimpanzee was likely to be present in the LCA structure as well. And in comparing the relations shared by the nonhuman hominoids, we can use these reflected forms as a kind of diagram for the reconstruction of the LCA form. Second, in line with the "regularity hypothesis" (to be discussed later in this chapter), the validity of the reconstructed ancestral form will require us to account for these novel patterns in terms of the selection requirements of particular ecological niches.

The relational data from the four ape genera can, when placed side by side in Table 1, offer a clue to the ancestral structure of hominoids. If we begin with a correspondence of the tie patterns *common to all* hominoids (that is, four out of four, or 4/4), we find the following regularities:

4/4  adult female – adult female: absent to weak ties

4/4  mother – young daughter: strong ties

4/4  mother – young son: strong ties

4/4  mother – adult daughter: absent to weak ties

4/4  father – adult daughter: absent ties

4/4  father – adult son: absent ties

In comparing the ties *common to most* hominoids (that is, three out of four, or 3/4), the following patterns are evident:

3/4  adult male – adult male: absent to weak ties (chimpanzee the exception)

3/4  father – young daughter: absent ties (gibbon the exception)

3/4  father – young son: absent ties (gibbon the exception)

3/4  mother – adult son: absent to weak ties (chimpanzee the exception)

Finally, in comparing the ties that show the *least common* correspondence (that is, two out of four, or 2/4), the following regularities are evident:

2/4 adult male—adult female: gibbon and gorilla have moderate to strong ties

2/4 adult male—adult female: chimpanzee and orangutan have weak ties

In looking over the hypothesized structure at the bottom of Table 1, two critical questions need to be addressed. First, is the reconstruction plausible? And second, is the reconstruction useful in helping us to better understand the foundations of human societies?

In addressing the problem of the plausibility of the hypothesized parent structure, it is important to consider first the null hypothesis that the tie patterns shared by hominoids all evolved independently for each ape genera *after* their divergence from the LCA. This hypothesis cannot be ruled out entirely, but several factors indicate that the social structures of current hominoids resemble one another to a degree that can be best accounted for through a historical connection. In looking over the hominoid tie patterns and comparing them with the ties from the Old World monkey "outgroup," for example, we find that the absent to weak ties between the adult ape females is a rare tie pattern for primates. This conclusion can be seen by comparing the tie patterns of apes in Table 1 with those of a sample of Cercopithecoidea (Old World monkeys) in Table 2 (Maryanski 1992).

Among the Cercopithecoidea, individuals live in relatively closed, discrete social groups where females normally outnumber males. In a harem group, a single adult male is usually present with a core of related females and young, whereas in a horde arrangement, multiple males and females and their young are present. For example, among open-country (Macaca) macaques and (Papio) baboons, group size may reach up to 200 individuals, with immigrant adult males organized into a hierarchy of dominant-subordinate relations. In turn, monkey females are usually lifelong members of their natal unit and are typically organized into high-density sets of strong cliques, especially with maternal relatives; in the case of macaques and baboons, matrilineages may include up to four generations of mothers, sisters, and daughters (see Fedigan 1982; A. Jolly 1985; Napier and Napier 1985; Cheney et al. 1986). Thus, related females with their immature offspring normally form the stable core of monkey groups, creating what are called in the literature "female-bonded societies" (Wrangham 1980; A. Jolly 1985: 123–27; Andelman 1986).

In contrast, hominoid mother-and-daughter ties remain strong only

TABLE 2

*Social Network Ties in Reproductive Units Among a Few Well-Studied Cercopithecoidea*

| Species | Adult kinship or voluntary relation | | | Adult-child procreation relations | | | |
|---|---|---|---|---|---|---|---|
| | Male-male | Female-female | Male-female | Mother-daughter | Mother-son | Father-daughter | Father-son |
| Gelada monkeys (Theropithecus) | Absent to weak ties | Strong ties | Weak ties (to most harem females) | Strong ties | Strong ties | Weak ties | Weak ties |
| Patas monkeys (Erytherocebus) | Absent to weak ties | Strong ties | Weak ties (to most harem females) | Strong ties | Strong ties | Weak ties | Weak ties |
| Most species of macaque monkeys (Macaca) | Weak ties | Strong ties | Weak to moderate ties | Strong ties | Strong ties | Unknown ties; most likely absent | Unknown ties; most likely absent |
| Most species of baboons (Papio) | Weak ties | Strong ties | Weak to moderate ties | Strong ties | Strong ties | Unknown ties; most likely absent | Unknown ties; most likely absent |
| **Last common Cercopithecoidea ancestor** | *Absent to weak ties | *Strong ties | *Weak ties | *Strong ties | *Strong ties | *Absent to weak ties | *Absent to weak ties |

NOTE: See Table 1.

until puberty and then usually revert to weak ties. In accounting for such major differences between female hominoids and almost all female monkeys (of which Table 2 is a small sample), this disparity would seemingly be linked to some strong underlying causal agent, or mechanism. One prominent mechanism is the migration pattern among ape females, who normally leave their natal unit at puberty. Since female dispersal at puberty is rare among primates (and rare among mammals in general; J. Moore 1984; Greenwood 1980), it seems unlikely that this highly deviant pattern evolved independently in each ape species. This conclusion is strengthened by the fact that among monkeys in general, and Old World monkeys in particular, male-biased dispersal at puberty is the normal pattern, with females remaining in their natal unit close to their mothers and other female relatives (Napier and Napier 1985: 71; Pusey and Packer 1987). By keeping the females together, most monkey societies ensure that the social group will reproduce itself and endure over time. Of crucial importance here is the continuance of the mother-daughter rela-

| Adult-adult procreation relations | | | | Gender dispersal from mother at puberty | Organiza- tional type | Residence type for offspring after puberty |
|---|---|---|---|---|---|---|
| Mother- daughter | Mother- son | Father- daughter | Father- son | | | |
| Strong ties | Absent to weak ties | Absent to weak ties | Absent to weak ties | Males | Harem group | Neolocal, males; matrilocal, females |
| Strong ties | Absent to weak ties | Absent to weak ties | Absent to weak ties | Males | Harem group | Neolocal, males; matrilocal, females |
| Strong ties | Absent to weak ties | Unknown ties; most likely absent | Unknown ties; most likely absent | Males | Horde group | Neolocal, males; matrilocal, females |
| Strong ties | Absent to weak ties | Unknown ties; most likely absent | Unknown ties; most likely absent | Males | Horde group | Neolocal, males; matrilocal, females |
| *Strong ties | *Absent to weak ties | *Absent to weak ties | *Absent to weak ties | *Males | *Horde group | *Neolocal, males; matrilocal, females |

tionship, which ensures that matrifocal units are self-recruiting and self-perpetuating. In contrast, the migration of hominoid females not only breaks down the bonds between mother and daughter but also discourages alliances among related or familiar females, with the result, as reflected in Table 1, that only weak ties, at best, normally prevail among nonhuman female hominoids.[8]

[8] Using living primates to reconstruct the lifeways of early hominids is an important area of inquiry that incorporates at least three perspectives. One approach is to consider how early hominids became differentiated from apes through ecological changes (Lovejoy 1981; Bartholomew and Birdsell 1953; Kortlandt 1972), new technologies (DeVore 1964; Washburn 1963), and dietary specializations (Lucas et al. 1985; C. Jolly 1970; Isaac and McCown 1975; Goodall and Hamburg 1975). A second approach is to study savanna-dwelling primates as representing the "ecological counterparts" of early hominid populations (Wolpoff 1978; see also Strum and Mitchell 1987). The third approach is focused on nonhuman hominoids in an effort to uncover their common affinities with each other and early hominids (Tanner 1987; McGrew 1981; Lancaster 1968; Zihlman and Lowenstein 1983; Goodall-Lawick 1975; Goodall and Hamburg 1975; Reynolds 1966; see also Kinzey 1987). We are aware of only two papers—by Robert Foley and P. C. Lee (1989) and

In addition to the females leaving at puberty, three of the four ape genera also have male dispersal at puberty, making it likely that all males and females will depart their natal unit. But unlike female dispersal, male dispersal is not crucial, for even if the males stay, patrifocal units cannot exist without a stable sexual relationship between a male and a female. It is possible, of course, for a mother and son to create a patrifocal unit through sex and reproduction, but since they rarely mate with each other (a pattern also seen in Old World monkeys), this tie is a dead end, reproductively speaking (Demarest 1977; Sade 1968; Pusey 1980). Hence, even when familiar males remain together, as chimpanzee males do, paternity cannot be known. Therefore, in chimpanzee society strong blood ties linking *adult* community members are normally limited to mother and son and male siblings.

A second pattern in the hominoid data is the lack of group continuity over time. Among gibbons, orangutans, and gorillas (and in contrast to the Old World monkeys), there is no group continuity over intergenerational time. In gibbons, the nuclear family structure dissolves with the death of the mated pair; in orangutans, there are no stable groups outside of a mother and her dependent offspring; in gorillas, the stability of the group rests with the leader silverback, and at his death, the group dissolves unless there is another silverback to replace him. But even with a second silverback present, females often individually disperse either to another group or to a solitary silverback (Stewart and Harcourt 1987). In chimpanzees, once again the only stable grouping is a mother and her dependent offspring. Yet at puberty, even among chimpanzees, offspring no longer remain in daily association with the mother. Moreover, the two genders have entirely different patterns of dispersal. Chimpanzee daughters move to another regional population, temporarily or permanently; sons continue to move within their natal ranging area, but not in their natal group. Among all apes, then, there is no reproduction of the natal group through time as is the case with Old World monkey groups.

Thus, in looking over the relational data on the living hominoids, there appears to be (1) selection against the continuance of the mother-daughter relationship, considered to be the primary building block for kinship net-

---

Richard Wrangham (1987)—where an emphasis is placed on the LCA hominoid structure as a model for understanding hominid organization. Although these authors emphasize a number of social features and use very different methodologies from the cladistic/social-network analysis outlined here, some of their conclusions lend credence to our LCA reconstruction. Foley and Lee suggest that the lack of female-female alliances in living hominoids suggests a trend toward a social system with a core of stable male-female relations and an elaboration of male-male alliances, especially among male kin, in early hominid societies; whereas Wrangham sees female dispersal and the lack of female-female bonding as conservative traits retained from the "ancestral suite" of the LCA.

works in most monkey societies; and (2) selection against social group continuity as a result of dispersal patterns. Since both are evolutionary novelties, and otherwise rare primate characteristics, it seems likely that they were also present in the LCA social structure.

Another consideration is ancestral organizational patterns. While population size is closely tied to environmental pressures and what this may have been in the LCA cannot be known, we might still consider the mating arrangements of extant hominoids to think about the LCA reproductive system. We can probably dismiss the monogamous mating pattern of the gibbons for the LCA, since it is rare, highly specialized, and inflexible, being faithfully observed among all six gibbon species. Instead, the multiple male–multiple female arrangement seems to us the most likely organizational pattern for two reasons: first, it is the most parsimonious and flexible pattern, and second, the weak tie patterns among apes suggest a fluid social structure indicative of transitory mating arrangements. Thus, it can be hypothesized that the LCA of hominoids was loosely organized into a horde arrangement, with mother-offspring ties being the only stable grouping tendency.

Finally, assuming that our representation of the LCA is a reasonable reconstruction, one striking configuration dominates all others: *the linkages among network members are weak with few strong ties.* As can be seen in Table 1, the LCA tie relations are fluid, creating a low density network since there are very few enduring connections among individuals. The only strong ties are among a mother and her dependent offspring until puberty, when it would appear that both males and females leave their natal unit. The LCA organizational structure appears as one marked by only occasional interactions among individuals, suggesting that the individuals making up the population moved about in space somewhat independently of each other and were, on the whole, relatively self-contained, highly individualistic primates.

## Conclusion

Applying the comparative method to the relational data on humans' closest living hominoid relatives argues for the following conclusion: the ancestral organization of apes and hominids was loose and fluid. Our reconstructed blueprint of the LCA social structure suggests a societal portrait of individuals with weak ties and few enduring strong ties beyond the stable grouping of a mother and her dependent offspring. Seemingly, there was selection against matrifocal units, thereby selecting against kinship alliances. Further, with male and female dispersal at puberty, there was also selection against group continuity, ruling out the kind of tight-knit "female-bonded" structure typical of most monkey societies (A. Jolly 1985). And perhaps the most intriguing finding is the selection for high individuality, since apes are rather self-contained individuals with few strong tie networks.

In order to substantiate this conclusion, a final step is to consider each ape genera as it branched from the LCA. The goal here is to account for the idiosyncratic variations among hominoid social structures. As mentioned earlier, the few remaining ape genera are often viewed as the evolutionary leftovers of a very widespread hominoid radiation in the early Miocene. We should emphasize that fossilized postcranial materials of early Miocene hominoids are considered at odds with contemporary apes because they lack the specialized ape locomotor morphology; instead, they are suggestive of the quadrupedal locomotor activity of Old World monkeys (Conroy 1990: 256; Andrews 1981; see also footnote 3, above). In turn, Old World monkeys, while rare during the early Miocene, proliferate during the middle to late Miocene, roughly concurrent with the decline and extinction of many hominoid genera from both Africa and Eurasia (Conroy 1990; Andrews 1981; Harrison 1989).

Why did Miocene hominoids decline and monkeys proliferate? This is not the place for a lengthy discussion of the ecological background and paleobiology behind this development (for details, see Temerin and Cant 1983; Andrews 1981; Harrison 1989), though we might mention one hypothesis, proposed by Andrews (1981): that cercopithecoids developed a clear competitive edge over hominoids by evolving a specialized digestive tract that allowed them to consume foods, especially unripe fruits, much earlier than apes, who had to wait for such foods to mature. Losing this dietary competition, some apes evolved forelimb dominant locomotion that allowed them to forage in novel ecological zones, such as the terminal branches of trees, where quadrupedal monkeys could not firmly step. Whatever the explanation, there is solid evidence that hominoids were being replaced by monkeys by the middle Miocene, with the fossil record confirming that during this replacement phase, ape species were undergoing modifications for the unusual limb proportions and skeletal features that characterize apes and humans today (Andrews 1981; Tattersall et al. 1988).

What of the LCA? We can assume that forelimb-dominant locomotion played a decisive role in the survival of apes, since this innovative trait is retained in all living descendant hominoid populations. And if the reconstructed form of the LCA social network is correct, we should expect that at one point in time this structure also facilitated survival and reproductive success. At a later point, however, descendant populations branched off from the LCA population and moved to new ecological zones, where selection seemingly favored the building of social network ties. Yet, in creating stronger relational ties, the problems of female dispersal at puberty and the consequent lack of group continuity over time remained. If we assume that the hominoid lineage was rather constrained by the dispersal of natal ape females around puberty, a hominoid trend of building network ties would have had to work around this dispersal problem and would still be evident in the social structures of the present-day apes. In keeping with the "regularity hypothesis," then, the highly novel organizational structures of extant apes can be viewed as compromise solutions, representing an effort to forge social ties that were compatible with specific niche requirements (e.g., group size, predation pressures, dietary adaptations) and sidestepped the biologically based constraint of female dispersal—a trait that is, seemingly, a derived character from the last common hominoid ancestor.

In profiling the organizational structures of contemporary nonhuman hominoids, we find that all genera (with the partial exception of the orangutan) have elaborated social network ties in distinctive ways that are consistent with the phylogenetic stumbling block of female dispersal. Among gibbon genera, the rare and highly specialized monogamous structure prevails; it is essentially a nuclear family structure, in which social relations are limited to the mated pair and their dependent offspring. Since the offspring disperse at puberty, gibbon social structure pivots on the strongly tied heterosexual pair. Seemingly, the co-dominance of the male and female in all activities works to strengthen the pair bond. Among gorillas, the harem structure, while superficially resembling harem monkey groups where females are linked closely together, is essentially structured around moderate to strong ties between the leader male and mothers with dependent offspring. Seemingly, this tie depends on the participation of the male in the care of dependent offspring. And among chimpanzees, the community structure is built around male relationships and around a mother-son bond that continues after puberty. Even in orangutans, which have the weakest ties of any higher primate, the strongest adult ties are between a male and female, although orangutan networks seem to be the least modified from the ancestral social structure. In every hominoid social structure, then, the efforts to build network ties seem to be the result of selection pressures for increased sociality and group structure in the face of female migration at puberty. To overcome this problem of migration and dispersal, apes had to fashion ties that are peculiar—and rare—in the primate world. For in creating social relationships, they had to operate within the ape phylogenetic framework derived from the LCA structure.

Thus, by using cladistic analysis to reconstruct the LCA structure, we are able to add some credence to our earlier suggestion that the habitat where the forerunners of modern apes evolved created selection pressures against large, rigid, and cohesive structures. Transfer at puberty and weak tie formation were the mechanisms that seemingly facilitated this process. But as we will attempt to show, genetic propensities that were adaptive for forest-living apes would be a liability for terrestrial, open-country apes. Consequently, early *hominids*—if they were to survive in a predator-ridden savanna environment—would have to develop more cohesive and tightly knit social structures. The result was the development of human culture, or systems of symbols. But it is important to keep in mind that the use of culture to construct ties could potentially contradict humans' primate legacy for rather weak and fluid social bonds.

# 3 /  THE ORIGINS OF
## HUMAN CULTURE

Humans are often regarded as unique because of their ability to use systems of symbols for representation and communication. Language is, of course, the cardinal example of this symbolic supremacy, and all scholars are in agreement that humans vocalize in a unique way. But as Edward Sapir (1933: 13) recognized long ago, human speech is merely the channeling of more fundamental cognitive processes into a suitable modality for symbolic communication. For "while speech as a finished organization is a distinctly human achievement, its roots probably lie in the power of the higher apes to solve specific problems by abstracting general forms or schemata from the details of a given situation" (Sapir 1933: 14). Subsequent research on chimpanzees and gorillas shows that even though apes cannot "speak" in a vocal sense, they are able to acquire and manipulate arbitrary symbols to communicate. Indeed, they appear capable of announcing their intended actions to humans and each other at what appears to be an elementary "linguistic level" (Savage-Rumbaugh 1986; Gardner et al. 1989; Linden 1986).

Although the data are now conclusive that apes are capable of sophisticated symbolic communication, the heated controversy surrounding this line of research is, itself, rather revealing since it reflects the centuries-old effort to keep humans apart from the animal world.[1] For example, in

[1] Few topics in the behavioral sciences have generated as much controversy as ape language research. If language is equated with speech, it can only be viewed as unique. But once language is viewed not as an oral but as a symbolic process that can manifest itself in a variety of modalities (Poizner et al. 1990; Bellugi et al. 1989), the door is opened for research on apes using American Sign Language or artificial languages (e.g., computer buttons or the manipulation of plastic disks). Skepticism about this approach surfaced when H. S. Terrace (1979) and his associates (Terrace et al. 1979) claimed that their linguistically trained chimp, Nim Chimsky, failed to acquire the rules of a grammar and the ability to

1871 Max Müller, the great comparative linguist, wrote: "The one great barrier between the brute and man is *language*. . . . Language is our Rubicon, and no brute will dare to cross it" (p. 403; emphasis in the original). Thus, whether conceptualized as a unique and autonomous "language organ" (e.g., Chomsky 1975, 1980) or as a cognitive capacity that marks a major "discontinuity" with nonhuman primates (e.g., Sebeok and Umiker-Sebeok 1979; Lenneberg 1971), for some scholars language remains the great divide between humans and nonhumans. The intensity of the debate and the level of acrimony among its antagonists signal that perhaps something telic is involved.

For those who are willing to look objectively at the evidence, however, it is apparent that apes (and monkeys and perhaps other higher mammals as well) have the ability to represent objects symbolically and intentionally. Even H. S. Terrace (1985: 1021), whose efforts ignited and fueled the ape language controversy, now contends that "there is little question that apes overlap with human beings . . . with respect to their ability to learn arbitrary rules regarding the use of symbols. . . . Both species learn to make requests by using arbitrary symbols, and both species are able to use symbols to communicate intentionally." Terrace now views the continued criticism as unfortunate, since it only diverts attention away from "the important aspects of an ape's ability to communicate symbolically, however primitive that ability may be" (Terrace 1985: 1011).

The altercation over the "language of the apes" cannot be easily resolved until agreement is reached on what language is. Because the pos-

---

create new sentences with a learned vocabulary. While there are clear methodological problems with Terrace's research (Nim, for example, had over 50 trainers and an unstable environment), and Terrace did *not* conclude that apes are incapable of language, his research was hailed as definitive evidence that language is unique to humans, despite protests from ape language researchers that language capacity may vary by degrees and by ape species (see Savage-Rumbaugh, Rumbaugh, Hopkins, et al. 1986 for a review). Essentially, critics of ape language research do not question that apes can associate symbols and objects, merely whether they can use rules of grammar and vocabulary to create new sentences or use language in a "meaningful" human sense, since apes must be cued and rewarded by researchers. Although this controversy cannot be resolved so long as ape linguistic abilities are equated with "full-blown" human linguistic abilities, new research methods have eliminated most of the ambiguities of the past in interpreting the ape data. Beyond any reasonable doubt it has now been established that (1) apes can learn (after extensive training) large vocabularies of arbitrary symbols and use these symbols referentially for objects not present; and (2) apes can utter learned symbols spontaneously without depending on the cueing of their trainers. They can also learn words from each other, and they can use words to coordinate their joint activities, to alert other apes to new information, and to announce or comment on their intended actions. During the 1980's, a young pygmy chimpanzee (*Pan paniscus*) began to use symbols spontaneously (without explicit training) just by exposure to a linguistic environment, and it also comprehended many spoken English words (for discussions, see Savage-Rumbaugh 1986; Gardner et al. 1989; Savage-Rumbaugh, Rumbaugh, and McDonald 1985).

session of language is typically viewed as an "all or nothing" phenomenon (see Savage-Rumbaugh, Rumbaugh, and McDonald 1985 for a discussion), some scholars believe that a change in emphasis from language per se to the cognitive prerequisites of language is in order (Muncer et al. 1982). They argue that less stress should be placed on language as communication (where humans obviously excel), and more on the cognitive capacities that underlie language production. For whether an animal "has cognitive abilities similar to those required for language is more important than whether it can produce strings that can be given meaning" (Muncer et al. 1982: 1181). Indeed, whatever the underlying cognitive abilities that produce language and culture may be, we should not consider it peculiar that our closest hominoid relatives reveal neurological, cognitive, and "linguistic" capacities similar to our own.

But what are these capacities? Our answer to this question may, at first, seem rather bizarre: the biological basis for language and human culture resides not just in increases in the size and reorganization of the hominid brain but, more specifically, in the elaboration of the association cortex that placed the cortical sense modalities—vision, touch, and hearing—under cortical control and integrated them under cortical processes dominated by our visual sense modality. The biological basis for language, we argue, is not the result of some large mutation, for a break of any magnitude, as R. A. Fisher (1930) noted long ago, would in all likelihood prove maladaptive, especially given the complexity of primate neuroanatomy. Nor can the capacity for culture be explained solely by selection pressures for a primate that could speak and organize itself in terms of symbols, for selection processes must work on small mutations that deviate from what is already genetically present in a species; and in the case of brain physiology, changes must be relatively small but, as we will see, nonetheless decisive. Rather, we must seek the origins of culture in (1) the gradual expansion and reorganization of the neocortex over the older limbic cortex, and (2) the emergence of intra- and cross-modal associations among the cortical sense modalities—touch (somatic in the broader sense), vision, and hearing—that govern higher cognitive functions. Nonhuman primates, notably the Great Apes, went only so far in this evolutionary sequence; and even the earliest known hominid genus, Australopithecus, was more apelike than humanlike in cranial anatomy as reproduced in fossilized endocasts (Falk 1986; Falk, Hildebolt, and Vannier 1989; Fleagle 1988: 416).[2] But endocasts of our own genus, Homo, reveal relatively subtle changes in cerebral evolution, reflected in the ex-

[2] Casts, or endocasts, of the inside of fossilized braincases reproduce the size, shape, and surface patterns of most primate brains. Evolutionary trends can be mapped by comparing these casts to existing primate brains (see Radinsky 1975; Holloway 1978).

pansion of certain regions of the neocortex; and these small quantitative changes produced, under selection pressures, humans' cognitive capacity for language and its elaboration into systems of symbols, or in a word, human *culture* (see Tobias 1987).

## Evolution of the Mammalian Brain

The survival and reproductive success of any organism are dependent on its ability to detect and respond to crucial aspects of its environment, such as meeting food requirements, finding mates, and avoiding predators; and from a neurological perspective, this continual exchange with the environment can be defined as the ability of an organism to receive information and to organize this information in ways that elicit behavioral responses that meet essential physiological demands. And the only possible way an organism can perceive the physical world is through its sensory equipment, which is of course why the sense modalities evolved in the first place (Gans 1986; O'Connor and Hermelin 1981; Coleman 1990).[3]

Throughout most of biological evolution, many organisms have been little more than mechanical sight-and-smell machines with sparse sensory equipment. As a result, they have had little ability for rapid responses or adaptation to environmental change. For example, during the Mesozoic or age of reptiles, the dinosaur detected and responded to environmental stimuli at such a slow pace that as Lord Brain (1965: 703) puts it: "If one had trodden on the tail of a prehistoric dinosaur, it would have taken so long for the resulting nerve impulses to reach its brain that one would at least have time to take one's foot away before it knew what had happened."

### Elaboration of the Brain

A most dramatic change in sensory capacities came about with the rise of placental mammals, beginning about 65 million years ago. This change was represented by a novel six-layered "neocortex" that appeared right on top of a phylogenetically older "limbic lobe" of interconnected neural tissue. A useful metaphor, following Paul MacLean (1990), is to divide

---

[3] The information received through the senses determines how the world appears to any organism. In the words of W. O'Connor and B. Hermelin (1981: 322): "Whatever one thinks about the nature of space perception, our movement in space and manipulation of objects in space are restricted by the development and structure of the appropriate sensory systems and by the nature of the physical world." Thus, an animal that makes primary use of a sense modality that is not dominant in humans, such as the olfactory organ, will form a very different internal representation of the world from ours. (See Passingham 1982: chap. 2 for a discussion of primate sensory equipment.)

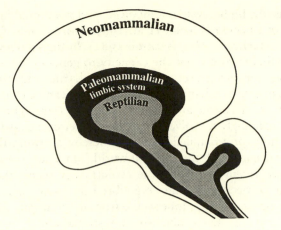

*Fig. 3.* The evolution of the neomammalian brain over the limbic system and the reptilian brain. Adapted from MacLean 1990.

the brains of mammals into the three basic divisions shown in Figure 3: a *protoreptilian brain* (reptilian complex); a *paleomammalian brain* (limbic complex); and a *neomammalian brain* (neocortex and connected thalamic structures). The protoreptilian brain can be characterized as a complex of ancient anatomical structures inherited from early mammal-like reptiles.[4] This most ancient cortex is thought to be involved in stereotyped behaviors such as displays and other primal behavioral patterns (MacLean 1990). The paleomammalian brain, or limbic system, can be characterized as a heterogeneous collection of specialized structures that include the subcortical gustatory modalities and the olfactory organ.[5] In

[4] We know little about the evolution of mammal-like reptiles of 250 million years ago, because there are no extant descendants representing a reptile-to-mammal evolutionary sequence. The consensus is that these lost transitional forms had only a rudimentary neocortex with few subdivisions. The turtle (which has only a cap of general cortex on the dorsal surface of its brain) is thought to have changed least from the basic reptilian stock from which mammal-like reptiles evolved (Haberly 1990; Kass 1987; Romer 1972). The Cenozoic era marked the "Age of Mammals" with the spread of eutherian (placental) mammals, a radiation that peaked during the Miocene, followed by a rather noticeable mammalian decline ever since. (For a detailed discussion of early mammal-like reptiles, or therapsids, see MacLean 1990.)

[5] The brain tissue making up the limbic system was first referred to as "the great limbic lobe" in 1878 by the French anatomist Paul Broca because it formed a border around the brainstem of all mammals. In 1952 the term limbic system was introduced to designate this cortex and directly related structures of the brainstem (MacLean 1990; Isaacson 1982). While a debate exists on which inner-core structures actually compose the limbic system and on whether or not these structures should even be considered a coherent system at all, the term is firmly entrenched in the literature; most scholars describe their results under that rubric. (For discussions, see Isaacson 1982: 2; Horel 1988; L. Swanson 1983.) Although somewhat redundant terminologies are used to characterize the limbic lobe, it includes the

general terms, the limbic system is involved in motivational functions and expressions of emotion (Lovilot et al. 1989; Horel 1988; O'Keefe and Nadel 1978; MacLean 1990; Isaacson 1982). In the words of MacLean (1990), "the limbic cortex has the capacity to generate free-floating, affective feelings conveying a sense of what is real, true, and important." In contrast, the neomammalian brain, or neocortex, can be characterized as the "mother of invention and father of abstract thought" (MacLean 1978: 332). Seemingly it evolved to serve as a better means for problem solving, learning, and detailed memory, thereby allowing the brain to cope more efficiently with the external world (MacLean 1982, 1990).

As the most recent arrival on the evolutionary scene, the neomammalian brain, or neocortex, can be pictured internally as a vast neural landscape composed of four lobes—the frontal, temporal, occipital, and parietal (see Fig. 4).[6] Each lobe contains specialized sensory cells and tissues that process information (Gans 1986; Shepherd 1988). Whereas the limbic zones generally monitor the internal environment and guide behavior for preservative and protective responses, the cortical senses are specialized to monitor and process information about the outside physical world (Mogenson, 1977; MacLean 1990; Isaacson 1982). A principal task of the mammalian sense modalities is to signal the different properties of objects in space, for the ability of an animal to recognize a physical stimulus is vital to its survival (Sutherland 1973: 157; Coleman 1990). In the mammalian case, all four of the major sense modalities are sensitive only to particular kinds of stimulation. The visual system has receptors in the retina that respond to different wave lengths of light; the auditory has receptors in the ear that are sensitive to the frequencies of vibrations activated by sound waves; the generalized somatic sense (especially the tactile sense) has receptors on the skin sensitive to vibrations and to touch; and the olfactory system, which is a noncortical sense and part of the limbic system, has receptors in the nose and is sensitive to airborne chemical substances. Thus, at the sensory level all modalities are quite unlike one

---

amygdaloid complex, septal nuclei, cingulate gyrus, hippocampal complex (including the hippocampus, dentate gyrus, and subicular structures) and olfactory structures (Horel 1988). Our usage is intended in the most general and uncomplicated way to distinguish most of the phylogenetically older "limbic" cortex from the higher order "neocortex." It is important to emphasize, however, that the limbic cortex and the neocortex are highly interconnected systems with ever more complex integrative abilities owing to the elaboration of higher-order association areas, especially in higher primates.

[6] There is no consensus among scholars on what precisely constitutes a cortical area or what criteria should be applied in identifying such areas and distinguishing among them (Van Essen 1985; Phillips et al. 1984). Essentially, regions of the neocortex are defined on the basis of distinct functions on myelinated fibers and on the local organization of cell bodies (see E. White 1989). Most scholars work with the notion that more or less discrete borders exist among cortical zones. In fact, through a variety of research techniques, more and more borders are becoming evident (Rapporteur et al. 1988).

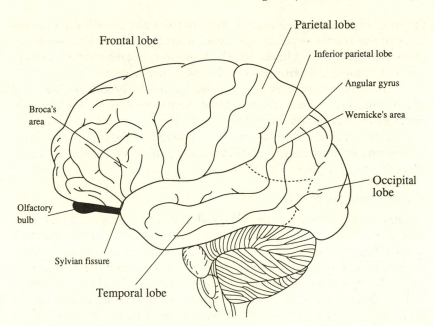

Parietal lobe

Frontal lobe

Inferior parietal lobe

Angular gyrus

Broca's
area

Wernicke's area

Occipital
lobe

Olfactory
bulb

Sylvian fissure

Temporal lobe

*Fig. 4.* Some key areas of the human brain

another; each evolved to detect different qualities of an object, which must then be integrated for object recognition (for discussions see Somjen 1983; Shepherd 1988; D. Wilson and Leon 1989).

Of course, an organism's ability to construct the properties of physical stimuli is highly variable; and the degree of sophistication of sensory equipment seems directly related to the perceptual demands of an adaptive zone (Hodos 1986).[7] But no matter how complex the sense modality, no organism, including the human animal, is capable of perceiving all possible qualities of objects.[8]

The fact that all organisms are so limited has led to the recognition that

[7] The idea that the anatomy of a species' brain might reflect its adaptation to a particular habitat, especially for such major regions as the sensory and motor centers, has received increasing support from both ecologists and morphologists (see Stephan et al. 1988). But it has also become increasingly evident that the neocortex of different species, including humans, is structured and built according to a common, basic plan (see E. White 1989; Passingham 1985).

[8] Research in neurophysiology has increasingly led to the rejection of the notion that our sensory experiences are either identical with or even similar to objects in absolute space (Brain 1965). For example, though the human visual system is a highly evolved sensory organ, the optic nerve can pass only a limited number of signals to the brain for further processing (Werblin 1976: 21). Since it is not possible to detect absolute reality, our construction of physical space may indeed be largely a product of the complexity of our central nervous system, as K. W. Craik (1943) suggested long ago.

the sense organs may "choose" to transmit what is of biological importance to the animal, especially in regard to its behavioral adaptation to a
given ecological niche (Julesz 1976).[9] Moreover, because of their perceptual limitations, the sense organs do not concern themselves generally
with the absolute features of an object (absolute brightness, absolute
sound, etc.) but instead abstract from environmental stimuli the relational properties of objects by focusing on the more constant and stable
characters. Thus, it is the *pattern of arrangement* of the parts, rather than
their absolute properties, that allows an organism to recognize objects
(Rensch 1967; Sutherland 1973: 161).

## The Operation of the Neocortex

In trying to understand the biological basis of language and culture, a
little working knowledge of the neocortex is necessary; for this structure
is what sets mammals apart from other organisms and humans apart
from other mammals.[10] Although the neocortex varies by species in size,
regional proportions, fissures and sulci patterns (i.e., infoldings or clefts),
and specialized areas, in an elementary and traditional sense it can be
classified into (1) *primary* cortex that encompasses the primary motor,
auditory, visual, and somatic sense organs; and (2) *association* cortex
that encompasses the remaining areas (Pandya et al. 1988). In simple
mammals the neocortex is composed mostly of primary tissue, whereas in
advanced mammals the bulk of the neocortex is composed of association
tissue (Kass 1987). For humans, association tissue makes up almost
95 percent of the neocortex (McGeer et al. 1987: 596).

As the neocortex expanded in primates, the association cortex itself
became more specialized and involved in a variety of functions. For
example, the association tissue in the vicinity of primary sensory cells
is specialized to provide additional or supplementary information that fa-
cilitates the complex processing of "unimodal" sensory information
(Shepherd 1988: 628; Horel 1988). Other zones of association cortex are
also specialized for "multimodal" sensory processing (where information
from several modalities converge) and "supramodal" processing (where
information from multimodal areas converge). While the complete layout
for even the simplest neocortex is still uncharted, the progressive differ-

[9] Some experiments have documented a kind of "selectivity" in what the human visual
system perceives. The failure of the visual organ to transmit many properties of objects suggests that these attributes were seemingly irrelevant to the survival of the very remote ancestors of humans (Julesz 1976: 37–38).

[10] Few scholars would disagree with the conclusion that what sets humans apart is the
elaboration of the neocortex, especially the association cortex (Rakic 1988). Investigators
have found a strong relationship between the prominence of the neocortex and greater neural plasticity.

entiation of neocortical areas is related to a concomitant elaboration of intracortical connections.[11] Thus, the phylogenetic trend for some mammalian lines has been toward a higher-order cortex with regions that communicate and interact with each other. This trend culminated in humans, where the neocortex can be viewed as a structure "that speaks primarily with itself" (Braitenberg 1977).

In discussions of cortical functions, the sensory modalities assume a crucial importance because they are the vanguard for the representation of information at the cortical level (Cook 1986: 160). In mammals like higher primates, when a cortical receptor is excited by an appropriate environmental stimulus, it stimulates a nerve fiber, which then carries a nerve impulse to the sensory zone concerned with the processing of that stimuli. Once this relatively "raw" input reaches a primary sensor, it cascades through a chain of cortico-cortical connections where incoming sensory information is processed sequentially through connecting association cortex. Finally, in order to be provided with meaning and emotional significance, all sensory information must eventually be conveyed to areas that link up with limbic structures (Horel 1988; Amaral and Price 1984; Mesulam 1983). In neurophysiological terms, this connection can be called a cortico-limbic association. For example, a cortico-limbic association takes place when a monkey is presented with a visual stimulus, such as pressing the correct button, in order to receive a food reward. Here, the animal performs a cortico-limbic cross-modal connection in that the visual (a cortical modality) is in a direct association with a limbic modality (a gustatory modality). Moreover, any higher mammal can learn to respond to multimodal stimuli, such as those activating both the visual and the auditory organs, so long as it makes a parallel visual-limbic and auditory-limbic association (Geschwind 1965: 250).

Humans easily make cortico-limbic associations. For example, any human can associate a refrigerator (a cortico-visual) stimulus with a food reward (limbic-gustatory), and a young child can associate the touching of a hot stove (cortico-touch modality) with burnt fingers (pain-limbic modality). Moreover, like all primates, humans emit limbic controlled vocal responses, such as screaming, crying, and laughing, that are laden with emotion (and when they are not, such as when someone forces laughter without genuine affect, people are usually aware of the difference). But human cortical modalities (and those of some higher primates,

[11] Neocortical expansion in advanced mammals has been well investigated in domestic cats as well as in New and Old World monkeys (see Kass 1987). For example, among macaque monkeys, which have the distinction of being the most investigated primate in neuroanatomy research, the primary sensory cortices send "cortico-cortical" projects to, and receive projections from, the monkey's supplementary association cortex; in turn, these secondary areas project to more distant cortical areas (Pandya et al. 1988).

especially apes) are not confined to making associations only with limbic modalities. For in addition to cortico-limbic associations, the human neocortex allows the sense organs to intermingle by exchanging information through cross-modal matching and transfer in the specialized multimodal zones discussed earlier. That is, the human neocortex has the capacity not only to integrate sensory information in order to present a unified picture of the world, but also to manipulate and elaborate incoming sensory information by making direct *intramodal* (e.g., visual-visual) and *intermodal* (e.g., visual-auditory) associations. Thus, while the olfactory modality in humans is directly linked to limbic structures, neocortical nerve signals first project through masses of association cortex, undergoing a variety of complex transformations within the neocortex, before connecting with limbic structures in order to be tagged with an affective or emotional label (see Horel 1988; McGeer et al. 1987).

In summary, the elaboration of sensory and association cortices appears to be crucial to the emergence of language and culture. For over time the evolutionary trend for some mammals has been to increase the capacity to associate the sense modalities directly with one another. This development led to cross-modal sensory equivalence, so that an object recognized in one modality could be represented in another.

## Evolution of the Primate Brain

As we noted in Chapter 2, problems of interpretation abound in the reconstruction of primate evolution. To some degree this is true of most reconstruction dependent on fragmentary fossilized material, but documentation of the primate order is especially onerous because a forest niche is highly unfavorable to fossilization. Yet, on the basis of large samples of dental remains and some skeletal materials, the fossil record suggests that the primates first appeared in the Paleocene epoch about 60 million years ago (Covert 1986; R. Martin 1990b; Gingerich, 1990), having evolved originally from a group of long-snouted mammalian insectivores (C. Campbell 1969; W. Hill 1972; Szalay and Delson 1979). The present-day tree shrew (Tupaia) probably resembles this ancient primitive Insectivora. Because of its tiny size and phyletic distinctiveness, the position of this small mammal in the primate order is debated (see Zeller 1986; Simmons 1988; R. Martin 1990a), but from a neurological perspective, the tree shrew is an early example of the evolutionary trend for neocortical expansion and "cortex-centered behavior" (Mayr 1963; Simmons 1988; Stephen et al. 1988), for it has such neuroanatomical primate features as a reduced olfactory apparatus, an enhanced visual apparatus, a distinct temporal lobe, and a noticeable expansion of the neocortex—all of which clearly separate it from the basal insectivore (Simmons 1988; Lavelle et al. 1977). Seemingly, ascendance into an arboreal niche initiated dramatic neurophysiological changes.[12] As Stanley Cobb (1965: 556) and others have emphasized, this primate adaptation involved a neocortical expansion that allowed for rapid adaptation to new situations and avoided the problem of developing a highly specialized body form. This elaboration of the new cortex also created connections within, and among, the tactile, auditory, and visual sensory paths.

The rise of the primate order thus represents a trend against highly specialized morphological structures and toward neurological specialization for the cortical processing of information. Since this evolutionary trend started when prosimians (pre-monkeys and apes) took up an arboreal lifestyle, the evolution of a brain that could produce culture began some 60 million years ago.

One of the oldest primate endocranial casts is *Tetonius homunculus*, a small, early Eocene prosimian approximately 55 million years old (Tattersall et al. 1988; Radinsky 1979). According to Harry Jerison (1973: 38), this endocast is broader and more spherical than that of other Paleocene and Eocene mammals, a development that enables a species like *Tetonius* "to pack a larger volume of brain within a given volume of skull." Jerison further notes (p. 372) that these differences indicate that "some of the earliest of the primate specializations were specifically related to the expansion of the brain." L. B. Radinsky (1970: 209) has similarly emphasized that *Tetonius* was "remarkably advanced for its time [with] enlarged occipital and temporal lobes . . . and reduced olfactory bulbs." Indeed, Radinsky argues that "the presence of these sensory specializations in such an ancient primate as *Tetonius* [suggests] that they may have been among the critical adaptations responsible for the Eocene radiation of primates" (Radinsky 1970: 210–11; see also Radinsky 1975). Finally, K. D. Rose and J. G. Fleagle (1987: 62) concur that the presence of expanded occipital and temporal lobes suggests "a visually, rather than olfactorily, oriented animal" because in living primates much of the temporal lobe, and all of the occipital lobe, are devoted to processing visual information (see Allman and McGuinness 1988).

After *Tetonius*, another fossil prosimian for which endocranial anatomy can be determined is *Smilodectes gracilis* (middle Eocene and about

[12] The evolutionary origins of major taxa are normally discussed in terms of new adaptive features and new adaptive zones. Although some extant primates are terrestrial, the scholarly consensus is that all primates are descendants of arboreal ancestors. Following Jenkins 1987, an arboreal habitat is considered an innovative adaptive zone for primates because, unlike some mammals that move between ground and trees, ancestral primates specialized by restricting themselves to an arboreal zone. For an alternative "visual predation" theory of primate evolution, see Cartmill 1974.

50 million years old). Compared with other fossilized Eocene mammals, this primate has very advanced features, including the expansion of the visual cortex (Radinsky 1975). Radinsky also notes that this prosimian was "extraordinarily specialized for its time in the degree to which the neocortex was expanded and the olfactory bulbs reduced" (Radinsky 1970: 211; see also Radinsky 1977; K. Rose and Fleagle 1987). We might also consider the available casts of other early primates such as *Adapis parisiensis* (late Eocene, 45 to 40 million years ago), *Necrolemus antiquus* (contemporary of *Adapis*), and *Rooneyia viejaenis* (early Oligocene, about 35 million years ago), but we need only state that all these fossils underscore a continuing expansion of the neocortex and its cortical senses, with a concomitant reduction in the olfactory bulbs (for comprehensive discussions, see K. Rose and Fleagle 1987; Falk 1986; Radinsky 1970, 1975; Conroy 1990). The essential point is that an expanding neocortex, especially in regard to the amount of area devoted to visual cortex, is a distinguishing primate characteristic.

While endocasts of extinct prosimians provide direct evidence of early primate development (see Holloway 1978: 182), we are forced to study the brains of existing prosimians to interpret subsequent evolutionary trends (Radinsky 1970: 209, 1975). Such interpretation assumes a "basal insectivore" as represented by the tenrecs (Tenrecidae), hedgehogs (Erinaceidae), and shrews (Soricidae; see Stephan and Andy 1970). Since these animals show the very least degree of change since their first appearance, they provide a point of reference for comparing subsequent evolutionary trends in primates, especially in regard to the development of the primate neocortex (Lavelle et al. 1977: 30).[13]

A comparison of the brains of present-day prosimians with those of a basal insectivore reveals a general heightening and expansion of the cortical senses, especially in the parietal area (Critchley 1969: 2; see also Fig. 4). In fact, on average, prosimians have fourteen and a half times as much neocortex as a basal insectivore of comparable body weight (Ste-

[13] The significance of relative brain size and its usefulness as a measure of intelligence and other parameters have been a subject of controversy (see Radinsky 1982 for a cautionary discussion). Also, the dearth of primate fossil endocasts prevents a clear picture of primate brain evolution. Insectivore brains are small, with a tiny neocortex and almost nonexistent neocortical folds. We should stress that we are not suggesting that prosimians have advanced or even large brains (which is untrue relative to carnivores and ungulates); rather, we are trying to document what is clearly a primate trend in the expansion of the neocortical lobes for particular sensory specializations. That is, following Kaas and Pons (1988: 458), the trend in the primate order from prosimians to humans reflects "successively higher levels of behavioral and neural development," especially at the cortical level. Fossil endocasts of early primates in conjunction with brain research on basal insectivores and living primates are able to provide direct evidence on these sensory trends in primate evolution (e.g., an increase in the visual cortex and a concomitant decrease in olfactory cortex). See Allman and McGuinness 1988 for a lengthy discussion.

phan and Andy 1970; Radinsky 1975). This early and sudden elaboration of the parietal area in the lower primates was sufficient to change the arrangement of the brain, pushing the visual cortex backward and the auditory area downward. Concomitant to the increase in the size of the neocortex was a general decrease in the olfactory system, although the prosimians still retain, as do most mammals, bulbus olfactorius as the chief sense organ (see Stephan and Andy 1970). Moreover, Radinsky (1968) finds an outbulging of certain areas of the neocortex in indriids (a family of lemur prosimians), which he attributes to an enlargement of the motor hand area compared with other lemurs. In conjunction with this change, indriids have more advanced frontalization of the eyes for stereoscopic vision than other lemurs and, interestingly, also have the greatest reduction in the olfactory bulb of any prosimian (Sanides 1970: 158; Stephan and Andy 1970: 120). Friedrich Sanides interprets these evolutionary changes in indriids as marking an early indication of a trend towards a prehensile hand and stereoscopic vision (prosimians have only limited stereoscopic vision, to 10 feet, and do not have prehensile limbs), and suggests that this first occurrence of integration (hand-eye coordination) "is bound to the steadily growing parietal integration cortex of primates, culminating in man" (Sanides 1970: 158).

To summarize, the first primate radiation is evidenced by an expansion of the neocortex reflected in a general heightening of motor and sensory zones, along with a decrease in olfactory bulbs. Although we do not know what specific selection pressures brought about these changes, the increase in motor cortex for movement and feeding in a three-dimensional environment would have facilitated adaptation. Some scholars suggest that early prosimians were relatively unspecialized in locomotion (e.g., R. Martin 1990a: 477), but others argue on the basis of hindlimb morphology that ancestral prosimians evolved a form of locomotion known as vertical clinging and leaping, or jumping locomotion, similar to the form widespread among their living descendants (Walker 1974: 376; Conroy 1990: 92ff; Napier and Walker 1987). This type of precise muscular movement, an indicator of an arboreal lifestyle, would place enormous emphasis on vision and perfected coordination of body movement; it would also require the perfection of a grasping foot, a feature that, as J. W. Gidley (1919) long ago contended, was in place before the prehensile hand.

There is limited fossil evidence on the radiation of higher primates— that is, simians (monkeys and apes)—out of prosimian stock (Simons 1990).[14] The data suggest that primitive simian forms first appeared in the

[14] The origin and history of anthropoids remain elusive and controversial. F. S. Szalay and E. Delson (1979: 189) suggest that a tarsier form gave rise to the anthropoids. The

late Eocene or early Oligocene (about 35 million years ago), and that anthropoids are African in origin (Kay and Simons 1987; Simons 1984, 1990; Tuttle 1988). In studying the few available endocasts from Fayum Oligocene deposits (about 32 million years ago), Radinsky (1975, 1979) concludes that, relative to prosimians, early anthropoids reveal an enlargement of the visual cortex and a reduced olfactory bulb, suggesting "an increased emphasis on vision and a decreased emphasis on smell" (1975: 156). These features have remained characteristic of living monkeys and apes (see also Simons 1990). With the displacement of prosimians by anthropoid forms (i.e., the prosimians became either nocturnal or confined to Madagascar), the primate order was further distinguished from ground-living mammals in a number of important ways. First, there was an elaboration of neocortex. For example, the neocortical structure of living monkeys is on the average about 45 times as large as that of basal insectivores (Stephan and Andy 1970: 113). Second, the olfactory bulb, as noted earlier, became measurably smaller than in prosimians. Although the olfactory system does not necessarily have to be reduced as the neocortex expands (the modern elephant, for example, has both a well-developed neocortex and a large olfactory system), it is likely that the anthropoid snout inhibited guidance in an arboreal world. Third, there was a marked shift in sensory modes as selection pressures favored the continued expansion of the visual modality and the reduction of the olfactory (Stephan and Andy 1970; Valverde 1985: 210). This trend represents a most extraordinary and revolutionary event, involving much more than the eventual supplanting of one sense modality by another. Recall that the olfactory organ in all mammals projects directly to the limbic system, and thus information received in this older forebrain center is primarily used to guide the behavior of an animal with regard to two life principles: the preservation of the self and the preservation of the species (MacLean 1990: 17). In contrast, information received from the visual modality is projected directly to the neocortex, a structure primarily geared toward understanding a variable and changing external environment, not internal emotional states. Thus, an emphasis on visually guided

---

oldest catarrhines (Old World monkeys and apes) are represented by newly discovered fossils from the Fayum badlands of Egypt, probably of late Eocene age (Simons 1990). The collection includes a crushed cranium with a postorbital closure, suggesting an emphasis on the visual modality. Although fragmentary specimens that are perhaps anthropoids have been found in Burma (see Ciochon et al. 1985), the Fayum late-Oligocene deposits remain the only rich early anthropoid site. A major problem is how to link these primitive anthropoids to later "true" Miocene monkeys and apes. M. G. Leakey and colleagues (1991) have proposed that recently discovered Fayum cranial materials provide the first good evidence of a strong phenetic link (i.e., based solely on similarity of phenotypes) between Oligocene and Miocene hominoidea.

behavior would tend to suppress species-specific emotional behavior, while promoting purposeful responses in dealing with the external environment (MacLean 1990: 17).

This dramatic change in the nature of sensory input made the primates a cortical step removed from most other mammals. What began as an increasing dominance of the visual organ over the olfactory in information processing was to culminate in the capacity to represent the world symbolically and use language. This neocortical expansion among contemporary monkeys can be demonstrated by comparing a New World genus called Callithrix (or marmoset) with two prosimian genera, Tarsius and Galago. While individual body size remains constant among the three, the marmoset's *absolute brain weight* is three times greater (Lavelle et al. 1977: 7; see also Stephan et al. 1988). Thus, despite the paucity of fossil material, we can reasonably posit a trend in primate evolution toward increasing development of the cortical modalities, particularly the visual. The neurological effects of this trend can best be assessed by reviewing the available data on each of the modalities in present-day Old World monkeys (especially since the neurological data on primates is largely drawn from experiments on macaques).

Let us take up the auditory system to begin with. If the absolute size of a cortical zone is any measure of its importance, the auditory cortex would seem to be of secondary importance for information processing. Although precise boundaries are unknown, nonhuman primate auditory fields are seemingly restricted to the banks of the Sylvian fissure (Masterton and Diamond 1973: 416; Kass 1987: 366; Heffner and Heffner 1990).[15] The data suggest that the primate auditory cortex has had a "conservative evolutionary history," with most higher primates sharing a basic structural design, despite different primate radiations (see Newman 1988 for a comprehensive discussion). A primary function of the ear in both human and nonhuman primates is to serve as a wide-ranging "early warning device" that localizes sounds, and in turn, alerts the visual system (Khanna and Tonndorf 1978). The visual system then normally attends to the object in space. For example, the primate auditory system is specialized to aid in the detection of abrupt and brief sounds like the

[15] Although larger cortical regions usually indicate more complex functioning, we should emphasize that the auditory system is a delicate and elaborate organ that is crucial for primate survival, in part because of its inherent tendency to respond to brief and abrupt sounds. This alerting function is believed so essential to primate survival that "it is virtually impossible to truncate the central auditory system in such a way as to make an animal completely incapable of responding to a brief sound. For if even a few fibers . . . are left intact and the remainder are sectioned completely, auditory evoked activity can still reach motor structures throughout the central nervous system (Masterton and Diamond 1973: 431). Thus, auditory stimuli activate a wide network of intricate neural pathways (see Strominger 1978).

thumps, snaps, cracks, thuds, and pops that mark animated movement and potential danger. All primates respond to brief, abrupt sounds as if their source were animate, whereas they tend to assume that continuous, periodic, or legato sounds are part of general background noise and, hence, not worthy of a response (Masterton and Diamond 1973: 419–20). Additionally, the primate auditory cortex is used to identify vocal sounds such as macaque monkey "coo" calls (Heffner and Heffner 1990).

An important change in the primate auditory organ is a loss of high frequency sensitivity and a corresponding increase in sensitivity to low frequencies (B. Campbell 1985a: 220). William Stebbins (1971: 187) feels that this loss of sensitivity is one of "the most striking changes in the evolution of the primates." He also argues (p. 186) that, in regard to the hearing potential of all higher primates, the "final stages of human hearing have taken place in the primates, and thus, it is not surprising that the difference in auditory sensitivity between man and nonhuman primates is small" (see also Khanna and Tonndorf 1978; Newman 1988).

Turning to the visual modality, we note the two principal features of the higher primate visual system in monkeys, pongids, and humans: stereoscopic perception and retina specialization for detailed and fine-tuned color perception. Although many mammals have some binocular vision, the phenomenon of viewing objects as separated from one another by air space, as in the stereoscopic experience, reaches its maximum development in the higher primates (B. Campbell 1985a: 84). Yet the actual experience of simple depth perception is a rather mechanical process, created when two eyes in a particular geometrical relationship to each other both perceive the same object in space, causing a visual disparity.[16] But this mechanical process set into motion a host of complicated neurological changes in the visual cortex. One important change was the expansion of the cortical motor zones for precise coordination of the two eyes, with the disparity of images leading to the overlapping or fusion of images (Ogle 1962a, b).[17] Moreover, because binocular vision provides for only the relative distance between two externally perceived objects, selection pressure must have been intense for visual association zones to store visual memories on the distances of objects from each other and ego.[18]

[16] The forward set of the eyes, which makes such disparity possible, is associated with a decrease in the size of the muzzle and a reduction of the olfactory bulb (Lavelle et al. 1977: 53).

[17] Experiments show that the two images need not fuse for the stereoscopic experience. This is one reason why we have a dominant eye; one eye must perceive the "real" image to prevent spatial disharmony (Ogle 1962a, b).

[18] Learned experiences provide secondary depth cues, especially critical in the recognition of objects as stable over time. Since the seemingly fluctuating size of an object according to

Binocular vision is activated when a two-dimensional stimulus of light falls on the two retinas (Robson 1975: 82–3). The kind of image, and how well objects in the real world are perceived, will depend on the number of rods and cones to detect and distinguish the details of form and shape. In primates the rich number of cones signals very high daylight acuity (Noback and Laemle 1970: 57). Additionally, color perception allows primates to perceive contrasts or differences in brightness in adjacent areas, and it is for this reason that higher primates can perceive the intricate details of objects and scenes (F. Campbell and Maffer 1976: 30). The fovea (which among primates is a specialization found only in tarsiers, monkeys, apes, and humans) is another important feature of the primate retina, for it is highly specialized to detect fine detail, especially near the eyes (Fleagle 1988: 24; Rodieck 1988). This component of the primate visual system is considered to be the "anatomical basis for visual acuity" (Le Grand 1975: 10; for discussions of the retina, see Werblin 1976; Rodieck 1988).

Thanks to these elaborations, the visual system became the primates' paramount sense (Wolin and Massopust 1970: 1; Noback and Laemle 1970: 55; Valverde 1985; B. Campbell 1985a: 86; Forbes and King 1982). In fact, binocular vision and a highly specialized retina made vision in primates so powerful that "most primates . . . depend almost entirely upon their vision both for orientation in space and for recognition of objects" (De Valois and Jacobs 1971: 108). Anatomically, this dependence on vision is confirmed by the very large proportion of information fed into the primate central nervous system from the optic nerve.

Turning to the generalized somatic system, we find that touch is only one of the very general body senses related to the expansion of the parietal lobe in primates. Sensitive somatic receptors are located in the skin, muscles, and joints; and they transmit necessary information to the parietal lobe for fine sensorimotor coordination. With the higher primates came selection pressure on the somatic senses for greater maintenance of balance, probably because the arboreal zone of anthropoids required a repertoire of navigational skills beyond those possessed by prosimians. Prosimians reveal a hand-and-foot locomotion adaptation, in which the hand is used only for grasping (Napier and Walker 1987; Walker 1974). In contrast, monkeys evidence a hand-and-foot locomotion best suited to gripping branches and a quadrupedal form of propulsion. The adaptive radiation of higher primates from a prosimian lineage was probably a function of their movement onto the branches of trees. This movement

---

its distance from the observer would create perceptual disharmony in an already precarious arboreal environment, learning and memory for secondary cues would seemingly have great selective advantage.

would, in turn, stimulate selection for anatomical changes as well as the expansion of cortical motor zones necessary for the coordination of quadrupedal locomotion (see von Bonin 1952: 137–38; W. Hill 1972; Vilensky 1989). Additionally, the evolution of the prehensile hand in anthropoids argues for the initial beginnings of finely tuned touch discrimination. Monkeys are noted for their precise manipulation of the prehensile hand in grooming conspecifics, whereas prosimians groom only with the mouth. This greater grooming ability requires an expansion of motor cortex for the very delicate motions involved in grasping and plucking small insects and other objects.

In sum, then, the rise of higher primates saw the reduction of the olfactory bulbs and a dramatic heightening of the visual modality and its eventual establishment as the sovereign organ (Radinsky 1974; see also R. Martin 1990a: 354; Wolpoff 1980: 47). This shift in dominance meant most information from the environment would be projected to a cortical organ rather than the olfactory limbic organ. This alteration was seemingly produced by adaptation to an arboreal niche, a transfer that activated selection pressures for greater sensitivity to a third dimension—depth. The move into a new habitat set into motion a host of highly intricate neurological changes that not only gave primates the ability to discern the pattern and composition of their environment, but allowed them very precise data about the properties of objects occupying space in a three-dimensional world. These transformations represented an extraordinary evolutionary advance with unprecedented implications for the continued expansion of association areas of the cortex. All of these changes required increased reliance on learning and memory, which in turn meant more purposeful, flexible, and voluntary behavioral responses.

As measured by a greater capacity to learn complex tasks and to demonstrate more flexible behavioral patterns, apes are more intelligent than monkeys (Lavelle et al. 1977: 32; Temerin and Cant 1983). At least two structural features account for this difference. For one thing, in vertebrates, larger species have absolutely larger brains and are able to learn more complicated tasks than related species of smaller size (Rensch 1956: 91). For another, apes have complex anatomical traits that clearly distinguish them from all monkeys. As discussed in Chapter 2, the early Miocene apes of approximately 20 million years ago (i.e., the earliest true hominoids) resembled contemporary monkeys in many postcranial features (see Conroy 1990: 200ff; Fleagle 1988: 363–73). Anatomically, monkeys are rather generalized in skeletal structure, with a tail for balance and short fore- and hindlimbs—a morphology that works to support above-branch locomotion. In contrast, modern apes (and humans), as discussed earlier, are rather specialized in skeletal anatomy, with a short trunk, no tail, relatively free movement of the wrist for rotation, and long limbs of unequal length—an unusual morphology that promotes below-branch locomotion and the use of the forelimbs for suspension and propulsion (see Andrews 1981; Temerin and Cant 1983; Swartz 1989).[19]

The ability of hominoids to support themselves by the front limbs (all monkeys require some other support) required, first of all, rather strong finger flexion, for if the hand is to suspend the body like hanging fruit, it must be formed into a kind of hook (Oxnard 1963: 166). Second, the hand (instead of the foot in monkeys) must be capable of propelling the body through space. Third, feeding or locomotion using forelimb suspension alone required an extreme range of supination (Gregory 1916), which made necessary a specialized and distinct wrist joint (Fleagle 1988). Finally, the loss of the substantial support of four limbs and reliance on the scant support of two limbs would favor increased cortical control over motor movements (Holloway 1968; Corruccini et al. 1975). Forelimb dominance would also favor a refined sense of touch. Cues to surface texture—that is, to temperature, roughness, elasticity, stickiness, slipperiness—and a general recognition of size, form, weight, and what lies under the surface of objects would be of great advantage to an arboreal animal dependent, for example, on determining the support capacity of a tree branch.

These changes in locomotion, especially of hand, wrist, and haptic sensory capacities, are seemingly associated with changes in hominoid brain size and structure. For all that essentially distinguishes the nonhuman hominoid brain from the monkey brain is the elaborate fissuration that buries 25–30 percent of the cortical surface (B. Campbell 1974: 262), and allows a very large quantitative expansion of neocortex (Stephan et al. 1988: 24). Of special interest in this connection is a large cleft on the external surfaces of the hemispheres called the Sylvian fissure, where the mean length on the left side is greater than on the right side. This asymmetry, characteristic of all apes and humans, is present also in the brains of some New and Old World monkeys (LeMay and Geschwind 1975; P. Heilbroner and Holloway 1989; LeMay 1985; Yeni-Komshian and

---

[19] Whereas brachiation is a novel and highly specialized form of locomotion and is associated with gibbonlike ricochetal arm swinging, animals with forelimb-dominant locomotion must have very efficient, mobile grasping forelimbs to suspend themselves entirely by two limbs and, if necessary, to perform hand-over-hand movement with the trunk held vertical. Although some New and Old World monkeys can move about using only their forelimbs, they must also use their tail for balance, and their anatomy still reflects a basic quadrupedal skeletal structure. The hominoids are distinct and represent nonquadrupedal locomotive movement in the ancestral lineage (see Napier 1963; see also Corruccini et al. 1975 for an analysis of wrist morphology and locomotor behavior).

Benson 1976; Falk 1978, 1986). But the asymmetry is less pronounced in monkeys (P. Heilbroner and Holloway 1989: 210), and only in apes and humans is there a further asymmetry in the height of the Sylvian point, suggesting an evolutionary trend in cortical complexity.

What makes this asymmetry so intriguing is that the major language areas in humans (i.e., Broca's area and Wernicke's area, to be discussed shortly) lie along the borders of the left Sylvian fissure. Additionally, the adjacent inferior parietal lobule appears to be a "supramodal" processing area for cortico-cortical connections in higher primates (see Fig. 4). For example, a recent study of several regions within the inferior parietal lobe of macaque monkeys (*Macaca fascicularis* and *M. mulatta*) revealed "a densely interconnected network of connections between large numbers of brain regions" (Andersen et al. 1990: 66; see also Horel 1988). In humans, an architectonic analysis of the inferior parietal lobule suggests an asymmetry in favor of the left hemisphere in the angular gyrus, a subregion that is relatively small in apes compared with humans (Galaburda 1984: 17; B. Campbell 1985b: 341). This zone contains multimodal sensory neurons and sits at the junction of the neighboring occipital (for visual), temporal (for auditory and visual), and parietal (for somatic) areas. Seemingly it functions as a kind of "association of association" zone, or integration region for all sensory systems; and it is believed to be important in aiding cross-modal associations (Noback and Maskowitz 1963: 156; Geschwind 1965; B. Campbell 1985b: 341; Dunaif-Hattis 1984: 43). Evidently, the angular gyrus region in humans is necessary for vocal language, serving as a "connecting station" for the linking up of an auditory sound with a visual object in space (B. Campbell, 1985b: 341).

Such sensory linkages in the anthropoid brain probably began with enhanced associations between the visual and haptic senses. This progressive trend in neocortical expansion can be seen in the cross-modal abilities of monkeys and apes. Although monkeys can make cross-modal associations, Great Apes have a dramatically greater capacity for doing so; and it is this additional capacity, we argue, that allows them to represent the world symbolically (Ettlinger 1977; Jarvis and Ettlinger 1977; Passingham 1982: 51–52).[20]

Subsequent to the pongid-hominid divergence, the brain tripled in size

---

[20] It is likely that a shift to a suspensory form of locomotion initiated further selection for cortical development in apes. Forelimb-dominant locomotion requires much greater motor control for precise movement because, unlike the relatively routinized motion of monkeys (Corruccini et al. 1975: 251), the ape pattern requires much greater emphasis on individually learned navigational skills. Such learning would depend on remembering the distance of objects and interpreting the significance of touch and feel; as a result, the visual and haptic senses would need to be better integrated in order to prevent sensory disharmony. This integration would, in turn, necessitate an expansion of association areas in the neocortex.

during a very brief evolutionary period—from 1.8 million years ago, with the ascendance of early Homo (*Homo habilis*), to the emergence of *Homo sapiens* in the vicinity of 100,000 years ago (Poirier 1987; Relethford 1990; Tuttle 1988).[21] Even with this enormous expansion in the size of the brain in hominids,[22] no new structures have been discovered in the human brain. Rather, as Stephen Gabow (1977: 647) points out, "there is abundant evidence of the restructuring of size relationships and functional interactions between different brain parts." Clearly, the magnitude of the increase in the size, complexity, and evolved integrative functions of the association cortex in humans made vast differences in the amount of information that could be stored and processed and in the sophistication of behavioral responses.

To understand the emergence of speech, language, and culture, however, we need not explore in detail the Homo brain. Rather, we will focus on the mechanisms of cross-modal connections among the sense modalities, especially vision, touch, and hearing. One such mechanism is a hierarchy of the senses, with the visual modality acting as the chief and guiding sense, and in so doing, having a strong influence on the information pickup of the auditory and tactile senses.[23] The visual sense in humans (and nonhuman primates) appears to be the most effective way to acquire spatial information, with the result that space is primarily represented in visual terms where objects exist within a three-dimensional visual field

[21] Many scholars recognize three species of Homo: *Homo habilis*; *H. erectus*; and *H. sapiens*. Controversy exists, however, on whether *H. habilis* is an advanced Australopithecus, an early Homo, or a transitional hominid (Fleagle 1988: 435). We consider *H. habilis* to be an early Homo because its average cranial capacity is between 600 and 650 cc, and new data hint at speech functions (Tobias 1987), though it otherwise retains many australopithecine features. *H. erectus* is not a controversial Homo and is normally characterized as having a cranial capacity of between 700 and 1,200 cc. Although the oldest *erectus* remains come from Africa, it was a widely distributed hominid. Seemingly its cranial morphology changed little over almost a million years (R. Leakey 1989). Dates for the emergence of anatomically modern *Homo sapiens* are still controversial; the best-dated remains come from South Africa (Tuttle 1988; Stringer 1989).

[22] The use of hominid here refers to any early taxa on the Homo lineage or side branch of this lineage after the divergence of Pan and Gorilla.

[23] Preference for the visual modality over another modality in a sensory conflict situation is known as the "visual capture" phenomenon. Irvin Rock (1966) has demonstrated that when pitted against each other, vision dominates touch. In fact, Rock argues that even when the visual system provides discrepant information in experimental situations, subjects tend to report "that objects felt precisely the way they looked" (p. 243). Subsequent studies support these findings (Freides 1974; Bower et al. 1970). Preference for vision over auditory takes place when a spatial discrepancy exists between a visual source and an auditory source. Both signals are usually perceived as coming from the visual source. This is what occurs, for example, when a ventriloquist's dummy "speaks" and is the basis for the illusion (Cloe et al. 1975). However, the degree to which vision will override another modality in sensory conflict depends on the task required. For example, vision is superior for spatial processing on the size, shape, or location of an object, but in fine-texture discrimination, touch may complement or even capture vision.

(O'Connor and Hermelin 1981). While important in their own right, the auditory and tactile modalities serve as complementary systems for recognizing the attributes of objects in space, especially when the processing capacity of the visual modality cannot by itself provide enough information. For despite some earlier opinions that stressed the equality of the senses, vision is clearly dominant for object recognition over touch, hearing, and smell (Rock 1966; Posner et al. 1976; Friedes 1974).[24]

What, then, accounts for visual superiority? Michael Posner and his coauthors (1976) argue that humans are biased toward the visual system because, unlike the auditory modality, which is automatically activated by sound, or the tactile modality, which is automatically activated by touch, the visual modality requires attention. That is, since the visual system is so inferior in its alerting capacities and in its ability to signal automatically the presence of objects or other environmental stimuli, humans are biased toward the visual modality and will attend to it unless there is instruction or some incentive to the contrary.

This "attention theory" of visual dominance is correct in its basic assumption that the visual system is less automatically alerting than the auditory and tactile systems. But it does not go far enough: the authors have not accounted for the dominance of the visual system: they have merely described its key property. We suggest that vision is dominant in humans because primates have been visually oriented mammals for at least 35 million years, and a major postulate of evolutionary theory—the "principle of conservation of organization"—decrees that it would likely remain dominant. As G. L. Stebbins (1969: 125) has phrased this principle:

Whenever a complex, organized structure or a complex integrated biosynthetic pathway has become an essential adaptive unit of a successful group of organisms, the essential features of this unit are conserved in all of the evolutionary descendants of the group concerned.

In short, if visual dominance was essential to the successful adaptation of ancestral higher primates in arboreal niches, this principle forces the conclusion that it would be retained in their descendants.

Another pragmatic reason for sensory bias in general and visual bias in particular is a need for perceptual constancy. The elaborate development of the cortical senses and the fact that they remain distinct systems for picking up particular properties of objects may create sensory disharmony where an animal is receiving conflicting information on the same object from different modality inputs. Thus, sensory information about

[24] On touch, see Peck et al. 1969; Bower et al. 1970; Reeve et al. 1986; Freides 1974. On hearing, see Colavita 1974; Lackner 1973; Platt and Warren 1972; Howard 1973. And on smell, see Batic and Gabassi 1987.

the properties of objects must be integrated, since intersensory disharmony can disrupt an organism's capacity to respond to its environment
(Freides 1974). Kenneth Ogle (1962a: 216) phrased the matter best when
he said: "Whatever relation exists between objective physical space and
subjective visual space . . . it must be stable if the individual is to act
effectively in his physical surroundings."

In most mammals, object recognition is dominated by a finely tuned,
discriminative olfactory sense organ (Jerison 1973: 268; Fleagle 1988:
23). For mammals like the bat and the dolphin that also migrated to a
three-dimensional adaptive zone, object recognition is dominated by the
auditory modality or sonar (Howard 1973: 278). In the same vein, object
recognition for humans and other higher primates is dominated by the
finely tuned visual modality. This conclusion helps explain why in experimental situations of intersensory conflict, the visual modality would exert
such an overriding influence. And it also explains why most spatial information among primates is given over to the visual modality, with little
perceptual influence from the other organs.

## The Emergence of Speech and Language

In trying to understand the emergence of human speech, the interaction among the cortical senses affords us some important clues—the most
important being that vision is primary in information processing. For at
least in its most basic form of object-naming, speech requires the integration of temporal-spatial properties so that an acoustic pattern and a visual pattern become functionally equivalent (e.g., a three-dimensional visually seen orange vegetable and the acoustic temporal sequence of
phonemes producing the word, "carrot"). How, then, do humans create
such sensory integration?

One important type of sensory equivalence in humans is nonlimbic intramodal agreement of stimuli where individuals match two objects for
equality. It has been clearly demonstrated that visual-visual matching of
forms is the easiest and most efficient (Cashdan 1968; Rudel and Teuber
1964; B. Jones 1981; Abravanel 1971; Rudnick et al. 1972). Intramodal
haptic-haptic comes next, and auditory-auditory is the most difficult of
all (Freides 1974). A second type of sensory equivalence is nonlimbic
cross-modal performance. For a long time, it was believed that speech itself was responsible for the equivalence of perceptual qualities across
sense modalities. But the data now show that prelanguage infants, apes,
and monkeys can perform cross-modal matching and transfer of stimuli
between touch and vision (Ettlinger 1973; Weiskrantz and Cowey 1975;
Bryant et al. 1972; Davenport et al. 1973). Thus, most researchers agree

that though language certainly accelerates cross-modal functions, it does not by itself allow for sensory equivalence (Abravanel 1968; Freides 1974). This supports Norman Geschwind's (1965) initial thesis that cross-modal sensory integration preceded the human capacity to acquire vocal language. The capacity for cross-modal integration, in short, made human speech possible.

One reason for cross-modal integration could have been environmental overload. When the visual system cannot handle environmental stimuli in the pickup or processing of information, it calls on the auditory and somatic (notably haptic) systems to enhance perception. One inherent weakness, for example, in the visual organ is in the processing of stimuli that must be integrated over time (Freides 1974: 295). An effect of this compensatory enhancement may have been spatial-temporal integration, seemingly first acquired between the visual and haptic systems because this kind of temporal analysis is best suited for haptic processing and because this association is common to humans, monkeys, and apes. Visual-auditory vocalization or propositional speech, however, is species-specific to humans, and so, our task now becomes one of considering the powerful selection pressures that produced the capacity for visual-auditory equivalence and integration.

As we have emphasized, primate evolution occurred mostly in an arboreal zone, and this specialized niche seemingly placed strong selection pressures on greater neocortical autonomy. For a tree-living niche requires precise and flexible behavioral responses to deal with a variable and changing three-dimensional physical world. In particular, the primate order on an ascending scale acquired the elaboration and expansion of the visual and haptic organs, with the concomitant expansion of sensory-association regions that permitted intended and rational responses for successful adaptation. In contrast, the auditory organ is uniquely specialized as "an early warning device" (Khanna and Tonndorf 1978: 23), with the primate ear exquisitely tuned to recognize and localize sounds (Howard 1973). The auditory cortex is seemingly also important in distinguishing primate vocalizations (Newman 1988). However, the neural mechanisms that control nonhuman primate vocalizations only overlap partially with those in humans, being mostly confined to limbic structures, where the stimulation of specific subcortical regions can elicit most species-specific calls (see Sutton and Jürgens 1988; Snowdon 1990).[25]

---

[25] Recent experiments have confirmed that primate vocalizations are far more structurally and functionally complex than previously reported. Some monkey calls are learned and used to transmit very specific information and, in some cases, to "signal about things" (Cheney and Seyfarth 1990: 138). This suggests that primate vocalization is not entirely emotional or instinctual but has volitional components (Steklis 1985; Sutton and Jürgens

Thus, in considering the first proto-hominids that sought to adapt to a parkland or open habitat, it is reasonable to assume that they carried with them those neurological mechansims that had facilitated adaptation to an arboreal niche: (1) they possessed (for mammals) large brains, with neocortical control over visual and tactile responses; (2) they evidenced a hierarchy of the cortical sense modalities, descending from the visual to the tactile and auditory; (3) they revealed an auditory modality that, while clearly a part of the neocortex, was linked to a vocal-call system largely regulated by motivational states with limited volitional control; and (4) they carried a series of hominoid skeletal features that, like their neurological legacy, were to shape their adaptation to a savanna or open-country ecological zone.

This legacy placed heavy constraints on the nature of that adaptation. As G. L. Stebbins (1969: 103–4) has emphasized, highly complex animals have an equally complex and precisely programmed pattern of gene and gene products that must be integrated with any new adaptive responses. Thus, proto-hominids were greatly circumscribed by the neurological and anatomical legacy acquired through the 60 million years of primate evolution. This fact requires that we stress several points. First, the evolution of hominids was influenced less by dramatic mutations than by extensions, elaborations, and alterations of the pongid biological heritage. Radical mutations would be too disruptive to these batteries of genes, their programmed sequences, and their associations, for as R. A. Fisher has argued, "the probability that individual mutations will contribute to evolution is in inverse correlation to the intensity of their effect on the developing phenotype" (quoted in G. Stebbins 1969: 104). Second, proto-hominids were not as "generalized" as is frequently assumed. While their skeletal features were certainly labile and allowed considerable flexibility, their neurological structure was highly refined and placed severe restrictions on adaptations to the savanna niche. And third, hominids did not undergo an increase in brain size until the rise of early Homo (specifically, *H. habilis*); the brain of the bipedal australopithecines remained within the range of the Great Apes for as long as five million years (Falk 1986). There was, then, a "hominid adaptive zone" on the savanna long before there was an explosive growth of the neocortex in the ancestral hominid brain. Thus, we need to ask: what dramatic event occurred to initiate the genus Homo?

---

1988). Essentially, the neural connections underlying primate calls are found in a number of regions within the brain (Sutton and Jürgens 1988), permitting some capacity, however rudimentary, for voluntary and semantic signaling (Steklis 1985; Cheney and Seyfarth 1990). However, the anterior cingulate gyrus (a limbic zone) retains control over vocal production (Snowdon 1990).

As has been frequently argued, open-country conditions favored bi-pedalism, the first acquired hominid trait and one that students of the origins of language consider crucial, prompting a change in the vocal-tract anatomy to allow for an apparatus that would produce a large variety of acoustic sounds (J. Hill 1972; see also Duchin, 1990). But this insight has not been systematically linked to a series of neurological changes in the neocortex of hominids. For it is in the selective pressures of the savanna as they operated to change the sensory patterns and the integration of relations between cortical and limbic structures that the origins of language are to be uncovered. Indeed, the origin of language is not found in radical mutations, as Noam Chomsky (1975) and others would have it, nor is it to be found in such fanciful notions as "babbling babies" or "singing australopithecines" (see Hewes 1975 for a bibliography of language-origin theories). Rather, from a neurological perspective, glottogenesis resides in a further integration of the auditory and vocal apparatus and in the changes in the organization of the cortical modalities as circumscribed by the pongid biological legacy.

A most significant constraint was the domination of vision. Proto-hominids, like human and nonhuman primates, were visually oriented creatures. Most spatial information was received and interpreted through visual sensations. Indeed, as proto-hominids became bipedal, reliance on the visual modality probably only increased. First, the tactile organ would have become of less importance in the extraction of environmental stimuli, for it requires actual physical contact with objects. In the context of a tree-living niche this has obvious advantages, but in a ground-dwelling niche, vision alone can guide the forelimbs. Second, once bipedalism became a way of life, the haptic modality would be further removed from actual physical ground contact, for a hindlimb-dominant creature moves through its habitat on the basis of visual cues alone (Johannson 1976: 75). This is probably why such a highly evolved complex organ as the tactile modality, even with its superior abilities for temporal processing, has so receded in importance among humans as a means of extracting environmental stimuli for object recognition. And third, the auditory system still served as a wide-ranging early warning system, "breaking" in automatically to alert the visual modality to environmental stimuli. But there can be little doubt that such warning only placed increased reliance on the visual system for an appropriate behavioral response to an open-country habitat rife with predators (see Maglio and Cooke 1978).

Contemporary terrestrial monkeys rely primarily on the visual modality for both spatial orientation and social communication (Marler 1965; see also Passingham 1982: 36). And the reliance on the dominant optic system no doubt placed powerful selective pressures on hominids to represent their world in visual terms. But unlike monkey terrestrial primates, hominids had a biological legacy that gave them a far-greater capacity for manipulating visual stimuli, as is illustrated by the ease with which present-day apes make intramodal visual-visual associations (indeed teaching chimps linguistic skills involves for the most part visual-visual symbolic connections). Such visual representations increasingly became mediated by symbols in order to better interpret, remember, and order stimuli received from visual receptors.

Such extensions in the functional use of the visual modality did not represent a radical spontaneous mutation. It is a latent capacity in hominoids who can acquire and use sign language; moreover, the visual system already had a built-in bias for the concern with ordering and patterning environmental wholes. Just as humans can take in scattered fragments of parts and construct the complete contours of a shape (Nebes 1977: 103), so it is likely that early proto-hominids could take parts of a visual stimulus, such as paw prints, and generalize to the contour of the animal. Thus, to the extent that speech is but expressed thought and an auditory form of symbolic behavior, we can conclude that the origin of language ultimately resides in the initial extension of visual symbolization in the savanna environment. And thus, those hominids who could best abstract, generalize, and visually remember aspects of their environment were more likely to survive and reproduce.

We should emphasize again that such capacities did not require great increases in brain size or dramatic mutations. Nor did they follow from the "generalized" capacities of pongids. Quite the reverse is true; they were forced on the early hominids, who had little choice but to rely on the dominant visual modality, especially as the tactile modality would have become rather dormant for the pickup of environmental stimuli (although later, of course, it became highly useful in adept tool-use in interaction with the visual organ). Moreover, as long as the auditory-vocal channel remained largely under limbic control, its usefulness was pretty much limited to emotionally based responses. Rational and intended responses to environmental stimuli were mediated primarily through the visual and tactile systems. This means that most intended communication about the environment between group members had to be channeled through the visual or the tactile modality. Recent experiments show that the visual system is directly used by chimpanzees for intended messages about the environment, for as E. W. Menzel (1971: 220) notes: "One chimpanzee can convey to others, who have no other source of information, the presence, direction, quality, and relative quantity or preference value of distant hidden objects that he himself has not seen for several minutes." This conclusion, in conjunction with the fact that human and chimpanzee perceptual processes are nearly equivalent (Matsuzawa 1990), suggests that early hominids extensively relied on the visual modality for social communication and for the extraction of environmental stimuli.

We are now faced with the intriguing question of how and why the auditory cortex became linked to the process of symbolization. Such a question cannot be answered solely by the recognition that bipedalism freed the speech centers. We must also consider the complex neurological transformations involved, including (1) the removal of most of the auditory-vocal machinery from limbic control, thereby placing it primarily under cortical or voluntary control; (2) the full association of the visual and auditory organs for the sensory equivalence of stimuli; (3) the creation of temporal patterns in a modality that, unlike the tactile modality, is not geared to recognize structural sequences (rather, it is geared to differentiating short and discrete sounds);[26] and (4) the reorganization and expansion of the brain that would be involved in all three of these developments. For such alterations to occur, there must have been selection pressures over a period of time for the placement of vocalizations under voluntary control. What were these selection pressures?

We argue that there were at least two related sets of environmental pressures: those having to do with selection for an increased control of sounds under the conditions of the savanna habitat; and those concerned with increasing sociality under savanna conditions. Let us take up each of these points in turn.

## Controlling Noise on the Savanna

A bipedal hominid, relying on its dominant visual organ, is probably handicapped by a call system primarily linked with neural mechanisms that largely regulate instinctual and emotional behavior. In the trees, an emotional species-specific call and other acoustic sounds can be highly advantageous, for they alert group members to danger under the protective forest canopy. This successful relationship of the auditory system to the other cortical organs is evident by the well-adapted arboreal apes and monkeys. In open country, however, where predators abound and where potential prey can easily move about, uncontrolled acoustic sounds can

---

[26] The human auditory sense is not equipped biologically to retain well or even recognize the temporal ordering of sounds. Instead, it is an organ specialized to differentiate and localize sound waves—not string them for the detection of a temporal pattern. Speech is seemingly a special and small subset of sounds sensitive to the auditory receptors that reach the brain in an auditory temporal code. According to Richard Warren and Roslyn Warren (1976: 173), the recognition of a temporal ordering of sounds may be possible "only for sequences that resemble those enncountered in speech and music." (See also M. Jones 1976; Freides 1974.)

alert predators and scare fresh food away. Much as some contemporary primate savanna-dwellers move quietly across their terrestrial habitat, so hominids probably exercised considerable auditory control. For though the early hominids' group size is unknown, if we imagine a large grouping of ape-sized open-country primates—a formidable amount of biomass—it seems implausible that such big mammals could always feed in spatial proximity. Instead, it would seem that early hominid groups during times of scarce and scattered resources (and much like hunters-gatherers of today) would break down into smaller (and more vulnerable) foraging parties, where selection would favor vocal silence.[27] This silence is not difficult to maintain, since most spatial information is controlled by the visual system, which can override limbic responses unless the sensations become too intense. Yet selection pressures must have favored, over a long time, those individuals who were able to suppress limbic vocal responses even when emotions ran high, for the dangers of emitting acoustic signals on a savanna where sound travels without obstruction would be great. And just as arboreal niches had placed selection pressures for freeing the other cortical modalities from limbic control, so the demands of an open-country habitat favored the separation of vocal-auditory mechanisms from direct limbic control.

This initial separation did not alter in spectacular ways the neurological structure of hominids, since the temporal lobe already housed the auditory system. On the contrary, the increased separation really represented only a quantitative change that produced dramatic qualitative differences. With the vocalization system under cortical control, vocal emissions would increase and undergo changes, especially if, as is supposed, bipedalism had already opened up the vocal tract. But as George Miller (1972: 76) has emphasized, selection for vocal variety must have evolved very slowly, because the human vocal apparatus is species-specific and "several important anatomical innovations had to evolve before a vocal mechanism adequate for speech was available." And, as with the visual and tactile modalities, volitional control favored the concomitant growth of cortical association areas to store memories of acoustic

[27] Patas monkeys (Erythrocebus) inhabit woodland and savanna zones and organize into harem, one-male reproductive groups. According to K. R. L. Hall (1967), patas have a vocal pattern of "adaptive silence": their vocalizations are usually muted, and the group's location is never given away by a vocalization. In contrast, common baboons (Papio) move about in large hordes and present an intimidating challenge to predators. They vocalize more than patas do and make no effort to hide themselves, though baboons are much noisier when in a wooded area than on the open savanna (R. J. Rhine, personal communication). It is important to emphasize that monkeys are considerably smaller than apes or hominids, which is one reason why common baboons can remain together as a cohesive grouping despite the scattered food supply of a savanna habitat.

associations and other cognitive processes for learned and intended vocal responses.

At this point, one must pause to ask how a neurological leap was made from a nonhuman primate call system of emotional communication under limbic control to a human system of propositional speech under neocortical control. The prevailing view has been that language cannot be studied from an evolutionary perspective because human language function had no anatomical correlates in other species (e.g., Chomsky 1980). On the surface, there is some justification for this conclusion, for extensive research has confirmed that human speech production is primarily dependent on two neural structures: Broca's area, on the frontal lobe adjacent to the motor cortex, which is believed to control the muscles for speech production and to contain the rules governing articulate speech production (i.e., successions of phonemes); and Wernicke's area, on the temporal lobe, which is specialized to give speech its content and comprehension (Damasio and Geschwind 1984; Shepherd 1988; Somjen 1983). Broca's area as *functionally* defined is unique to humans and involves species-specific rules for coding language into an articulatory form (Noback 1982; Snowdon 1990).[28] Wernicke's area is situated near a supramodal area (i.e., the inferior parietal lobule) that receives inputs from multiple cortical areas, perhaps making it a more generalized neural mechanism (see Fig. 4).

As discussed earlier, it is intriguing that the apes and some New and Old World monkeys reveal left-hemisphere asymmetries similar to those in humans along the Sylvian fissure where Broca's and Wernicke's areas are found. Indeed, Geschwind (1985: 272) was moved to comment that "if the [cognitive] abilities possessed by the chimpanzees were in fact earlier stages of linguistic ability, then it would be reasonable to expect them to have an anatomical localization similar to that of human language." In light of this finding, the symbolic capacities of apes using a visual-spatial modality are compelling, since these cognitive abilities probably rest on a "technical" development in primate neural circuitry that permitted linguistic processing in humans.

We can assume that these neuroanatomical changes evolved before human speech became possible, and the initial growth of the brain in early Homo (or *H. habilis*) over the small-brained australopithecines may have involved an expansion of the auditory zone (in the temporal lobe), a concomitant expansion of association zones, and, with the partial release of the vocal channel from subcortical control, the capacity for learned and

---

[28] In monkeys, the association cortex cytoarchitecturally homologous to Broca's area does appear to mediate facial and laryngeal motor muscles, but this region does not have a vocalization function (P. Heilbroner and Holloway 1989; Jürgens 1974).

stored vocal associations. Again, we do not need to speculate about mutations for language as Chomsky (1975) does or about some dramatic change of the sort. To assume that human language arose spontaneously without forerunners and solely for communication runs counter to evolutionary theory. Indeed, we subscribe wholeheartedly to the view that "something so complex as language could *not* have evolved from 'nothing' just to support the human enterprise" (Rumbaugh and Savage-Rumbaugh 1990: 490; their emphasis). Besides, as Geschwind (1985: 272) states, it is difficult to imagine that "simultaneous mutations would take place in many individuals so that communication could take place between them."

What, then, were the selection pressures producing these changes? And we might ask, why would language be verbal rather than visual (visual-gestural, for example), especially since vision is the primary sense modality and since such major neurological changes were necessary to relocate the vocal system primarily within the neocortex and to integrate the auditory modality with the visual and the tactile? It is conceivable that some populations did have a primal language that was visual-gestural, as Gordon Hewes (1973) contends. The chimpanzee and gorilla certainly reveal how easily proto-hominids could have handled a visual-gestural language. This language system has some major disadvantages, however: (1) the system requires relatively close visual contact, with any obstruction preventing receipt of the message; (2) a bipedal creature certainly carried weapons, food, babies, and other things, somewhat inhibiting the use of the hands for signing; and (3) the visual system is so low-alerting that an auditory sound would first have to break through and alert the recipient to pay attention to a gestural sign—a complex sequence that would probably be selected out. Thus, Jane Hill (1972) is probably correct in her argument that hominids were unlikely to have used a gestural language despite the fact that Great Apes can perform this symbolic activity.

In trying to understand the selection pressures for speech, we must temper somewhat the long-held assumption that the "need" for social communication among group members was the *only* stimulus for language (see next selection). Clearly, the distinct advantages of speech were evident at some time in hominid evolution, but this realization was not possible until the initial neurological changes that caused hominid vocalizations to rely primarily on cortical structures had already occurred—probably independently of any selection pressures for human speech—in the same way as the selection pressures for visual-visual associations in chimpanzees and gorillas have occurred independently of any "need" for language. One plausible hypothesis is that the cognitive processes involved originally developed early in hominoid evolution solely for inner communication, and that later, with selection pressures on hominids, the function shifted to social communication (see the discussions in Barlow 1983; Geschwind 1965). Indirect support for this hypothesis comes from sign-language research suggesting that the left cerebral hemisphere is specialized not just for spoken language but for signed language (Bellugi et al. 1989; Poizner et al. 1990). Hearing and speech functions, then, are not crucial to language, nor are they necessary for the development of hemispheric specialization. It is the neural-processing operations, not the form of the signal, that underlie language functions (Poizner et al. 1990).

Still, all this does not explain why the vocal-auditory channel in hominids was transformed for propositional or symbolic speech. Imagine for a moment an open woodland or savanna plain with little protective refuge, except perhaps for scattered and dispersed trees and the cover of tall grasses. In this predator-ridden environment, selection would have favored increased knowledge about its dangers. Yet these savanna-dwelling primates had long since lost a major source of information available to most mammals—the keen long-distance olfactory sense, with its automatic alerting and lingering chemical cues about the location of predators and prey. To be sure, the visual system is also a long-distance sense; and along with the stereoscopic experience, it is a valuable mechanism for determining the distance of objects (such as predators) in space. But vision cannot always detect the presence of objects, because it is often in reduced alertness, or preoccupied; and where visibility is low (such as at dusk) or absent (such as at night), it is completely deficient as a sensory organ. Thus, early hominids were biologically "stuck" with few built-in defense weapons, a low-alerting visual sense, and a greatly reduced olfactory organ. The auditory modality, however, is a splendid long-distance receptor, with fine low-frequency discrimination and a specialization for sound localization. Thus, it is not unreasonable to see a heightened auditory modality as useful in compensating for the deficiencies of the visual system.

Still, changes to the auditory organ had to be very selective because the visual system was already highly specialized to be the prime sense organ in primates. The auditory organ could not replace the visual organ for object recognition by evolving sonar or echolocation, for organs competing for object recognition would pick up different perceptual qualities of absolute space and create sensory disharmony. More important, as Stebbins (1969: 105) has argued, "once a unit of action has been assembled at a lower level of the hierarchy of organization and performs an essential function in the development of organization at higher levels, mutations that might interfere with the activity of this unit are so strongly disadvantageous that they are rejected at the cellular level and never appear in the adult individual in which they occur." Thus, in the hierarchy of sensory organization among primates, vision would greatly restrict the range of possible changes in the auditory organ. Despite selection pressures for heightened auditory cues, the auditory system could only change in ways that would not disrupt the prime function of the visual organ. It could not compete with it in regard to spatial matters, and only where the visual modality was deficient in some way would selection pressure modify the auditory organ. Perhaps Jerison (1973) is correct in his assumption that vocal sounds initially served in some capacity to enhance visual imagery. The environmental demands of an unstable and dangerous Pleistocene environment could expose points of vulnerability in the optic system; and so, perhaps before there was selective advantage in hominid evolution for vocal sounds revolving around symbolic communication and culture, much of the neurological work had been done.

## Communication and Sociality

Subsequent to, or perhaps alongside of, these selection pressures for increased control of auditory senses were those for communication and sociality. Whether or not the latter pressures were involved in the neurological changes that placed vocal responses under cortical control cannot be known. The sudden increase in the brain size of early Homo suggests that these pressures could have had their effect 1.8 million years ago, but it is also possible that the increase was solely due to selection pressures for vocal control.

There is, of course, nothing original about the argument that there were selective advantages for speech and communication. A hominid with vocal communication under volitional control could become more efficiently and flexibly organized for defense, hunting, gathering, and other activities on the open savanna. But we want to add a different twist to this conventional line of argument.

In Chapter 2, we stated that the fossil record strongly suggests that habitats of early Miocene apes were filled by monkeys in the middle Miocene. Until monkeys began to take control of the arboreal niche, ape species were very abundant and were not greatly differentiated from monkeys in locomotor patterns (Fleagle 1988: 363–73). But seemingly as a result of competition hominoid species dwindled. Those that survived underwent dramatic morphological changes, such as the capacity for forelimb-dominant suspension that we associate with modern apes. But more than skeletal changes must have been involved. Locomotion patterns reflect foraging strategies; and these locomotion patterns allowed apes to maneuver to the pendulous branches where monkeys could not venture. Foraging patterns also greatly influence group organization;

and if hominoids were pushed to the extremes of the arboreal niche (as the declining Miocene ape population suggests; Fleagle 1978), their patterns of social organization were likely altered away from the monkey (and general mammalian) pattern of cohesive and large group structures held together primarily by female bonds and intergenerational matrifocal networks. If for no other reason than the inability to sustain large numbers at the arboreal extremes—much like the present-day gibbons—social structure changed. And it changed, we argue, to a system where high sociality *was selected against* and where social attachments and bondings of kin *were reduced* (see Chapter 2). The current ape pattern of male and *notably female* transfer out of the natal group at puberty is, we argue, a phylogenetic holdover from the pressures that operated to break down group structures among those ape species pushed to a niche that could not sustain such structures.

Yet what would be an advantage at the extremes of the trees—lack of close bonding and of group structure—would be a severe handicap in an open environment. The "isolationism" and "self-reliance" of apes would expose them to dangers that a tight-knit group structure of the macaque and baboon sort would mitigate (Alexander 1974). Indeed, it is now well established that conspecifics with a high rate of predation are likely to mass close together as one spatially bound group (C. Anderson 1986). Thus, there would be extreme selection pressures for group organization, but these pressures would be operating on apes that, if not "rugged individualists" or "social isolates," were not inherently disposed to create matrilineages and tight-knit groups (as is the case today with gibbons, chimpanzees, orangutans, and gorillas). Ecological pressures, then, could not operate on already existing genetic tendencies to form groups to impel even more tight-knit and cohesive groupings, as has been the case for savanna-dwelling baboons (Rhine et al. 1985). Rather, selection would work on the genetic structure of a creature with more individualistic ways and a greater integration of visual, tactile, and auditory senses than any monkey.

Our view is that initially the easiest genetic path would have found selection for the transfer of the auditory-vocal apparatus from limbic to cortical control. To be sure, a bipedal hominid with merely voluntary control over its vocalization is still very far removed from a hominid with linguistic-based vocalizations. But purposeful communication using the auditory-vocal channel would have permitted much greater social interaction among group members and opened the evolutionary door for the later expansion and reorganization of the brain in ways that promoted symbolic communication through logically based speech. In short, since social bonds could not be easily built genetically—as with monkeys—

they had to be built through symbolic communication, a process that would eventually entail a radical departure from the vocalization of any known animal. The sudden increase in the brain size of *Homo habilis* and *Homo erectus*, then, may have involved more than neurological groundwork for speech; it may signal the actual use of a rudimentary vocal language for symbolic communication and sociality. Clearly, the competitive advantages of a hominoid that could form group structures through symbolic communication would be great, enabling it to outcompete hominoids who did not have this capacity and to at least hold its own with ground-dwelling savanna monkeys.

## Conclusion

Our hypothesis, as we mentioned in Chapter 2, has a further implication: there may be less of a genetic basis for human sociality than is often presumed. One of sociology's most unquestioned and sacred assumptions is that humans "need" groups and "naturally" seek social solidarity with others, but in our view, this is an unsubstantiated claim. Needs for groups are perhaps more of a cultural product than a biological one, although there was in all probability some genic selection for group bonding (especially in early hominids), until the emergence of speech and language allowed for organization through the easy movement of ideas from one human brain to another. However, the very fact that group solidarity could be achieved through more cultural processes would mitigate against selection pressures for it at the genic level. For if culture can achieve the same consequence, the need to alter hominids' complex neoanatomy genetically is dramatically reduced.

We will make further comments on these matters throughout this book. But we begin our review of human organization with at least this presumption: humans are far more individualistic than is commonly supposed; and if there was a "genetic reprogramming" of our ancestors for group formation, it was laid over earlier programming among forest apes for self-reliance, spatial mobility, and transfer. Many of the emotional, political, and social conflicts among humans over freedom, individualism, and autonomy, on the one hand, and group solidarity, embeddedness, and control, on the other, are perhaps manifestations of a conflict within our biology, or between our biology and sociocultural constructions.

Our speculation on the origin of language views humans' symbolic capacities in somewhat less grandiose and self-congratulatory terms than is often the case. Human language and culture are based on neurological capacities for the integration of sense modalities under cortical control; and only under the selection pressures of the savanna did such control of the auditory vocal channel emerge. It may have emerged simply because a loud savanna-dwelling primate with few natural defenses is soon a dead one, although selection for communication and organization of apes without strong genetic tendencies for bonding was, in all likelihood, also involved.

Thus, human culture is but an extension of the neurological capacities of all apes; and "the social bond" that has been the centerpiece of sociological wisdom may not be genetically based but cultural. We do not want to push this last point too far, but sociologists, who from the very beginning of the discipline have had a "communal" and "collectivist" bias, should subject this bias to further scrutiny. Let us, at the very least, keep an open mind about this conclusion as we begin to examine the evolution of human societies.

THE FIRST HUMAN

SOCIETY: Hunters

and Gatherers

According to the fossil record, the first hominids appeared in Africa around five million years ago (Boaz 1988; Johanson and White 1979). Though their origins are unknown, these Pliocene hominids no doubt evolved from an ancestral population of African hominoids that, in the face of drier climactic conditions during the Miocene, abandoned the shrinking forests and settled in the expanding open woodlands and savannas (Malone 1987).

The earliest hominid fossils are classified in the genus Australopithecus, which contains four species. In order of their appearance, these are *Australopithecus afarensis*, *A. africanus*, *A. robustus*, and *A. boisei*. In terms of their facial features, brain size, and cranial anatomy, the australopithecines were very much like apes, but there was an important difference: they were fully bipedal.[1] Since the australopithecines had to adapt to a new ecological niche, their ranging, dietary, sleeping, and organizing behaviors underwent modification from their ape ancestors. And one of these "apelike" australopithecine lines, moving about the savanna as habitual bipeds, was to establish the Homo lineage, culminating in present-day humans.[2] In all likelihood, australopithecines were food foragers (Fleagle 1988: 427) and opportunistic scavengers (Shipman 1986) who wandered around in relatively loose groupings in search of edible plants and fresh carcasses left by predators (Speth 1989; Cavallo and Blumenschine 1989).

[1] See Grine 1988; Washburn and Harding 1975; M. Leakey and Hay 1979; Johanson 1980; Isaac and McCown 1975; Isaac 1978; Rak 1983; Stringer 1984; T. White and Suwa 1987; Susman 1989; Fleagle 1988; Boaz 1988; Falk 1983; Stern and Susman 1983.

[2] The finding of preserved hominid footprints in northern Tanzania dating to at least three million years ago provides strong evidence that bipedalism was the first distinct hominid trait (see T. White and Suwa 1987; Latimer and Lovejoy 1990).

Yet despite the growing understanding of the physical characteristics of early hominids, their patterns of social organization are hard to discern in the fossil record.[3] If australopithecines had evolved from cercopithecine ancestors, the large number of predators on the savanna would have surely favored selection for tight-knit social structures (Maglio and Cooke 1978). For example, present-day terrestrial baboons (Papio), which live mostly in a savanna habitat, are organized into large, dense, and hierarchical networks, presumably because such organization deters predators and lessens the chances of any one individual becoming a target (Alexander 1974; Hamilton 1982; see also Rhine et al. 1985 for a discussion of the regularities in baboon progressions). It is unlikely, however, that these same selection pressures could have molded early hominids, who probably looked much like bipedal chimpanzees, into the biological equivalent of terrestrial monkeys. Too much selection against rigid structure had occurred in the hominoid line; and so, if a more close-knit and stable social structure was to be achieved, selection would be more likely to work on the neuroanatomy of hominids in ways that facilitated social bonding indirectly through increased facility for communication.

The effects of these selection pressures can be seen in the late Pliocene and early Pleistocene fossil record. The genus Homo first appears in the form of *Homo habilis* (2.0 to 1.5 million years ago), successively followed by *Homo erectus* (1.6 million years ago) and *Homo sapiens* (in the vicinity of 100,000 years ago). The significant increase in the brain size of Homo over that found in australopithecines is the best evidence of how selection worked to produce a cultural or "proto-cultural" basis of organization. The earliest known Homo, *habilis*, was similar in size and appearance to australopithecines, but its cranial capacity was on average near 650 cc, with one specimen measuring over 750 cc (Tobias 1987; Conroy 1990: 326). This represents an increase of nearly 50 percent in brain volume over an australopithecine brain, and equally, if not more, important to this size difference is endocast evidence that the *habilis* brain differs from the australopithecine brain in having (1) a humanlike cortical sulcal pattern in the frontal lobes, which in modern humans is associated with the development of Broca's (speech) area (Falk 1983, 1989); and (2) a developed inferior parietal lobule, which is associated with the development of Wernicke's area, the part of the human brain that gives speech its content and comprehension (Tobias 1987; Conroy 1990: 326). Moreover, the cortical endowment of *Homo habilis* is evidenced by the literal meaning of its name—"handy man." *Homo habilis* may have been using its expanded neocortex to manufacture crude stone

[3] For general references, see Foley and Lee 1989; Goodall and Hamburg 1975; Johanson and White 1979; Isaac 1978; Kinzey 1987.

choppers and scrapers, for these artifacts also first appear in the archaeological record in the late Pliocene / early Pleistocene of 2 million to 1.5
million years ago (Harris 1983; M. Leakey 1971; Foley 1987b).

Unlike the short-lived *habilis*, *Homo erectus*, the next Homo to appear, looked more like a human than an ape (Rightmire 1988). Its brain
size ranged between 727 cc and 1,200 cc, and its skull was closer to that
of humans in the frontal and posterior lobes than its predecessor's was
(Wolpoff 1980), especially with regard to those areas linked to linguistic
abilities. In addition to neurological changes, some specimens of *Homo
erectus* show modifications of the upper respiratory tract toward a more
humanlike pattern, with a lowering of the larynx and hence an increased
ability to produce laryngeal sounds (Laitman 1985: 285). Seemingly,
changes in the neuroanatomy of the *erectus* brain had also brought the
vocal-auditory channel under cortical control and increased the capacity
for intra- and cross-modal associations, changes that in turn expanded
the capacity for symbolization. Although the evidence clearly suggests
that *erectus* was moving in the direction of a capacity for language and
speech (Conroy 1990: 328), just when "full-blown" language evolved is
still unknown. In any case, it is likely that *Homo Erectus* used some
kind of crude linguistic system, possibly using vocal sounds to designate
objects.[4]

The increasing capacity of *Homo erectus* for complex cognitive processes was surely linked to new cultural adaptations. The number and variety of artifacts made and used by this hominid (such as hand axes) suggest both an increased refinement and specialization of tools and an
expansion of activities involving tool-use (Fleagle 1988: 439). Moreover,
although *Homo erectus* probably relied on plant foods for basic subsistence, there is evidence for two major cultural innovations by this hominid—hunting and the use of fire (Shipman and Walker 1989; Fleagle
1988: 438; Isaac 1989: 107).[5] There would be advantages for an open-
ranging hominid that could organize and hunt (rather than just scavenge)
game—fewer competitors plus extra amounts of protein, fat, and other
nutrients. But a bipedal primate would need to be an organized tool-user
to undertake such activity. Selection would thus favor a primate capable

[4] Evidence that *Homo erectus* was a speaking hominid of some sort has been strengthened by the recent find of a Neanderthal skeleton (i.e., an archaic *H. sapiens*) from the
Middle Paleolithic. Materials included a complete hyoid bone (the first hominid hyoid bone
ever found), providing clues to the position and shape of the upper respiratory structure in
Neanderthals. Some scholars have argued that Middle Paleolithic peoples were not capable
of producing the full range of human vocal sounds (see Lieberman 1984; Crelin 1987). But
these new data strongly suggest that they were as capable of speech as modern humans (see
Arensburg et al. 1990).

[5] Although the importance of vertebrate flesh in the diet of *erectus* is unknown, a major
dietary shift toward meat eating began with this hominid.

of planning, calculating, and cooperating in stalking and trapping big game. Such capacities would only be possible with an expansion of the neocortex. In turn, cooperation through the use of symbols would strengthen social bonds, with the result that groupings would become more complex and enduring. There would also be clear advantages for an economic and sexual division of labor to strengthen bonds between males and females. Males could leave the group to hunt; females could gather food close to a home base and, at the same time, care for children (who would, no doubt, suckle for almost four years, as is the case among both the Great Apes and modern-day hunters and gatherers).

*Home erectus*'s other important cultural innovation, the harnessing and use of fire, only reinforced these selection pressures.[6] Fire could be used for light and warmth, as well as for cooking and the softening of animal flesh. It could also be used in hunting (to panic game animals and drive them to their deaths, perhaps off a cliff), and it could be developed as a technique for hardening the tips of wooden tools and weapons. Equally important, the use of fire encouraged communication and social bonds by drawing members of *Homo erectus* groupings together to warm themselves and spend time together beyond the daylight hours.

*Homo habilis* lived only in Africa, but *Homo erectus* migrated out to parts of Europe and Asia (Foley 1987b: 261; Rightmire 1990), testimony to the increased reproductive fitness of a fire-using, tool-making, game-hunting, and group-organizing hominid to adjust and adapt to various habitats. At this phase of hominid evolution, such fitness was not the result of individual selection alone, but also the result of cultural selection operating on social groupings. Selection worked at the individual level to create more efficient tool-use and social organization by favoring those individuals with expanded neurological capacities, but once these capacities could be harnessed for symbolization and organization, the social network also became a crucial unit, or mediator, of selection processes. Those groupings that could best organize to hunt, gather, and reproduce would be most likely to survive. Equally important, in light of the weak ties common to all hominoids, those hominid groupings with even the slightest linguistic edge over others would have a decided advantage: the capacity to share ideas would plainly promote more complex and stable ties among individuals, thereby increasing individual reproductive fitness. And a linguistic-based system with a fixed set of arbitrary symbols,

[6] The consensus among scholars is that *Homo erectus* was a fire-using hominid by the Middle Pleistocene, about half a million years ago. However, there is considerable debate on the earliest use of fire; some scholars even suggest that the controlled use of fire began before *erectus*, some 1.7 million years ago. (See James 1989 for a critical review of the evidence; see also Straus 1989.) It is important to emphasize that few scholars doubt that *erectus* populations used fire; what is controversial is whether or not they *made* fire (Relethford 1990).

no matter how crude, is always a product of group activities because it is created and preserved through culture and social organization. In our view, then, the increasing complexity of hominid social organization was achieved through selection for a neurobiology that, in turn, could create cultural (rather than genetic) codes for male-female bonding, reciprocity, and other forms of sociality. Thus, those populations that could create values, norms, traditions, and other symbol systems that encouraged (1) an efficient division of labor between age and sex classes, (2) a stable set of bonds among males, females, and offspring, (3) a strong sense of obligation to relatives and group members, and (4) an enduring attachment of both males and females to the young were more likely to survive and reproduce themselves. Once the large brain allowing elaborate symbol-use was created, few of these processes required selection at the genic level. Moreover, once cultural selection processes became operative, selection would favor increased development of the association cortex to improve the capacities for symbolization and communication still further.

In fact, contrary to the arguments of some human sociobiologists, for a somewhat individualistic hominid, the easiest path to increased organization was to expand cortical functions so that a tradition of culture could be used to increase sociality. To genetically reprogram a hominid to be like a hierarchical, matrifocal, terrestrial monkey would be far more difficult than to work on brain functions in ways that allow for flexible patterns of social organization, especially since much of the difficult neurological work had already been done in the arboreal niche. In short, hominid evolution did not involve selection among "selfish genes" ruthlessly pursuing the maximization of fitness; rather, it involved selection for neocortical expansion and reorganization so that hominids could be better culture-producers and culture-users. By the time *Homo sapiens* appeared about 100,000 years ago, this process of increasing communicative capacities was well developed; and with *Homo sapiens sapiens*, social organization by cultural codes was clearly a more important adaptive process than selection at the genic level.

Figure 5 models the selection pressures that produced hominid sociocultural organization revolving around hunting and gathering. A model like ours emphasizes the cycles of selection processes at both the individual and the sociocultural level. One cycle revolves around selection pressures for bipedalism. Exactly what those pressures were is unknown, but if a visually oriented ape was to survive on the savanna, one crucial need was to see predators and prey over the high grasses; and this ability would be facilitated by upright stance. With this change, tool-use and increased manual dexterity would have selective advantages for gathering, hunting, defense, and carrying.

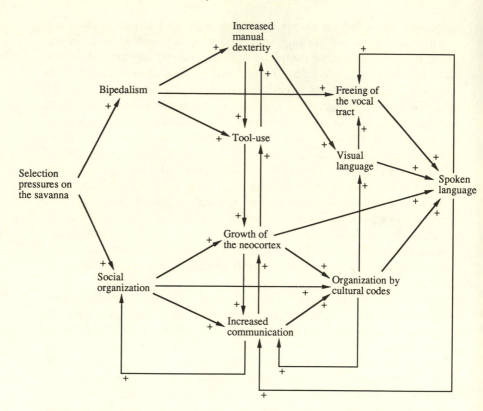

*Fig. 5.* The evolution of culturally based patterns of social organization

Tool-use also feeds into the other selection cycle initiated by savanna conditions: increased social organization. An organized primate on the savanna is better able to find prey and to fend off predators; and as we have emphasized, symbolic communication would have selective advantages in that it would give flexibility to such patterns of social organization. Thus, as the larger brain of *Homo erectus* signals, a mutually reinforcing cycle revolving around an expanded neocortex, increased levels of communication, and escalated use of cultural codes was initiated. And once started, the cycle increased the selection pressure for more brain capacity, communication, and organization in terms of culture (that is, smarter, more communicative, and flexibly organized groups were more likely to survive in competition with other groups of primates and under the harsh dangers of an open plain and, later, the diverse habitats of Asia and Europe).

Initially a visual language may have been used, but for the reasons discussed in Chapter 3, this form of symbolic communication would be far less adaptive than a spoken language. Here again, bipedalism feeds into the selective processes favoring organization by culture. For bipedalism helped open the vocal tract, making an oral language possible if there were sufficiently strong selection pressures for more efficient communication. Such selection for speech had to wait until the auditory-vocal channel could be brought under control. Once this happened, there would be selective advantages for a speaking primate, encouraging the ever more fine-tuning of the neocortex in ways creating the capacity for language as we know it today. The increase in brain size between *Homo erectus* and *Homo sapiens sapiens*, whose brain measures 1,300 cc on average (Fleagle 1988: 440), reflects the operation of these selection pressures.

At some point in the cycles portrayed in Figure 5, sociocultural selection began to operate on hominid groupings as much as on individuals. Once the neocortex was developed to the point of organization in terms of symbolic codes, networks of individuals were selected for their increased capacity to organize in terms of cultural codes, causing the expansion of the neocortex at the individual level, a development that led to stable and flexible social groupings. By the time of *Homo sapiens sapiens*, we believe, selection was working disproportionately on collectivities; those populations that could use culture to organize in ways that created a set of stable bonds, a viable division of labor, and a capacity to learn and adjust organizational patterns to new or changing habitats could outcompete any hominids who were not so flexibly organized (see, for example, the discussions of the complex communal hunting strategies among Upper Paleolithic populations in Olsen 1989; Kehoe 1990). Moreover, once cultural codes could be used to organize populations, the diffusion of ideas about how best to organize became possible, enabling hominid populations to learn from one another.

Up to the point of humans' current capacity for language and culturally based social organization, selection favored cultural as opposed to biological programming in hominids. Otherwise the rapid growth of the brain and its increasing complexity make little sense.[7] Competition among hominids and other primates may have been intense; and direct competition among culturally organized hominids may also have ex-

[7] As B. Smith Holly (1990: 365) points out, an increase in brain size for a hominid species would incur substantial costs, namely, (1) an increase in energy requirements for a given body size; (2) a further commitment to fewer offspring, since larger brains would require greater parental investment because of slower maturation and longer socialization; (3) an increased sensitivity to maternal blood pressure and perhaps to brain chemistry; (4) an alteration of circulatory pathways to oxygenate and cool a larger brain; and (5) an increased difficulty for females giving birth to larger-brained infants. Selection for increased brain size, then, had to outweigh the sizable costs.

isted.[8] But it is important to note that the very nature of organization for hunting and gathering does not demand cultural mechanisms to integrate large collectivities, for in nomadic food-foraging societies, population densities are low, groups are dispersed, conflicts within and between groups are relatively infrequent, and resources are easily secured, even in difficult habitats. Thus, we suspect that there was little chronic "warfare" in the Spencerian sense among human hunters and gatherers to reorganize in some other pattern—at least for 30,000 years of human history. But as we will see in later chapters, once new forms of social organization beyond hunting and gathering were created, selection on patterns of collective organization worked against hunting and gathering, so forcefully in modern times, indeed, that within a generation hunting and gathering societies will probably disappear. The "first society" will have been "selected out" by its successors—horticulture, agrarianism, industrialism, and post-industrialism. Before examining these evolutionary developments, however, we should consider the generic organizational features of human societies and look at the specific features of the root form, the hunting and gathering society.

## The Organizational Features of Human Societies

In order to analyze the evolution of human society from its hunting and gathering origins, it is useful to have a conceptualization of societal social structure that can allow for comparisons among varying societal types. Our view is that societies are organized along six dimensions: (1) demographic, (2) spatial, (3) institutional, (4) stratifying, (5) categoric, and (6) corporate. Let us look at each of these in turn.

1. *Demographic dimensions.* A social system must always consist of a population whose members are distributed and organized. As we will see, the absolute number of actors—that is, population size—is crucial to understanding the organization of a society (H. Spencer 1874–96; Carneiro 1967), and related issues are the population's rates of growth and social mobility.

2. *Spatial dimensions.* The members of a society are distributed in physical or geographical space. There is not only an internal aspect to this distribution, but also an external geopolitical one. Internally, the relevant issues are the degree of concentration or dispersion of the popu-

---

[8] A case in point are archaic *Homo sapiens*, especially a population known to us as the European Neanderthals. Many scholars feel that Neanderthals were overwhelmed or replaced by more advanced and expanding populations of *sapiens*, perhaps because of sociocultural differences. Indeed, in modern times the invasion of one human population by another turns on organizational and technological superiority (see B. Campbell 1985b: 423).

lation, the rates of geographic movement and redistribution, and the physical features (mountains, waterways, bodies of water, etc.) that influence a population's distribution in space (Hawley 1950, 1986). Externally, populations must confront each other and develop relations that can range from war and conflict, to mutual immigration/emigration, to negotiated peace and exchange.

3. *Institutional dimensions.* Populations are organized in ways that allow their members to persist and reproduce themselves. The organizational forms that harness and channel human energy to these ends are the institutional dimensions of a society (J. Turner 1972). These institutional structures reveal varying profiles, depending on the nature of the activity among their incumbents. Institutional arrangements are universal in three domains: economy (gathering, producing, and distributing resources), kinship (ordering blood and marriage relations), and religion (interpreting and ordering relations to the supernatural and nonempirical). Even these most basic institutional forms are not clearly differentiated in simple societies, but they increasingly become so as societies grow more complex. And with further differentiation, other institutional structures emerge: polity (mobilizing power, making decisions), law (specifying and sanctioning activities and relations), education (formalizing cultural transmission), medicine (systematizing approaches to physical health), and science (articulating procedures for acquiring knowledge). To a great extent, the overall structure of a society reflects the level of differentiation among institutional forms as well as their specific structure and patterns of interrelations.

4. *Stratifying dimensions.* In all societies, some valued resources are unequally distributed. Some members always get more of what is valued than others. The nature of the resources, the profile of their distribution, and the consequences of this distributional profile for the cognitions and behaviors of individuals are among the most important aspects of stratifying processes in a society.

5. *Categoric dimensions.* In all societies, individuals are seen as representatives of distinctive categories by virtue of certain shared attributes and qualities (Hawley 1986; Blau 1977). And on the basis of these perceptions, they are responded to in varying ways. Age and sex are universal categories, but with increases in the size and complexity of a population, many new categoric distinctions emerge: ethnic (distinctive cultural and behavioral attributes), race (perceived distinctions in biology), class (attributes associated with varying shares of resources), regional (distinctive features ascribed to place of residence or origin), occupational (features associated with different types of economic activity), educational (distinctions based on incumbency in, and credentials from, educational

structures), and religious (differences stemming from beliefs and ritual practices centering on the supernatural). The number and kind of categoric distinctions in a society are among the most significant organizing dimensions of a population.

6. *Corporate dimensions.* The organization of individuals for the pursuit of specific ends constitutes the corporate dimension of a society. The number of such corporate units, their size and complexity, and their involvement in different institutional and stratifying dimensions are, as we will observe, crucial to understanding the organization of a society (Hawley 1986).

When analyzing a population of individuals as a "society," then, it is useful to think in terms of these six basic dimensions of organization. But it is also important to keep in mind that these dimensions are not totally discrete; indeed, they often overlap and always have causal effects on each other. They constitute a matrix of forces that shape the organization of a population into a society; and as we now approach human hunters and gatherers, we will describe this societal type along these six dimensions. Later, we will use the same dimensions to depict the key organizing features of horticultural, agrarian, industrial, and post-industrial societal types; and in this way, we can compare societal forms with one another.

## Hunting and Gathering Social Organization

Hunting and gathering societies are typically small, usually consisting of a band of 50 to 80 people.[9] Each band tends to be autonomous but to be in contact with other bands sharing the same language and region (a larger unit that can be viewed as a deme or the actual intrabreeding population). The largest single grouping of hunters and gatherers ever discovered was a settlement in a highly fertile area of France; by the archaeological evidence, it numbered about 400 to 600 people. Spatially, a band of hunters and gatherers wanders a region or territory, often in a somewhat circular pattern. The band settles for a time—perhaps several weeks—in one area, extracts the available resources, and then moves on to exploit a new location. Eventually, when resources have replenished themselves, the band may return to its starting point and initiate a new round of movement to and from favored locations. Band members appear to have a sense for their own and others' home range, and as a result, bands tend to wander within a delimited area, respecting the domains of others. If resources are scarce, the band may disperse for a time (and even permanently), with some members seeking a new area to exploit. This demo-

[9] The description in the text is based primarily on the sources listed in Table 3 (p. 87).

graphic and spatial profile requires low population densities, so that the environment is not overtaxed. The bands themselves seek to maintain their population size to an optimal level through a combination of infanticide, abortion, and birth control (which includes women nursing children for prolonged periods and maintaining a low level of body fat and weight; see Kolata 1974).

With respect to institutional structure, hunters and gatherers reveal a very low degree of differentiation among economy, religion, and kinship. These societies possess only a minimum of the basic elements of an economy—for our analysis, technology, capital, labor, entrepreneurship, and land (J. Turner 1972). Technologically, they possess limited albeit highly useful knowledge about how to exploit the environment. This knowledge revolves around such practical matters as how to gather various food sources at different times of the year; how to hunt with spears and, for some, bows and arrows; and how to search for hidden water sources in times of drought. Capital formation in the economy is extremely limited, consisting of the equipment for hunting and gathering (e.g., digging sticks and baskets) and perhaps a few utensils for preparing food. Labor is strictly divided between men and women, with men performing almost all the hunting, and women virtually all the gathering, which normally involves picking or digging for food, as well as carrying it back to camp for processing. Contrary to earlier opinions, most studied hunters and gatherers do not have to work hard to meet their nutritional requirements, even under what appear to be extreme environmental conditions (Lee, 1968; Woodburn 1968). Men normally provide far less food with their labor than females, primarily because hunting is not always successful but also because men spend considerable time talking, gambling, and smoking when possible. Women and their offspring are much more likely to secure the necessary food through their activities, but generally they too do not need to spend long hours in gathering fruits, nuts, berries, roots, and other edible foods. Hunters and gatherers generally live what has been called a "leisure-intensive" lifestyle (Eibl-Eibesfeldt 1991: 55). Entrepreneurship, or the organization of other economic elements, is performed by the band and nuclear kinship units. Finally, hunters and gatherers have relatively limited access to the last economic element—land, or more accurately, to its resources—since they tend to extract only the readily available foods and rudimentary building materials (sticks, grasses, leaves, roots, etc.) from their territories.

Turning to religion, we can define this institutional structure as consisting of beliefs about supernatural realms and forces, coupled with cult structures that organize ritual practices directed at the supernatural (Wallace 1966). Hunters and gatherers do not reveal much complexity in their beliefs about the supernatural, rituals directed at the supernatural, or specific structures beyond the band and kinship for organizing ritual activity. We can term their religion "simple shamanic" because it does not reveal a well-articulated belief system consisting of explicit religious values and cosmology, and because religious rituals and cult structures are sporadic, individualistic, and only at times mediated by a shaman (Wallace 1966; J. Turner 1972).

In these shamanic religions, religious conduct tends to be circumscribed by certain rituals within which religious values remain somewhat vague and implicit. The cosmology of primitive religions, however, can display some degree of definition and complexity (Bellah 1964: 364–66). Supernatural beings can be objectified and viewed as clearly distinct from the natural world. Some of these beings willfully control and influence people's worldly activities. Usually supernaturals have specified and delimited spheres of influence. The relationships among these forces are a source of considerable speculation, and at times, an incipient hierarchy or pantheon of relations among such forces—who are often viewed as spirits—can emerge. But religious myths delineating the history of supernaturals are not elaborately developed.

The fairly clear differentiation between the natural and the supernatural in shamanic religions results in a set of rituals through which spirits and people interact. The locus of such rituals is the cult structure. But cult structures in shamanic religions are loosely organized (Bellah 1964: 363). Following A. F. C. Wallace (1966: 83–90), we can distinguish two general types of cult structures within these religions: individualistic cults and shamanic cults (from which we derived the label for this type of religion). In individualistic cults, there is no distinction between religious specialists and laymen; cult members engage in appropriate rituals addressed to the supernatural without a religious specialist as an intermediary. Shamanic cults, by contrast, display a clearly differentiated structure, with part-time religious practitioners serving as intermediaries between laymen and the supernatural. These intermediaries assume this status on the basis of family ascription, specialized training, and inspirational experience with the supernatural. General norms require that for a fee they act as magicians, witch doctors, medicine men, mediums, spiritualists, astrologers, and diviners. Depending on the society, the nature of religious beliefs, and the needs of the client, shamans can usually perform at least several of these services. It is thus with shamanic cults that the first religious division of labor emerges in a society. Both individualistic and shamanic cults in hunting and gathering societies are loosely organized, and since they are not clearly bounded, they display a transient clientele.

Also, in neither case, do adherents show any real sense of religious community; despite certain shared beliefs and rituals, there is little mutual identification and solidarity among cult members in food-collecting societies. Furthermore, few if any calendrical rituals are required of members; rituals are performed when needed, and quite often there is no stable locus of religious activity.

In conclusion, then, we can visualize shamanic religions as the most basic type. The religious belief system, while distinguishing between the sacred and the profane, as well as between the supernatural and the natural, does not display a clearly differentiated and systematized cosmology and value system. Structurally, cult organization displays at most a clear differentiation between two religious statuses: shaman and layman. And yet much religious activity occurs within individualistic cults.

Kinship is the pivotal institutional structure among food collectors. A band is normally composed of several nuclear units (parents and their unmarried offspring), each of which can stand alone as an independent foraging unit. However, nuclear families are often linked into larger household groups through parent-child relations (lineal relatives), sibling relations, or aunt, uncle, or cousin relations (collateral relatives). Polygyny (one male, multiple females) is normatively acceptable and even preferred in the vast majority of hunting and gathering societies, but as a practical matter, it is rather rare and usually limited to only a few influential males (Lenski et al. 1991: 101). The rule of descent among present-day hunters and gatherers is typically bilateral or cognatic (equal weight to both blood lines), a descent system that effectively isolates out the nuclear family.

In most bands, marriage must be exogamous (outside the band); on occasion, there are rules of endogamy (bands into which one must marry). These practices create network ties and alliances with neighboring bands that make for the easy movement of individuals or bands within overlapping territories and, in difficult times, for resource sharing. Further links may be forged among males where bands practice wife "sharing" or "lending" when a male guest visits (R. Spencer 1968). Upon marriage, in most contemporary band societies, couples are free to reside with either partner's band, although limits on band size can force them to emigrate to new bands. As we noted above, there is a clear division of labor in hunting and gathering families. But whereas females usually gather only for their own households, men often pool their labor for large-game hunting, with the meat shared among all camp residents (Lee and DeVore 1968). This division of labor does not seem to translate into significant differences in authority relations within the family; males and females appear to share decision-making more or less equally.

To sum up, if we were to ignore deviations and typify kinship systems in terms of various normative practices about family size and composition, residence, activity, descent, authority, and marriage (J. Turner 1972), then hunters and gatherers of today would reveal a profile of small groups, a clear division of labor for males and females, truncated bilateral descent, little if any difference in authority among adults, and relatively limited marriage rules.

We are now compelled to consider the merits of two strikingly different models of hunter-gatherer band formation. So thoroughly divided are scholars on this point that, in the words of Richard Lee (1972: 350), the field is now faced with the problem of "an apparent chaos of hunter social arrangements." In the classic model, first proposed by A. R. Radcliffe-Brown (1930), bands are constructed, integrated, and maintained by a core of related males (e.g., sons, brothers, and fathers), creating a "patrilocal residence pattern and a marriage rule of female exogamy" (Steward 1955; Service 1966; Lévi-Strauss 1969). Support for this hypothesis comes from George Murdock's *Ethnographical Atlas* (1967), in which 62 percent of the societies that relied primarily on hunting, gathering, and fishing revealed a residential pattern of patrilocality (C. Ember 1978; see also Murdock 1949). In the second model, originally proposed by M. J. Meggitt (1962) and B. Hiatt (1961–62), bands are flexibly assembled and maintained over time by a mixture of near and distant relatives, and married couples are free to live with either parent (bilocal residence) or establish an independent household (neolocal residence). Support for this model comes from studying present-day hunters and gatherers, most of whom have been found to lack both a patrilocal residence rule and explicit female-based exogamy. In response to these findings, proponents of the classic patrilocal-band model argue that contemporary band societies are mere remnants of once-viable populations now forced to live in marginal areas where the "composite" band is the only possible kinship grouping (see Service 1966: 33). Although many ethnographers agree that the patrilocal-band model is too strict and inflexible, they are unwilling to see a hunting and gathering camp as "a random assortment of unrelated individuals whom adverse circumstances have thrown together" (Lee 1972: 30). Rather, for ethnographers like Lee (who studied the !Kung of Botswana), a band is a network of kinsmen (blood) and affines (marriage) who "live and work well together."

Although this controversy continues to rage (see J. Martin and Stewart 1982), in fact, each model can be supported. By their very nature, food-foraging economies are intimately tied to environmental resources that dictate band size, while demographic processes determine the number of blood-related males (Howell 1988: 63). Given the high mortality rate, low birthrate, and "fission-fusion" flexibility of nomadic peoples, it seems unlikely that a strict patrilocal rule of residence could ever be maintained for more than a few generations. Still, a predisposition toward patrilocal residence whenever possible is, we agree, highly plausible on a number of evolutionary grounds (see J. Martin and Stewart 1982; Fox 1967; C. Ember 1978). First, to the extent that savanna-living conditions in *early hominids* generated selection pressures against lone individuals and temporary groups, while selecting for increased organizational structure, a trend toward the formation of stable male-female bonds seems likely, for in a food-collecting society, this allows for an efficient breakdown into smaller heterosexual foraging parties during times of scarce or scattered resources. Second, to the extent that a female dispersal pattern operated in early hominids (as it does in nonhuman hominoids), a system of dispersing the females after puberty would be the least disruptive arrangement, since in every primate group studied at least one sex leaves the natal unit after puberty (Pusey and Packer 1987). Thus, if only by default as females transfer, there would be a bias toward patrilocality. Third, to the extent that keeping related males together for defense and good fellowship promoted survival and reproductive success (as it does for our closest relative, the chimpanzee), a patrilocal unit would be favored, and it may also have inadvertently laid the cooperative framework for communal hunting, as evidenced in the Upper Paleolithic fossil record (see Olsen 1989). To band together as one large patrilocal group that could separate easily into smaller parties would seem advantageous for large primates living in an open environment. Fourth, in terms of sheer numbers, it is difficult to deny that human societies have overwhelmingly favored patrilocal residence (Murdock 1967; C. Ember 1978). Finally, to the extent that a patrilocal residence pattern eventually gave rise to a unilineal descent system (found among horticulturalists), it is interesting that patrilineal kin groups (to be discussed in the next chapter) combine almost inevitably with this residence rule (Murdock 1967).

Having strayed a bit from our original point, let us finish our review of the hunter-gatherers' institutional structure. In the political and legal domain, such societies have only the most rudimentary of institutions. There is little polity because there is little inequality in power and authority. There may be a "headman" who performs certain activities, such as meeting with outsiders and other bands, but for the most part, the headman does what other males do and possesses no exceptional authority.[10] Some band members do have a certain "influence" because they

---

[10] The exception to this conclusion is "Big Men" societies, where lush fishing or other abundant resources have led hunter-gatherers to settle down. These societies are examined in the next chapter.

are particularly skilled at hunting and gathering, or religious activity, or perhaps artistic expression, but these people have no capacity to tell or force others to do anything. And in cases of serious conflict within the group, the matter is usually settled by having one of the parties leave the band. Law, too, is a recessive institution, in the sense that legal codes are not clearly differentiated from kinship norms and general cultural traditions. Although a "council of elders" can occasionally be found to pass judgments on deviant acts, these "courts" are rare, and judgments are not clearly articulated with a separate enforcement agent (e.g., the "police"). And there are no explicit law-making (legislative) bodies, although informal agreements are often negotiated among band members and, at times, between bands. There is, then, little need for a legal institution in small bands where informal control and easy out-migration are possible.

Other institutional structures are virtually nonexistent in hunting and gathering societies. Education is purely informal, involving some explicit tutelage, but in general children learn by watching and helping their parents and practicing among themselves the rudimentary skills of hunting and gathering. Medicine is tied to religious activity or, more typically, to folk practices that most members of the band know. And science is unknown because individuals do not seek explicit ways to develop new knowledge. Instead, they perform tasks as their parents did, with knowledge coming from learning "the ways of the ancestors" and from experience and practice.

In terms of institutional structure, then, most activity is organized within the nuclear or household kinship units that make up the band. Only economic, religious, and occasionally political (headman) activity can be observed outside kinship units, and even here, this activity is generally ruled by kinship and is typically conducted by individuals as such or by individuals as members of a nuclear family.[11] What is distinctive about a food-collecting society is its fluidity. It does not compel and constrain individuals in significant ways, beyond the need to secure food, reproduce and socialize members, and perhaps appease supernatural forces. The most unifying force among hunter-gatherers seems to be the intraband obligations that are dictated by a generalized "principle of reciprocity." Overall, the hunter-gatherer lifeway is relaxed and harmonious; and although in general socialization and child-rearing practices place a strong emphasis on "individualism" and "self-reliance" (Barry et al. 1959), most hunting and gathering societies are loosely organized around norms and values that emphasize sharing and cooperation. This image of the first human society runs counter to old sociological stereotypes, as we

---

[11] Again, the exception here is Big Men societies.

will explore later. But we should keep in mind one obvious fact as we proceed to examine other dimensions of these societies: the fluid and minimal nature of social structure and constraints.

Turning to the stratifying dimension of societal organization, we can say that hunters and gatherers come close to being a fully egalitarian system (Lenski 1966; J. Turner 1984). There is no real inequality over material wealth, since all adults have access to the same resources. Of course, there is very little material wealth—bows, arrows, spears, pots, simple building supplies—to be accumulated, since all possessions must be carried to the next settlement site. Some individuals enjoy greater prestige because of their skill and talent, but this prestige does not give them either power or extra material wealth. And although a band may have a headman, he has no real power to compel individuals to do as he asks. Thus, there is very little in the way of unequal distribution of resources in hunting and gathering societies; and as a result, there are no categories or social classes based on varying shares of resources.

In regard to the categoric dimension of societal organization, the major distinctions are between age and sex classes, much as in the case of other primates. Men and women play different social, economic, and domestic roles. Generally speaking, male roles are given more status, honor, and prestige than female roles (Schlegel 1972), and the very young and old are typically assigned to special categories that free them from most labor. Thus, the few categoric distinctions that do exist in hunting and gathering societies are tied to institutional structures, primarily the overlapping economic and kinship systems.

Corporate dimensions of hunting and gathering societies are also extensions of the institutional system, primarily the nuclear family. The family unit is organized for two explicit ends: the procurement of food and the procreation/socialization of the young. The band as a whole might also be seen as a corporate unit, since it seeks to organize nuclear families in ways that facilitate movement to available resources. But unlike the corporate units of more complex societies, the bands are not elaborate, hierarchical, or highly constraining. They are simply places where individuals have considerable freedom to choose when and how they will pursue their various lines of activity.

Table 3 summarizes the organization of hunting and gathering societies across the six structural dimensions. As is immediately evident, the institutional dimension is the main organizing axis, especially the bilateral kinship system. If we compare this structure with our reconstruction of the last common hominid ancestor in Chapter 2 (see Table 1), it is evident that hunting and gathering societies have greatly elaborated tie-building between males and females to form stable conjugal units. Other adult

TABLE 3

*The Organizing Dimensions of Hunting and Gathering Societies*

| Dimension | Description |
| --- | --- |
| 1. DEMOGRAPHIC | |
| Population size | Small; 50–80 people |
| Population movement | Cyclical migration within a delimited territory; seasonal or occasional break-up of band or out-migration of individuals and families, depending on resource levels |
| Growth | Maintenance of stable numbers through abortion, infanticide, and birth-spacing |
| 2. SPATIAL | |
| Internal distribution | Low population densities; band that periodically relocates within a fixed territory in a cyclical pattern |
| External distribution | Acknowledgment of other bands, especially those with similar culture, and acceptance of respective territorial claims |
| 3. INSTITUTIONAL | |
| Economy: | |
| Technology | Knowledge of food resources and limited tool-making |
| Capital | Hunting equipment (spears and, at times, bows and arrows); cooking utensils |
| Labor | Clear sexual division of labor; males hunt, and females gather |
| Entrepreneurship | Band and nuclear family units organize economic activity |
| Land | Low access to resources, revolving around securing indigenous animal and plant life and simple building materials |
| Kinship: | |
| Size and composition | Nuclear units and extended units |
| Residence | Neolocal, bilocal, and patrilocal |
| Activity | Clear division of labor; males hunt, and females gather and do domestic chores |
| Descent | Usually bilateral, but truncated |
| Authority | Egalitarian |
| Marriage | Incest prohibited; exogamy and endogamy; considerable freedom of choice; divorce easily effected |
| Religion: | |
| Beliefs | Conception of a supernatural realm of beings and forces, but not clearly organized into a cosmology; some mythology; no clear religious value system |
| Rituals | Some calendric rituals, but most rituals performed ad hoc as needed; shaman directs some rituals, but many performed by individuals on their own |
| Cult structure | None that can be distinguished from band or its nuclear units; occasional "festivals" when bands come together |
| Polity: | |
| Decision-making | Mostly individual or family-based; some decisions by band as whole |
| Power-authority | Headman in some cases with no power but some influence; high-prestige individuals can also exert influence |

| Dimension | Description |
|---|---|
| Law: | |
|     Legal codes | Undifferentiated from kinship norms and general cultural traditions |
|     Enforcement | No coercive capacity |
|     Courts | None; occasional "council of elders" |
|     Legislative bodies | None |
| Education | Informal socialization and learning through observation and individual tutelage and practice |
| Medicine | No specialists, though shaman may use rituals to deal with ill health; most medicine practical and known by all members of band |
| Science | None beyond development of practical economic technologies, and here rate of innovation is very slow |
| 4. STRATIFYING | |
| Resource distribution: | |
|     Material | No inequality |
|     Prestige | Some inequality |
|     Power | None exists and, hence, no inequality |
| Class formation | None |
| Mobility | None, since there are no classes |
| 5. CATEGORIC | Young and very old; male and female distinguished |
| 6. CORPORATE | |
| Spatial units | The band, which at times decides when and where to locate or organizes a party for a gathering/hunting foray |
| Institutional units | Most activity organized in nuclear or household family units |

SOURCES: Roth 1890; Hose and McDougall 1912; Radcliffe-Brown 1914, 1930; Spencer and Gillen 1927; Steward 1930; Holmberg 1950; Childe 1951; J. Clark 1952; Elkin 1954; Goldschmidt 1959; L. Davis and Reeves 1990; Goodale 1959; Turnbull 1961; Washburn 1961; Service 1962, 1966; G. Clark and Piggott 1965; Lenski 1966; Lee and DeVore 1968, 1976; Sahlins 1968a, 1968b, 1972; Coon 1971; Bicchieri 1972; Earle and Ericson 1977; Rick 1978; Tonkinson 1978; Lee 1979; Winterhalder and Smith 1981; Hayden 1981; Hultkrantz and Vorren 1982; Riches 1982; Schrive 1984; Johnson and Earle 1987; Hart et al. 1988; Howell 1988; Lenski et al. 1991.

kinship ties may be weak or strong, since families and individuals are not locked into tight-knit cliques that would constrain movement, but are free to leave one band and join another. For contemporary hunter-gatherers, marriage rules are flexible and culturally defined, although in all studied band societies, incest within the nuclear family is taboo (Murdock 1949: 12–13), which represents a normative extension of mother-son (and to a limited extent brother-sister) sexual avoidance found among Old World monkeys and apes (Pusey and Packer 1987). Much like contemporary chimpanzees and gorillas, hunters and gatherers have a home range within which band members move about either as a single unit or as dispersed nuclear units. A major spatial difference between humans and their ape cousins is that hunter-gatherers have more clearly organized territories, so that each band has a home range of its own that is honored by others, whereas among chimpanzees and gorillas, a number of individuals (in chimpanzees) or groups (in gorillas) share a home range. Again, the structural organization of space is a modest, still crucial extension of the ape pattern. The presence of a headman among some hunters-gatherers is similar to the pattern of a "lead" silverback male in each gorilla group and an "alpha" male for the regional area in which chimpanzees group and regroup. But the lack of a dominant headman in many bands should not be surprising, if our reconstruction of the Last Common Ancestor is correct. Our distant ancestor was not, we have argued, a hierarchical group-oriented animal; rather these ancestral groupings were probably small, loose, fluid, and leaderless. The reason for this structure was seemingly the marginal habitat in which our remote ancestor evolved; for in this arboreal niche, there were not sufficient resources for large, stable, and well-structured groupings. The relative lack of dominance and hierarchy among human food collectors (and other hominoids), compared with monkeys, reflects, we believe, this distant ancestral pattern of leaderless organization.

To survive, then, hunters and gatherers have elaborated on the hominoid organizational pattern in minimal ways: they created cohesive bands, but these are loosely structured with little organization; they strengthened male-female bonds, to form stable units as the structural core of their societies (as is the case with gibbons and gorillas); they organized territory so as to ensure that each band could secure resources; and they avoided hierarchies. Thus, contrary to much speculation about "human nature," hominids are not "killer apes" (Ardrey 1966), nor are they hierarchical or strongly territorial (van den Berghe 1973, 1974, 1975). Certainly, there are strong bonds among males, females, and offspring; these were, no doubt, selected as the easiest way to build structure on the phylogenetic base left by our Last Common Ancestor. And to sustain viable groups, selection pressures probably favored bonds among close relatives, as well as attachments among females and among individuals of different nuclear units. But these are not the same as the tight-knit monkey cliques and hierarchical structures of female matrilines, especially among such terrestrial species as macaques and baboon troops, with their ranked lineages and ascribed statuses (A. Jolly 1985: 123). Instead, they are more like the "friendships" that develop among male chimpanzees: overall fluid and loose networks. Moreover, to the extent that we are willing to interpret social grooming behavior among primates as a bonding ritual, hunters and gatherers (and most apes) display little in the way of bonding rituals as compared with cercopithecines. There are some exceptions here,[12] but one does not observe a high degree of ritual

[12] The hunting and gathering societies of Australia present what appear to be significant deviations from our portrayal of the first human society. We would expect, of course, some deviations as a result of varying ecological conditions. Moreover, contact with more com-

activity among hunters and gatherers. Hence, to the extent that rituals create strong bonds, or at least reinforce social relations, the simplest human societies are not tight-knit structures outside of the nuclear family unit. They can become more cohesive, but food-collecting societies are not necessarily, inevitably, or universally inclined to elaborate social structure. Indeed, as "fission-fusion" societies, human bands are more inclined to divide and disperse if necessity dictates or if conflicts emerge. Thus, hunting and gathering societies emerge as a crucial link to both the evolution of human society from its hominoid roots and, as we now turn to horticultural societies, the evolution of more complex societies.

## Conclusion

The first hominid and then human societies revolved around hunting and gathering among relatively small bands of individuals. The elaboration of social structure in terms of codes from the phylogenetic legacy of the Last Common Ancestor was, in our view, minimal: strengthening the male-female bond into the nuclear family and creating more cohesive and longer-lasting ties among diverse kinfolk in well-defined territories. Thus, the last phases of humans' biological evolution—from *Homo erectus* through *Homo sapiens* to *Homo sapiens sapiens*—occurred in small and flexible social structures. A central manifestation of genetic change in Homo was the increase in size and fissuration of the brain. The most reasonable interpretation of this change is that selection favored the ever-more-efficient use of tools and communication in terms of culture. Any other presumed genetic changes—say, the human sociobiologists' emphasis on kin selection and inclusive fitness, altruism, and reciprocal altruism—are unwarranted speculation; and any presumption that humans are genetically aggressive, highly territorial, and hierarchical is contradicted by the evidence from hunters and gatherers (the only case that could be made is for territoriality, but even this argument seems overdrawn).

plex societies has influenced, to some unknown degree, the organizational patterns of contemporary hunters and gatherers. Yet the aborigines of Australia do reveal social patterns that signal far more structure and constraint on individual behavior than we have portrayed and far more elaborate ritual activities and constraining marriage rules. Indeed, they remain an enigma in this regard. Australian hunter-gatherers do follow the band pattern of small, wandering groups on a given territory, with an emphasis on the nuclear family, few material possessions, little or no hierarchy, and a generalized "principle of reciprocity." What is puzzling is that some aborigines have elaborate symbol systems, with an emphasis on totemic clans buttressed by complex marriage rules, that lack apparent utilitarian value in a stone-age economy. The original portrait of Australian aborigines as constrained by rigid kinship, marriage, and residence rules, however, has been challenged by several Australian scholars, who argue for more flexible and fluid patterns. (For a general discussion, see Hiatt 1961–62, 1966.)

A further implication is that humans' genetic predispositions are perhaps closer to other living hominoid relatives than is typically realized. Humans may not be, in a genetic sense, as social as is often assumed. There was no doubt some biological evolution toward increased sociality, but how much? Present-day apes reveal degrees of sociality: mother-child bonds (all hominoid species); father-child bonds (only gibbons and perhaps gorillas); adult male-female bonds (gibbons, gorillas in the case of a mother and a leader male, and mothers and sons among chimpanzees); male-male sibling and assorted friendship bonds (typically chimpanzees only); adult female-female bonds (no ape species); and lone or individualistic travelers without apparent bonds (all species except gibbons). Given these weak propensities for tie formation among nonhuman hominoids, how much dramatic genetic selection could we expect for increased bonding in the six to eight million years since our hominid line shared a common ancestor with chimpanzees and gorillas? Some, of course, but—we contend—not nearly so much as has often been assumed. Human social relations are, we believe, primarily generated through an elaboration of culture, a by-product of the increased levels of communication made possible by a larger brain. That is, the more individuals interact and the more depth and complexity of interaction allowed, the greater are the possibilities for social bonding through shared ideas and symbols. Moreover, while our ability to form lots of weak ties and to socialize in a constant variety of temporary groupings have been greatly extended through shared symbols and propositional speech, it is easy to see how our social ways still rather closely parallel our chimpanzee relatives, whose greeting gestures and fluid but friendly male interactions help weld members into a community. Thus, at a genetic level, humans are probably much like our ape cousins and the LCA ancestor: somewhat individualistic, self-reliant, and mobile. If we are willing to consider this prospect, then the elaboration of social structure into more constraining patterns violates humans' genetic tendencies. Coevolution has, therefore, produced a fundamental tension between humans' primate legacy and their sociocultural constructions. Human society as it has evolved is thus a kind of cage, but one of our own construction. Why, then, we must ask, would humans put themselves in a cage from which they would perpetually want to flee, at least in terms of their genetic propensities? We can begin to see the answer to this question in a review of horticultural societies and the creation of the cage of kinship.

# 5 /   THE CAGE OF KINSHIP:

## Horticultural Societies

There is good evidence that Upper Paleolithic hunters and gatherers beginning about 40,000 years ago had a sophisticated understanding of the principles of cultivation— seeding and the seasonal growth of "crops" (Kabo 1985; Harlan 1975; D. Harris 1977). And it is easy to imagine food foragers scattering seeds as they left a site in the hope that plants would grow and be available for gathering on their return. But long after the appearance of *Homo sapiens sapiens*, humans continued to prefer a hunting and gathering way of life: the archaeological record reveals that food collectors did not begin to domesticate wild plants until about 10,000 years ago (Blumler and Byrne 1991; Flannery 1986; Byrne 1987).[1]

The adoption of "horticulture," or simple farming without the benefit of the plow and animal power, was not rapid. But once adopted, it tended to deplete resources in an area. For while the object of horticultural farming is to increase the energy yield on a plot of land, the early practitioners relied on the nutrients already present in the soil, and after a few years, the soil was exhausted, requiring that garden plots be moved. Moreover, horticulturalists typically hunt and kill most of the game in an area, especially as the settled population grows. The result is that hunters and gatherers are often forced to leave those territories where horticulturalists have settled, or give up and join them in farming to sustain themselves.

[1] Although cultivation and domestication are related terms, it is important to distinguish them when considering the origins of horticulture (or early farming). You can cultivate *either* a wild or a domestic plant from seeds, bulbs, or shoots. However, a domestic plant (or animal) has been genetically altered by human hands and, unlike its wild form has become relatively dependent on humans to survive and reproduce (see Blumler and Byrne 1991). At present, the archaeological record points to the Near East, especially the southern Levant (Jordan Valley) area, for the earliest definite traces of domestication—around 10,000 years ago (McCorriston and Hole 1991; Bar-Yosef and Kislev 1989).

Horticulture thus pushes aside the older hunting and gathering system; and so, as the number of horticulturalists increased, there was a corresponding decrease in hunting and gathering. But why did this process of displacement occur in the first place, especially since humans appeared to have been content with hunting and gathering?

The answer to this riddle probably varied somewhat in different parts of the world, but it is reasonable to conclude that, by and large, hunters and gatherers were compelled to turn to farming when they could no longer support themselves by the old techniques (M. Cohen 1977; Mann 1986; Sanders 1972; Lewin 1988). Horticulture yields far more food than hunting and gathering, but it is also a lot more work (Bates and Plog 1991: 65). Moreover, it requires more control, regulation, and coordination of large numbers of individuals. Land for crop production must be allocated; crops must be stored and distributed; conflicts and tensions must be mitigated; and defense against neighbors must be secured. Indeed, defense may have accelerated the need for organization (H. Spencer 1874–96; Webster 1975), for as populations grew and settled, resource competition would emerge as a result of the greater population density, increased resource extraction, and depletion of many indigenous resources, such as fertile land and game animals.

To become horticulturalists, then, necessitates the elaboration of culture and social structure; and as a consequence, humans began to cage themselves in sociocultural creations. One probable historical sequence in this caging process is that improvements in hunting technology—more efficient bows and arrows and hardened spears, for instance—led to a decrease in big game animals in a region, forcing hunters to become farmers to support even small bands; and as they did so, their numbers grew and forced them to remain horticulturalists (Lenski and Lenski 1987: 131). Another possible historical sequence is that some bands established relatively permanent settlements near fertile rivers, where fish and plant life were abundant; and as a result of this "prosperity," they overbred themselves, creating a larger population that required increasing amounts of gardening to be sustained. Such a scenario would be particularly likely if big game in a region were hunted out, if once plentiful local resources were depleted, and if neighboring populations began to claim the remaining resources (Johnson and Earle 1987).

Whatever the precise sequence of events in different regions of the world, humans were probably forced to cage themselves, if they were to survive.[2] Hunters and gatherers of today—the few that still remain in the

---

[2] There are many theories on why hunters-gatherers shifted to a sedentary lifestyle. The consensus is that most humans were forced to take up plant cultivation because of certain pressures that very likely included population pressures (M. Cohen 1977; Binford 1968; Lewin 1988). It is important to recognize that demographic pressures on the food supply

most marginal habitats—are often asked why they do not take up agriculture; their answer is usually that farming is too much work and restricts their freedoms. A case in point are the !Kung of Botswana who, when asked why they did not take up plant cultivation, replied: "Why should we plant when there are so many mongongo nuts in the world?" (Lee 1968: 33). Humans did not rush to settle down and farm; they did so very gradually and probably reluctantly, because in tilling and harvesting the land, they had to relinquish most of their hunting and gathering cultural heritage, a lifeway that had easily accommodated biological propensities for freedom, movement, and individualism.[3] Only severe selection pressures would, we believe, push humans to genetically alter plants and animals (a time-consuming process that is physically arduous and restricts individuals to a fixed plot of land) and to create the restrictive structures that violated their inherent propensities. But once created, such structures would, in the long run, "push out" the more primordial hunting and gathering mode, or at least push it to the edges of territories or to isolated pockets in the gradually spreading structure of "civilization." If there was a "garden of eden" in human history, hunting and gathering comes as close to it as was ever possible (Sahlins 1968a). Obviously, wandering bands with few possessions and dependent on wild game and indigenous plants for food are not living in great luxury. But they had something that most humans have yet to recapture—equality (with respect to social, economic, and political rights), leisure, considerable freedom from sociocultural constraints, and relative insulation from the ravages of external war and internal conflict. The last two were to be the outcomes of human progress.

We can get some sense for the likely reluctance of hunters and gatherers to cage themselves in more elaborate structures by looking at populations that only settle in gardening hamlets for part of the year. They are perhaps a looking glass to the distant past, as hunters and gatherers were slowly pulled into full-time horticulture. Allen Johnson and Timothy Earle (1987: 63), for example, argue that "agriculture and pastoralism appear not as economic revolutions permitting a sedentary lifestyle, but as long and gradual transitions" in which people perhaps first created vil-

---

can come about either by an actual increase in population or by a decrease in resources for a stable population. The ideas of Ester Boserup (1965) have been especially influential; she proposed that population growth is the prime mover in triggering technological innovations aimed at increasing agricultural productivity at any stage of human social evolution. Robert Carneiro (1967) has also shown that larger populations are associated with more complex organization.

[3] Western civilization from the nineteenth century on has promoted an ideology of progress: that social change is both inevitable and desirable. It is often not recognized that among most traditional peoples the opposite is true: social change is viewed as mostly negative, and the ways of the ancestors best (see Bodley 1975).

lages simply as places to cultivate and store grain against lean times while retaining the nuclear family units and other structural arrangements of a hunting and gathering way of life. Early villages in the Middle East and Mesoamerica, for instance, indicate that families maintained domiciles in more than one place in these transitional societies. Similarly, the household units of the Machiguenga of the Peruvian Amazon often remain isolated from each other, with hamlets emerging primarily in response to resource scarcity and efforts at cooperation (Johnson and Earle 1987: 67). Among the Nganasan of Northern Siberia, animal husbandry does not force the elaboration of social structures beyond nuclear family units, for while there is some sharing among families, they retain a clear autonomy.

Thus, even when people use more advanced technologies, they resist imposing constraints. They remain in Johnson and Earle's (1987: 62) terminology "family-level societies," where kinship and polity have not created a social cage. They scatter across a territory, aggregating when needed (for fishing, herding, storing crops, and other cooperative activities) in seasonal hamlets, but always maintaining the autonomy of the family and the freedom of individuals. When possible, then, people preserved their individuality, as would be expected if our inferences about humans' genetic nature are correct.

As resource pressures mount, however, more permanent settlements become necessary, and conflict over resources begins to erupt. Yet even when needs for more intensive farming and defense escalate, local groups in hamlets and villages seek to disperse, if possible, and they try to avoid the elaboration of kinship structures and polity. For example, the famous and ferocious Yanomamö of South America (Chagnon 1983) often organize into permanent settlements, primarily for defense, but there are still many small and mobile groups, whose freedom and autonomy are admired by the settled population; and their household units, while extended, remain relatively autonomous. Moreover, although Yanomamö kin groupings have been described in the vocabulary of unilineal descent (Johnson and Earle 1987: 115), a full-blown unilineal kinship system has not developed. Instead, the Yanomamö system is considered bilateral but with a definite agnatic emphasis (i.e., relations through males) (Shapiro 1972: 9). Indeed, if it were not for constant warfare (Horgan 1988), even these emerging kinship structures would probably disband. This is suggested by the situation seen in smaller villages at the outer fringes of "Yanomamö Land," where bilateral kinship prevails, often without a strong patrilineal emphasis, in conjunction with a less-developed sense of male "fierceness" and a lower incidence of warfare (Shapiro 1972: 81–83, 170).

Thus, once again, we see a reluctance to construct a cage of kinship, even when, as in the Yanomamö case, resource scarcity, overpopulation, and war generate strong pressures for more rigid and complex kinship structures and patterns of political leadership. Kinship begins to enclose the individual, and dominating leaders become valued. Yet there is no headlong rush to elaborate these caging processes beyond what is minimally necessary.

In gradually abandoning hunting and gathering, however reluctantly, people faced new problems. How were their larger numbers to be organized and coordinated to ensure the food supply? How were territories to be maintained for farming and, in some cases, herding and fishing? How were territories to be defended? It is often assumed that humans "naturally" adapted to the new sociocultural creations that were constructed to answer these questions. Our view is that this was not an easy accommodation, for it violates "human nature." The increase in ritual, religion, external war, and sudden eruptions of internal conflict all signal that horticultural systems exist in a most volatile and uneasy tension with humans' more basic needs for greater independence and freedom (see Lenski et al. 1991). In leaving hunting and gathering, humans created a cage—kinship and the beginnings of polity—from which they have frequently sought to escape.

## Horticultural Social Organization

There is considerable variation in horticultural systems, leading most analysts to distinguish between "simple" and "advanced" forms, but the distinguishing characteristic of all horticulturalists is farming or gardening without the benefit of the plow and nonhuman sources of energy.[4] Table 4 summarizes in general terms the organization of both simple and more advanced horticultural societies; and below, we highlight the key features of this summary.

Demographically, horticultural societies vary in size, from an average of 100 to 150 people in simple systems to 5,000 or 6,000 in advanced forms. In simple horticultural societies, soil depletion usually forces some resettlement every few years, whereas in more advanced systems, permanent core cities can often be found, with only peripheral villages evidencing periodic resettlement. The population tends to grow in horticultural societies, up to the available resources and, at times, beyond these limits. Cycles of overpopulation may well have posed a problem for many horticulturalists, forcing them to expand their boundaries, resettle, or pursue the resources of other societies through war.

[4] The text discussion is based on the sources shown in Table 4.

## TABLE 4
### The Organizing Dimensions of Horticultural Societies

| Dimension | Description | |
|---|---|---|
| | Simple society | Advanced society |
| **1. DEMOGRAPHIC** | | |
| Population size | 80 to 5,000 people, but usually about 100–150 | 500 to 100,000 people, but usually about 5,000–6,000 |
| Population movement | Semipermanent settlements; movement when soil is no longer fertile; occasionally, a more permanent core or central "city" | Semipermanent settlements and movement on periphery; permanent settlements at core city, with movement in and out of it becoming typical |
| Growth | Variable; some societies remain stable, others grow | Tend to grow up to resource limits |
| **2. SPATIAL** | | |
| Internal distribution | Autonomous small villages, with surrounding gardens; at times, waves of political (through conflict) unification and dissolution of ties/alliances among villages; use of footpaths to connect villages; almost always kin ties among villages; relatively small amounts of territory used, even when interconnections among villages exist | Larger villages, often linked economically and politically to a core city, and connected not only by paths but by quasi-roads; larger amounts of territory are incorporated into the village-city network; kin ties almost always link villages and are basis for political and economic linkages |
| External distribution | Incessant warfare with other villages or networks of villages; some trade and exchange with other villages and societies | Incessant warfare with other societies; considerable amount of trade and exchange with other societies |
| **3. INSTITUTIONAL** | | |
| Economy: | | |
| Technology | Knowledge of herding, farming (planting, harvesting, storing, grinding, and cooking of grains), tool-making (initially with stone, then with metals), pottery-making (with kilns, which later lead to annealing, smelting, casting, and eventually, alloying) | Knowledge of herding, breeding, farming, fertilizing, and crop rotation, tool-making with metals (with exceptions, such as ancient China), pottery-making, metallurgy, and masonry |
| Capital | Tools, pottery, housing-storage sheds, negotiable items used (in most cases) in barter; unstable economic surplus; little ability to horde perishable commodities | Tools, pottery, housing-storage sheds, walled cities, and the beginnings of liquid capital—money; stable economic surplus, which can be used in exchange and horded |

| | | |
|---|---|---|
| Labor | Clear division of labor between males and females (with females doing most of the tending of gardens); specialized occupational "trades" in weapon-making, pottery, house-building, boat-building, and bartering; some use of proto-slaves captured in war | Clear division of labor between males and females; in-creased level of specialization in trades and occupations, especially in masonry, metal-working, weaving, leather-making, pottery-ceramics, boat- and house-building, and commerce; frequent use of slaves captured in war |
| Entrepreneurship | Community/village structure; kinship units in villages are principal organizing structure, though village leaders/head-man often allocate gardening plots and other resources, extracting some of the product to redistribute to village members; at times, a few trade specialists | Community structure; kinship and headman are principal organizing structure at village level, with leaders and head-man involved in resource allocation and redistribution; in-creased number of trade specialists; in larger core cities, merchants and markets become major entrepreneurial mechanisms |
| Land | Modest access to living resources; constant problem of resource depletion; limited access to nonliving, physical resources | Increased access to living resources; some problems in resource depletion, but increased ability to sustain land (through fertilizing and crop rotation); increased access to nonliving, physical resources |
| Kinship: Size and composition | Extended units | Same as simple societies |
| Residence | Patri- or matrilocal, but mostly patrilocal | Same as simple societies |
| Activity | Clear division of labor between males and females in economic, community, political, religious, and domestic tasks | Same as simple societies |
| Descent | Unilineal, generally patrilineal; organized to lineage and clan level, and at times, to moiety level | Same as simple societies |
| Authority | Male-dominated | Same as simple societies |
| Marriage | Incest prohibited; considerable exogamy and endogamy; dissolution allowed | Same as simple societies |
| Religion: Beliefs | Conception of supernatural realm of beings and forces; no clear organization of supernatural into cosmology, but con-siderable mythology; no explicit religious value system or moral code | Conception of supernatural realm of beings and forces; in-creased organization of supernatural realm into levels and a hierarchical pantheon of gods and forces; extensive my-thology often evident; some indication of explicit values and moral codes |

(Continued on next page)

TABLE 4 (*continued*)

| Dimension | Simple society | Advanced society |
|---|---|---|
| | | Description |
| Rituals | Clear and regular calendrical rituals, usually performed by individuals alone or in kin groupings, but at times led by shaman | Regular calendrical rituals, often led by shaman and, in more complex systems, by full-time priests; increased control and mediation of ritual activity by religious specialists |
| Cult structure | Explicit structures devoted to religious activity, involving (1) division of labor among lay participants, lay organizers-sponsors, performers, and religious specialists (shamans, magicians, and others deemed to have special capabilities to mediate with supernatural); (2) explicit symbols and artifacts representing various aspects of the supernatural, and at times (3), specialized buildings and places where cult members meet to perform religious activity | Explicit structures devoted to religious activity, involving (1) clear division of labor between religious specialists (often full-time) and increasingly less active lay persons, who assume role of worshipers; (2) hierarchy of religious specialists; (3) elaborate symbols and artifacts representing each aspect of the supernatural; and (4) specialized buildings and places (temples) for religious specialists to perform religious activity for lay persons |
| Polity: Decision-making | Explicit headman or chief at village level empowered to make decisions, sometimes consulting with kin elders and religious specialists; often paramount chief who, in consultation with local village/kin leaders, makes decisions for larger network of villages | Explicit king or high chief empowered to make decisions for all community and kin units, sometimes in consultation with local village/kin leaders and religious specialists |
| Power-authority | Coercive capacity, but limited by kinship networks and alliances; power to extract surplus, but there is usually a redistributive requirement, and with redistribution of what is extracted basis for prestige and legitimacy; sometimes village headman and almost always paramount chief has staff and army, typically composed of his own kinsmen and selected kinsmen of other lineages or clans | Clear coercive capacity, allowing for the extraction of labor, material surplus, and property of others; usually, a well-developed taxation formula and administrative bureaucracy (composed of kinsmen and selected individuals from other kin groupings and villages) for collecting taxes and performing other administrative chores; typically an administrative power and prestige hierarchy emanating from king and close advisers to paramount chiefs, village headmen, and kin leaders; legitimacy based on acts of redistribution and, at times, religious beliefs and ritual |

| | | |
|---|---|---|
| **Law:** | | |
| Legal codes | Permeated by custom, tradition, and kinship norms, but some differentiation between substantive law (rights, duties, obligations, prohibitions) and procedural law (administration, adjudication, and enforcement); all legal codes unwritten and not clearly codified | Explicit codes, often reflecting custom, tradition, and kinship norms; growing differentiation between substantive and procedural law; legal codes still unwritten in most cases but more clearly codified |
| Enforcement | Many laws explicitly enforced by kin, village leaders, or paramount chief; usually some form of restitution required, but in extreme cases, banishment from the society imposed | All laws explicitly enforced by kin, village leaders, and representatives of paramount chief or king; restitution, banishment, imprisonment, loss of property, demotion to slave status, and death are all possible sanctions |
| Courts | Ad hoc and created to deal with a particular dispute or deviant act; the roles of judge, aggrieved parties, and defendant emerge, but usually there are no permanent "judges"; typically, headman or council of elders, but at times, third parties from another village or kin group, adjudicate disputes and decide on sanctions | Ad hoc courts at local village level, but more formal and permanent courts begin to emerge in core city and adjudicate disputes and deviant acts in a territory; explicit judge positions exist (even if only part-time) |
| Legislative bodies | At village and intervillage level, councils of elders, kin leaders, religious specialists, and village heads often make laws | Superimposed on councils at village and intervillage level are more extensive bodies of paramount chiefs and the king, whose edicts usurp local laws |
| Education | Some explicit tutelage for religious and political specialists, as well as for particular crafts; few, if any, education structures outside kinship and community structures | Explicit tutelage for religious, political, and military specialists, often in clearly defined structures outside kinship and community; apprentice-like tutelage of economic/craft specialists, most often by kinsfolk |
| Medicine | No specialization, though religious specialists often ritually seek cures; most medicine is folk techniques and known by most adult members | Some medical specialization, though often tied to religion and kinship structures; some specialized knowledge beyond folk techniques known by all adults |
| Science | None beyond practical and military technologies; rate of innovation slow | Little beyond practical and military technologies, but some efforts to learn and understand aspects of physical (astronomy) and biological (medicine) universe; perhaps a few specialized practitioners; rate of innovation still slow but considerably faster than in simple systems |

(*Continued on next page*)

TABLE 4 (*continued*)

| Dimension | Description | |
|---|---|---|
| | Simple society | Advanced society |
| **4. STRATIFYING** | | |
| Resource distribution: | | |
| Material | Moderate inequality; headmen, religious specialists, heads of kin units, some craft specialists and paramount chiefs receive surplus material goods (food, lodging, weapons, land), though redistribution requirements on political leaders mitigate degree of material inequality | High inequality; headmen, religious elite, paramount chiefs, military elites, successful craft specialists, and especially king and his court receive surplus material goods; accumulation of wealth becomes possible as more material surplus becomes durable and redistribution requirements begin to recede somewhat |
| Prestige | Moderate inequality; chiefs, headmen, heads of kin group, shamans, exceptional warriors, and some craft specialists receive honor and deference | High inequality; king, his court and kin, local headmen, some craft specialists, and religious, military, and administrative elites receive considerable honor and deference |
| Power | Moderate inequality; chief with staff can coerce conformity and have right to extract surplus resources; chief and local headmen have legitimated rights to regulate and administer village activity, especially in economic sphere | High inequality; king and his army possess considerable coercive ability and can extract labor, property, and other material surplus through well-developed taxation collection systems; there is also a stable bureaucratic hierarchy connecting king, village heads, paramount chiefs, and kin heads |
| Class formation | Some, but not developed into homogeneous ranks; clear differentiation of headman and religious elites from others; if there is a dominant kin group (lineage or clan), then some differentiation among kin grouping; also, at times, village differentiation, with one village dominating others; vast majority population forms a single class, with distinctions by kin group, sex, age, and at times, craft specialization being salient but not producing distinctive social classes | Several homogeneous subpopulations in a hierarchy of ranks; political leaders and their kin constitute distinctive grouping, as do religious specialists; military elites and economic specialists can become distinctive subgroupings; slaves, where found, constitute a distinctive class; vast majority of population forms a single class, with distinctions by kin group, sex, age, and age being salient but not producing distinctive social classes; however, craft specialties and other economic positions can produce identifiable classes, and ethnic distinctions can also create a new basis of class formation |

| | | |
|---|---|---|
| Mobility | Little mobility since class formation is tied to kinship; at times, members of kin groups can achieve power through military activities; some mobility also possible through craft and market activities | Little mobility, though special skill in military, economic, or religious sphere can lead to some mobility |
| 5. CATEGORIC<br>Age and sex | Young and old, plus increased numbers of intermediate age classes are distinguished; clear male-female distinctions in all activities | Same as simple societies |
| Ethnicity | Some distinctions at times, if there has been conquest or contact with other cultures | Frequent distinctions, since conquest and contact with other cultures are typical |
| Kinship | Kin-group affiliation at lineage, clan, and at times, moiety level highly salient and constraining | Kin-group affiliation highly salient but less constraining in more advanced systems |
| Economic | Some distinctions over craft specialization | Numerous distinctions over craft specialization |
| Religious | Some distinctions between shaman/religious practitioners and others | Clear and often fine-tuned distinctions of religious specialists from others and among those at different points in a religious hierarchy |
| Political | Clear distinctions between heads of village, networks of villages, and kin groups and others; distinctions among warriors also sometimes salient | Clear and complex distinctions between leaders and administrators at different levels of political hierarchies; extensive distinctions among warriors, and between warriors and general population |
| Class | Membership in homogeneous and ranked subpopulation, or class, can be bound with respect to power and perhaps kin group and craft specialty, but these are not as salient as other categoric distinctions | Membership in a class becomes highly significant basis for categorizing individuals; population can usually be divided into several classes: elites (high-ranking members of political, kinship, religious, military, and economic hierarchies), administrative functionaries in emerging governmental bureaucracy, and emerging trade specialists, craft workers, farmers, and slaves; not all these classes are necessarily well formed and used as a basis for categoric distinctions, but some are always salient |

*(Continued on next page)*

TABLE 4 (*continued*)

| Dimension | Description | |
| --- | --- | --- |
| | Simple society | Advanced society |
| 6. CORPORATE<br>Spatial units | Villages and networks of villages organize much activity; almost always influenced by kinship rules | Village organization supplemented by emergence of core cities revolving around trade, polity, and religion |
| Institutional units:<br>Kinship | Unilineal descent creating well-organized and highly constraining kin units organized at least to the lineage level and frequently to clan and moiety level | Unilineal descent creating well-organized units to at least the clan level, but with other corporate units beginning to supplement and supplant kinship units |
| Economic | Coextensive with kin units | Kinship begins to lose monopoly with emergence of specialized economic units, though these are often embedded in, or influenced by, kinship units |
| Political | Headman's kin unit, along with council of elders and military leaders, both also usually linked by kinship ties, organize activity | Quasi-state, army, and courts not wholly circumscribed by kinship begin to emerge |
| Religious | Cults but almost always extensions of kinship units | Cults not tied to kinship and organized by religious specialists and, at times, into quasi-bureaucratic structures; competing cults and sects sometimes evident |
| Education | None, outside of kinship | Some apprenticeship to craft and religious units |
| Associational units | Secret societies within kinship units, and usually only for males | Secret societies within kinship but also outside of kinship, especially with respect to religious and military activity; social clubs outside of kinship emerge, as do economic and political associations |

SOURCES: General features are drawn from Gordon 1914; Malinowski 1922; Landtman 1927; Childe 1930, 1952, 1953, 1960, 1964; Herskovits 1938; Goldschmidt 1959; Leach 1954; Schapera 1956; Murdock 1959; von Hagen 1961; Mair 1962; Chang 1963; MacNeish 1964; Hawkes 1965; Gibbs 1965; Lenski 1966; Mellaart 1965; Parsons 1966; Fried 1967; Chagnon 1968; Heider 1970; Goldman 1970; Flannery 1973; Bender 1975; Service 1975; M. Harris 1978; Kirch 1980, 1984; Earle 1984; Mann 1986; Johnson and Earle 1987; Lenski and Lenski 1987; Lenski et al. 1991; Bates and Plog 1991.

For descriptions and analysis of kinship systems, see Keesing 1975; Schneider and Gough 1961; Fox 1967; Pasternak 1976; M. Ember and Ember 1971; C. Ember et al. 1974; Graburn 1971. For basic references on this type of economy, see Lenski and Lenski 1987: 130–31; Sahlins 1968b; Boserup 1965; Sanderson 1988: 62–67; J. Turner 1972: 25–27. For basic descriptions and analyses of religion in these types of systems, see Wallace 1966; J. Turner 1972; G. Swanson 1960; Parsons 1966; O'Dea 1970; Norbeck 1961; Malinowski [1925] 1955; Lowie 1948; Goode 1951. References used to construct the description of the polity among simple horticulturalists and, then, the beginnings of a quasi-state include Schapera 1956; Mair 1962; Sahlins 1963; Fried 1967; Lenski 1966; Parsons 1966; Carneiro 1970; R. Cohen and Service 1977; Claessen and Skalnick 1978; Murra 1980; Haas 1982; Kirch 1984; Mann 1986; Lenski and Lenski 1987; Johnson and Earle 1987; Lenski et al. 1991. For discussions of legal evolution in these types of systems, see J. Turner 1972, 1974; Hoebel 1954; Gurvitch 1953; Diamond 1951; Lloyd 1964; Vaco 1988; Schwartz and Miller 1964.

In simple systems, small and relatively autonomous villages of huts surrounded by gardens are typical, although there are often ties and alliances among villages linked by kinship rules. In more advanced societies, villages are typically linked not only by kinship but by economic and political ties to a larger core or "capital" city. In both types, warfare with external societies is constant, and in advanced societies especially, there is considerable external trade and exchange.

Institutionally, the principal organizing mechanism is kinship. There is usually a clear unilineal descent rule, where descent is traced through one parental line only, and it is generally patrilineal with numerous exceptions. A unilineal descent rule can organize extended family units into a lineage, or a grouping of males and females who trace their blood lines through exact genealogical lines to a common known ancestor, either male or female; and if a more complex structure is to be constructed, the descent rule organizes lineages into clans, or groupings of lineages descended from a common ancestor without reconstructing the exact genealogical links. Even larger structural units can be created by organizing clans into moieties. Of course those transitional systems where gathering is still the principal activity and gardening only supplemental do not evidence clear unilineal descent.

The prevailing descent rule among horticulturalists often dictates the residence pattern (e.g., patrilineal descent calls for patrilocal residence, matrilineal descent for matrilocal residence), as well as the composition of family units and marriage rules of exogamy and endogamy. In all kinship systems, whether patrilineal or matrilineal, males dominate politically and domestically, despite the substantial contribution of women to subsistence activities (Fox 1967: 97). This declining status of women with a move to a sedentary lifestyle has been imputed to their greater confinement to near-home activities; women with increased household chores, garden-keeping responsibilities, and rates of reproduction could no longer enjoy the autonomy and mobility of their nomadic sisters (Draper 1975; Kolata 1974). In contrast, men perform most religious and political activities of the community and most away-from-home trade and warfare activities.

Full-fledged unilineal systems are complex and highly restrictive in that they use residence, descent, and authority to aggregate individuals and to constrain their social behaviors by dictating the rights and obligations of each kinship position within a greatly extended network of ties. As a result, many relations within and between lineages, clans, and other extended units are mediated by rituals to reduce potential tensions and, at the same time, to highlight the significance and overriding importance of kinship bonds for conjugal relations, defense, economic cooperation, and most other social activities. Thus, in unilineal systems, most social relations "are very largely regulated on the basis of kinship" (Radcliffe-Brown 1971: 89).

Unilineal descent has been viewed by some scholars as the natural way for humans to organize themselves (Radcliffe-Brown 1952: 48) because it is the easiest base on which to elaborate structure so as to organize larger numbers of individuals. Indeed, kinship is the most rational way and the only base available to populations that cannot produce sufficient material surplus to sustain non-kin organizations. Yet kinship involves humans' most intimate social ties and emotions, and its use as the major structuring principle of a society through extended family ties with high degrees of obligation and involvement creates potential tensions that need to be regulated and controlled. Such needs translate into additional constraints—norms, rituals, clear roles—in order to handle the burdens of using a structure that evolved to regularize sex, reproduction, and the socialization of the young for uniting and organizing larger numbers of individuals. Thus, in moving to horticulture, humans were compelled to create an emotionally charged sociocultural cage revolving around proscriptive kinship rules that circumscribed most attitudes and social relations; and in so doing, they limited their options and autonomy as compared with hunters and gatherers, while placing themselves in what often became an emotional tinderbox.

The use of kinship to cage and organize a larger population was inevitable in light of the nature of horticulture as an economic mode of adaptation to the environment. In terms of the basic elements of economic organization delineated in Table 4 (J. Turner 1972), the level of technology, capital formation, labor power, entrepreneurship, and access to resources (land) was still rather low. With respect to technology, knowledge of gardening, harvesting, grinding, cooking, and tool-making was not elaborate in simple systems. But there were some critical breakthroughs that were to be extended, especially with respect to using fire to make pots and, in some regions, to begin metallurgy. As a consequence, more advanced sytems could develop more efficient tools made of metal, while improving on potting and other kiln-produced products. Moreover, experience with gardening would "teach" the principles of fertilization (perhaps initially a by-product of herding) and crop rotation, allowing for larger and more consistent yields. In regard to capital formation, tools, pottery, storage sheds, and in more advanced systems, stone buildings and metal tools were the basic materials for production. In simple systems, economic surplus was perishable and, hence, not easily accumulated, but as new forms of production—ceramics, metal working, masonry—were developed, the level of economic surplus could increase and be used not only to create personal and permanent wealth but also to expand production. Such expansion would depend on the specialization of labor, which initially was limited in simple systems to sexual and domestic divisions; but increasingly, specialized trades and occupations greatly expanded the productivity of each worker, as well as the volume and velocity of trade and exchange. To some degree, the use of kinship as the major organizing mechanism of the economy would limit economic expansion, but the development of trading centers, markets, and merchants in more advanced systems all represented new entrepreneurial mechanisms that could supplement and later supplant kinship as the organizational base of the economy. Finally, land or access to resources was limited in both simple and advanced systems—being confined to crops, easily secured metals, and animal herds. Only with the adoption of masonry, refined metallurgy, and the use of crop rotation and fertilizers in more advanced systems could access to resources be increased. But even here, there was an upper limit as long as human energy was the source of power driving the economy. Only when nonhuman sources of power could be harnessed to tools would access to resources be dramatically increased.

In simple horticultural systems, religion is somewhat more complex and constraining than in hunting and gathering societies. We term these systems "communal religions" among simple horticulturalists (Wallace 1966: 86–87). With respect to beliefs, the cosmology of communal religions is only slightly more complicated than in shamanic religions. The pantheon is a loosely structured conglomerate of supernatural deities and spirits. However, the mythology surrounding these deities tends to be more elaborate than in the shamanic religions of hunters and gatherers. The values of the belief system of communal religions are not clearly articulated or systematized, and they are not codified into a moral code. The cult structure and its organization are considerably more complex in communal than in the shamanic religions of hunters and gatherers. In addition to individualistic cults, there are cults that can be termed "communal" (Wallace 1966: 87). These cults usually display a division of labor: lay participants; lay organizers, sponsors, and performers; and religious specialists (shamans, magicians, etc.). The rituals performed in these communal cults tend to be calendrical, with laymen organizing and often performing at least some of the prescribed rituals. Frequently, this organization of lay personnel begins to approximate a bureaucratic structure with regular technical and supervisory assignments for laymen. Yet no full-time priesthood or elaborate religious hierarchy can be said to exist (Wallace 1966: 87). Communal cults vary in size from small to very large, encompassing the whole community. Membership also varies and usually revolves around special social categories such as age and sex or around special groups like secret societies or kinship groupings.

Communal religions among simple horticulturalists thus display a level of structural organization beyond that evidenced in the shamanic religions of hunters and gatherers. Cult structures are more varied and begin to evidence bureaucratic organization. The belief system is only slightly more elaborate than that among simpler religions, although the mythology tends to be more extensive. But within communal religions are the seeds of the kinds of belief system and cult organization that become conspicuous features of what we will term the "ecclesiastical religions" of more advanced horticultural systems, as well as even more advanced agrarian systems to be discussed in the next chapter. These ecclesiastic religions display a marked increase in the complexity of both the belief system and cult structure.

The most notable difference between the belief systems of ecclesiastic and communal religions is the extensiveness and complexity of the cosmology (G. Swanson 1960). In some ecclesiastic religions, there is an elaborate pantheon, as well as a relatively clear hierarchical ordering of the supernatural beings in terms of power and influence. There is also usually a creator god—a supernatural being who created both the natural and the supernatural. The mythology of the cosmology is often well developed and can include episodes in the lives of gods, fraternal jealousies, sexual relations, and competition among various supernatural deities. In some traditional ecclesiastical religions, values begin to be codified into a code of rights and wrongs, although religious values more typically remain tied to and fused with ritual activity.

We have labeled such religions ecclesiastic because this label denotes a new, revolutionary form of cult structure: the beginnings of a professional clergy, which is organized into an emerging bureaucracy. These clergy differ from both shamans and lay officials, in the one case because they are not private and individual entrepreneurs, and in the other, because they are formally appointed or elected as more or less full-time religious specialists (or priests). Relations among these priests usually become somewhat hierarchical in terms of prestige and power. These professionals are also exclusively responsible for performing certain rituals, calendrical and noncalendrical alike, with laymen increasingly becoming passive respondents rather than active participants and managers (Wallace 1966: 88). Such rituals are performed in established and enduring temple structures. Furthermore, these religious specialists begin to exert tremendous nonreligious influence and perhaps authority in secular (as well as sacred) activities. The emergence of an ecclesiastic cult structure marks a major stage in religious evolution. Typically, even in the more advanced societies, this type of cult structure is just beginning to develop, though among some horticulturalists of the past, such as the Maya of the New World, a relatively well developed system existed.

The polity in horticultural societies is limited by the amount of economic surplus that can be produced (Lenski 1966). But the locus of power and decision-making is rarely ambiguous; and in most systems, particular kin groups (usually clans) have assumed power on the basis of territorial holdings. The authority and descent rules of these dominant kin groups determine who the political elite are. In more advanced horticultural societies, these elites make decisions for others in the dominant kin group, as well as for subordinate kin groupings. These elite leaders are usually called chiefs in simple societies; in more advanced systems, they can become kings. This points to the fact that the sphere of power and decision-making in these traditional polities can vary greatly. In some there are limited territorial boundaries encompassing various kin groupings and/or villages over which a chief or chiefs rule. In others, territorial boundaries are sufficiently vast and fixed as to approximate a nation. In either case, the polity maintains and defends its boundaries from outside encroachment. To do this, both chiefs and kings begin to appropriate part of the economic surplus of subordinate groups (usually through taxation) to finance the administrative and military organizations needed to maintain and control the territory or nation. Thus, the sphere of power and decision-making of the polity becomes increasingly more articulated, geographically bounded, and compelling on subordinate incumbents.

The basis of the polity's power to make decisions is a mixture of tradition, religious sanctioning, and force. In small, kin-based polities, the power to make decisions is based more on tradition and religion than on force. Leaders are sanctioned by their ties with the gods and by the fact that custom and tradition have always dictated who should rule. But as the territorial sphere of the polity increases, force often becomes necessary to maintain control. This is especially true if the polity is expanding its influence through the conquest of neighboring territories, a situation that forces the polity to expropriate surplus from conquered territories in order to maintain the military organization needed to enforce decisions. In principle, the acquisition of power and decision-making prerogatives in kin-based traditional polities is through hereditary succession in accordance with the authority and descent rules of the kinship subsystem. But in practice this is not always the case. Succession often involves considerable violence and bloodshed as fellow kinsmen jockey for the right to rule. And sometimes high-level and ambitious administrators or military leaders from nonelite clans become involved in power struggles. Such coups and usurpations of power from nonelite kin groupings become much more frequent and typical in advanced horticultural societies.

The exercise of power and decision-making involves both an administrative staff and a military organization. The administrative staff is composed of kinsmen from elite kin groups, but as the tasks of administration increase, incumbents from nonelite kin groups begin to be recruited. Military organizations are usually led by members of elite kin groups, while the rank and file tend to be drawn from the nonelite kin groupings. But exceptional performance in military activities can bring nonelites into leadership positions. The emergence of these kin-dominated military and administrative organizations marks the incipience of the state, which becomes the principal form of political organization in agrarian societies, generating a new kind of sociocultural cage—the cage of power and bureaucracy.

Law as an institution is tied to the polity, for as "a state" begins to emerge, clear legal codes, enforcement agents, courts, and legislative bodies become evident. Horticulturalists only initiate the transition to the state and, therefore, the institution of law is not fully elaborated. In simple systems, laws are so permeated by custom, tradition, and kinship rules that they do not exist, to any great extent, as a separable body of codes. With more advanced systems, the increased volume of economic transactions and prominence of political elites produce more explicit legal codes that articulate rights, duties, and obligations, on the one hand, and appropriate procedures and practices for implementing laws, on the other. Yet, even here, the codes are unwritten and heavily infused with custom, tradition, and kinship rules.

The enforcement of laws, even those merged with tradition and kinship, becomes ever more explicit among horticulturalists. In simple systems, fellow kinsmen, village leaders, or paramount chiefs enforce rules and mete out punishments; in more advanced systems, similar processes occur at the village level, but superimposed on this traditional form of enforcement are representatives of the king who are empowered to administer appropriate sanctions. The adjudication of disputes in simple horticultural systems is ad hoc, usually involving the village headman as judge and perhaps elders as a "jury," but as horticultural societies grow in size and complexity, these informal "courts" are supplemented in larger core cities by formal structures, often involving explicit judges and quasi-lawyers. Law enactment in simple systems usually involves some combination of village headmen, councils of elders, religious specialists, and kin leaders, who create laws as problems and disputes necessitate; in more complex systems, local entities are subject also to laws imposed by paramount chiefs and the king and, if the system is sufficiently large, by the council of the king. Thus, the institution of law, revolving around explicit legal codes, enforcement agents, courts and legislative bodies, becomes increasingly evident in horticultural societies as they grow to a size and complexity where the beginnings of a quasi "state" are evident. For the most part, then, much legal activity remains at the local village and perhaps intervillage level, but with advanced horticulture, the institutional base for a significant elaboration of a legal system is in place. With increased economic surplus created by agrarian technologies and the expansion of polity into an increasingly bureaucratic state, formal law as an institution increases in importance.

Other institutional structures in horticultural systems remain recessive or nonexistent. Education is perhaps the most visible, in some expanding horticultural societies involving specialized tutelage by political and religious specialists and, in more advanced systems, by military and various craft specialists. Medicine is still connected to religion, although some medical specialists, who practice various folk techniques, emerge in advanced systems. Finally, science does not exist in simple systems, but among more advanced horticulturalists, the beginnings of astronomy can be found, although this activity is highly infused with religious significance.

One of the most dramatic transformations in the movement from hunting and gathering as a way of life to horticulture is the growth of stratification (Lenski 1966; J. Turner 1984; Lenski and Lenski 1987). The unequal distribution of resources—material, political, and symbolic—increases slowly but steadily; and by the time a society is at an advanced horticultural stage, clear social classes are evident. Such classes revolve around political, religious, and military activities, kin affiliation (various kin groups often become ranked), craft specialties, trade and commerce, and unskilled work (ranging from free workers to slaves). Moreover, ethnic classes often exist as a result of war and conquest, although these are frequently co-extensive with a slave class. Thus, from moderate levels of inequality in simple horticultural societies, stratification becomes ever more elaborate and rigid as the population, the amount of economic surplus, the concentration of power, and the specialization of labor increase.

With increases in size and complexity, the number of social categories multiply. In simple systems, one's kin affiliation (lineage and clan), age, and sex are the most relevant categories, but in more advanced systems, these distinctions are supplemented by ethnic, economic, religious, political, and class categories. Each of these categories locates individuals in the social web, dictates the resources available to them, controls their perceptions and actions, and circumscribes how others respond to them.

In simple horticultural systems, the major corporate unit, organizing virtually all activity, is the kinship structure. As mentioned earlier, each person is a member of a nuclear unit embedded in an extended unit, which is connected to other such units to form lineages that can be grouped into clans (and at times moieties). Economic, political, military, religious, and social activities are conducted within the constraints of this kinship system. There are some additional kinds of corporate units—village structures, secret religious and military associations—but even these are often organized by kinship rules. Thus, the "cage of kinship"—the title of this chapter—is quite restrictive in simple horticultural systems, but as the population grows and economic productivity increases, kinship (though still dominant and very important) increasingly becomes only one of many corporate units—village, town, and city; economic, military, political, legal, and religious groupings; and various voluntary associations. As a result, the cage of kinship weakens, but as we will see in the next chapter, new caging structures revolving around power and stratification emerge.

## Conclusion

The abandonment of hunting and gathering involved the construction, we argue, of sociocultural cages that infringe on human needs for parity, freedom, mobility, and individualism. Of course, as big-brained hominoids, humans are remarkably flexible; and when forced to settle down in larger numbers, they could do so. The principal tool for this adaptation was the elaboration of kinship units from relatively autonomous nuclear (and at times extended) units into lineages that trapped individuals in a web of kinship. This line of structural elaboration was the easiest, especially when economic surplus was modest. But compared with the mobility and freedom of hunters and gatherers, the constraints of unilineal descent rules, dictating as they did family composition, residence, domestic and economic activity, authority, and marriage, represented a truly dramatic change. Perhaps the change occurred so gradually that people were unaware of the structural cage in which they were enclosing themselves, but once constructed, this highly circumscribed existence stood in contradiction to our ancestral heritage and its refinement during thousands upon thousands of years of hunting and gathering modes of adaptation.

Unlike some scholars looking at horticulturalists, we see this contradiction between human biology and social structure as rife with potential strain. The elaborate ritual activities—not just religious but the daily forms of address and response among kinfolk—signal that individuals are working very hard to reduce social tensions. The frequent outbreaks of violent feuds among individuals and between kin units and the compulsory rules of kinship that virtually force people into contractual obligations attest to a new level of volatility not generally found among hunters and gatherers. And the constant state of warfare with "external enemies" (Bates and Plog 1991) reveals not only a new level of violence in humans but perhaps a safe outlet for accumulated aggression inside the cage of kinship. Indeed, the almost ritual quality of some "wars" underscores their adaptive significance for displacing aggression and for promoting in-group solidarity under conditions of constant tension. For instance, contemporary horticulturalists quite commonly engage in what A. F. Vayda (1974) calls "nothing fights" that include "war" strategies with prearranged times, rituals, duels, and explicit game rules. And it is clear from the archaeological record that violent conflicts among early farming peoples in the Near East were an important aspect of a horticultural lifestyle (Boyden 1987: 114).

If our speculations are correct, then many of the so-called instincts of humans for "fighting," "hierarchy," and "territory" are not instincts at all, but adaptive sociocultural mechanisms for overcoming the contradictions between humans' biological propensities and the necessity of increased social organization. Even the more "benign" instinct theories emphasizing the need for intense group solidarity and high ritual reinforcement of such solidarity can be seen as denoting mechanisms in structures and cultural codes that contradict humans' basic biological needs. For it can be argued that intensified solidarity and constraining rituals are not instinctual tendencies of humans, or at least not as instinctual as is often assumed by sociologists and anthropologists.

Similarly, as the most recent manifestation of instinct theory, early human sociobiology imputed genetic propensities—"selfish" genes driven to survive—that seem to us unwarranted. In their unwillingness to entertain the notion that sociocultural entities can become units of selection, early sociobiologists were forced to view kin structures and other sociocultural arrangements as manifestations of human genetic programming. Hence, "reciprocal altruism" is not the result of socialization in groups but of genetic propensities for selfishness. So, in a manner very similar to other instinct theorists, sociobiologists see the emergent properties of groups—solidarity, sociality, ritual, altruism, kinship, and so forth—as somehow rooted in the human genotype.

More recent coevolution theories have provided an important corrective in recognizing that cultural codes and group structures can represent an independent basis for selection and evolution. While we prefer to avoid the analogies to biological evolution frequently offered by coevolutionists, our conclusions are similar. But we add an important point: many emergent structures contradict our biology, at least to some extent, and create strain for both individuals and social structures. Thus, the coevolution of biology and culture involves contradictions between the genic and sociocultural levels.

Hunting and gathering societies are as close as humans have ever come to constructing social patterns compatible with their primate and genetic legacy—a composite of both strong and weak ties, an egalitarian ethic, and a sense of community resting on cooperation and exchange among several interrelated but self-sufficient families that are free to disperse or come together depending on individual preference and available resources. But after this period of human evolution, social and genetic structures have often stood in contradiction, and therefore, it is unwise to assume that sociocultural arrangements will reflect biological propensities or that coevolution necessarily involves compatibility between the genic and the cultural. Indeed, we are still very much the product of our hunter-gatherer heritage both in our hominid physical traits that began with upright walking and in our social and emotional predispositions, for the last 12,000 years of sedentary living cannot have modified human genotypes except in small and insignificant ways (e.g., variation in skin color). People's efforts to break out of the sociocultural cage and recreate what was lost after the abandonment of hunting and gathering may reveal more about their biological heritage than the bars of the sociocultural cage itself. Let us pursue this metaphor, then, as we move on to see how humans have historically resisted and changed the nature of their confinement, and how they are doing so today.

# 6

# THE CAGE OF POWER:

## Agrarian Societies

Power is the capacity to direct and control the activities of others, and it is one of the most volatile features of human societies. Why, then, would people subordinate themselves, giving others the capacity to regulate their affairs and setting into motion a perpetual tension-producing machine?

As with the cage of kinship, the increasing concentration of power was, no doubt, forced on people by their circumstances. But "the state" and a full-blown bureaucratic cage of control and regulation did not suddenly emerge; rather, much as in the case of the extension of kinship in horticultural systems, humans were slowly pulled into this new form of constraint. All the same, the concentration of power can begin very early in societal evolution. For example, the Indians of the northwest coast of North America exhibited a "Big Man" structure of power, in which a population with essentially a hunting and gathering technology reveals strong leadership revolving around the usurpation of surplus by the Big Man, the accumulation of wealth, and the concentration of power. The key factor causing this seemingly premature development is an abundance of resources—fishing coupled with rich plant life in this case (Boas 1921). Indeed, the "conspicuous consumption" of the famous Potlatch ceremonies attests to the wealth that these stone-age peoples could, at times, accumulate.

Abundant resources encourage population growth and increased population density, creating needs for new mechanisms of social integration and control. One such mechanism is the extension of unilineal descent and the creation of a cage of kinship. As with the Yanomamö mentioned in Chapter 5, a complete unilineal descent system was never fully articulated among these natives of the northwest coast. But the forces that have historically created selection pressures for kinship are evident: relatively high population densities, settlements in villages, the potential for periodic resource scarcity, raiding, conflict, and war. Under these conditions, leaders who can coordinate economic activities, promote defense, negotiate peace or wage war, and regularize exchange are valued and allowed to impose themselves on the village economy and the incipient unilineal descent and kinship systems. The Big Man becomes the local group's spokesperson with other groupings, negotiating trade, intergroup ceremonies, political agreements and, if necessary, leading his village(s) in open conflict. Internally, the Big Man coordinates economic activity and may in fact "own" the land and rights to resources. He then extracts some of the surplus of each family, storing and controlling its distribution. This surplus can then be used in trade, prestige-giving festivals, and, most significantly, assistance in times of scarcity.

Thus, without a fully developed kinship system, power can become highly concentrated in societies that, in terms of their technology, are rather simple. Similar Big Men structures can be found among other gathering, herding, and fishing populations (see Johnson and Earle 1987: 160–93 for examples). The critical conditions producing such structures are the capacity to produce economic surplus, the need to control local territory, the growth of the population and of population density, and the lack of a fully developed unilineal descent system. The last condition is crucial, we think, because as kinship becomes more elaborated into clans and moieties that actually constrain and organize activity (as opposed to expressing certain relations symbolically), Big Men decline, and something closer to a chiefdom emerges. Here, leadership is more connected to the descent rules of kinship than to personal charisma. Moreover, a chiefdom system controls and administers larger territories and greater amounts of economic resources than a Big Man system.

## Building the "Second Cage"

Yet there are more similarities than differences between Big Men systems and simple chiefdoms, which can reveal the same dependence on a leader's personal qualities and display similar instability and fragmentation on his death. It is the rise of complex chiefdoms that sets the stage for the development of a cage of institutionalized power. As compared with the simple form, these chiefdoms generally (1) organize larger territories, (2) create clear lines of authority and hierarchy among the paramount chief, regional subchiefs, and local village/kin leaders, (3) undertake large economic tasks (capital improvements, exchange and trade, the coordination of labor, and the storage of surplus), (4) mediate internal disputes more closely, and (5) coordinate larger military operations.

These more complex chiefdoms emerge with larger population densities, and as a result, selection pressures for intensifying and expanding production through capital projects, storage facilities, the coordination of labor beyond nuclear and extended households, and trade arrangements beyond the local village dramatically escalate. Moreover, as population densities increase and production expands, war with neighbors becomes more likely, further escalating selection pressures for military organization and its inevitable by-product: the concentration of power. All of these conditions increase the likelihood of a highly centralized chiefdom that begins to take on the features of a state bureaucracy.

But subjugation to Big Men and chiefs was not something that people rushed to embrace. Giving power to others imposes constraints on a basically individualistic primate; and so, there must have been strong forces pushing people to exchange the cage of kinship for one constructed of power. Population growth, increased densities, conflict and war, and the need to expand production beyond what was possible in horticultural systems compelled people to submit to a new form of constraint. Once power becomes concentrated, it is used to accumulate more power and to concentrate wealth and privilege among the few. Thus, what was perhaps a necessity in the history of various populations soon became an exploitive and constraining cage as those with power sought to extend and consolidate their power and privilege (Lenski 1966). And once established, state power becomes a sociocultural juggernaut, seeking to colonize and control other types of societies and, in the process, destroying older forms of human organization. The dynamics producing the centralization and consolidation of power are modeled in Figure 6.[1]

As the left portion of Figure 6 emphasizes, population growth and density, as they create resource scarcity, operate to expand productivity (at least to the limits of a population's technology). Under conditions of scarcity, trade with other populations may be initiated. Moreover, coupled with population density and settled territories, this scarcity often leads to conflict and war, which, at times, can be mitigated by trade. Scarcity and population density also create the potential for conflict within a population, which, in turn, escalates selection pressures for the use of descent rules to structure a kinship system; and if such a system is not developed

[1] The processes outlined in Figure 6 have been discussed by a number of scholars. Herbert Spencer (1874–96) was certainly the first to see concentrations of power as related to size, density, internal and external conflict, and ecological constraint. (See J. Turner 1985 for a more extensive analysis.) There has been no dearth of subsequent conceptualizations on how and why power becomes concentrated in human populations. We have drawn from a number of sources, including Carneiro 1967, 1970; Carneiro and Tobias 1963; Claessen and Skalnick 1978; R. Cohen and Service 1977; Fried 1967; Haas 1982; Kirch 1984; Johnson and Earle 1987; Boulding 1978; Lenski 1966; Mair 1962; Mann 1986.

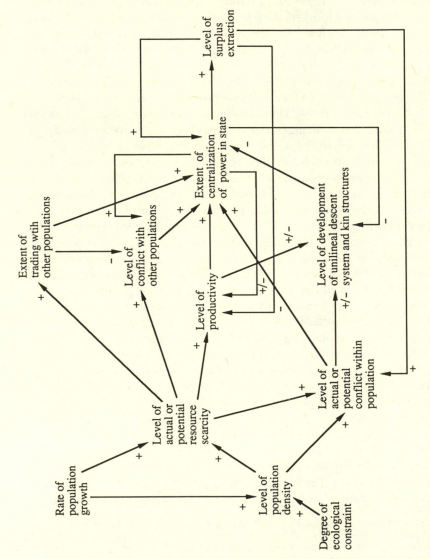

Fig. 6. The dynamics of political centralization

so as to organize activities in kinship groupings—that is, lineages, clans, and moieties—then this potential for internal conflict generates selection pressures for strong leadership, or a Big Man system. Unilineal descent, if established and effective in organizing economic activity, will decrease the likelihood of a Big Man system in favor of a simple chiefdom, where power is somewhat less concentrated. But over time, with increased productivity, war, and trade, a chiefdom will become more centralized and hierarchical. Hence, we posit a negative curvilinear relation between kinship and the centralization of power: a well-developed kinship system reduces the likelihood of a central Big Man system in favor of a kin-based simple chiefdom, but over time, with increased production and with expanded war and conquest, kinship becomes the basis for the concentration of power and for stratification among kin groups. War creates additional pressures for centralized power, whether of the Big Man variety or, more likely, a kin-based chiefdom where "armies" can be more effectively mobilized in terms of kin loyalties. Trade also encourages centralized power as leaders seek to establish and regulate flows of resources into and out of the society, but trade is not as powerful a force as either war or internal conflict for centralizing power. The centralization of power is used to increase productivity (through capital improvements, organization of labor, and the coordination of access to resources), but as power becomes an end in its own right in order to extract surplus and to support war, as well as the privilege of the ruling elite, then the rate of increase in productivity begins to slow and perhaps even stagnate as incentives for technological innovation decline. Figure 7 shows how this process works. Although the concentration of power initially has positive effects on productivity, the continual escalation in the extraction of surplus by elites and the corresponding impoverishment of nonelites produces disincentives for nonelites to innovate and increase production for the privilege of elites.

Other feedback processes are also crucial to understanding power in human societies. With the increasing use of power to extract surplus, not only is productivity potentially decreased, but the potential for internal conflict increases. To some extent, these problems of extraction can be mitigated by the successful conquest of a society's neighbors and the usurpation of their surplus (hence, the positive feedback arrow in Figure 7 between the concentration of power and conquest), but in the long run, empires engage in ever-greater levels of surplus extraction (to support larger armies, as well as increased administrative and logistical loads for controlling larger, more diverse territories), and as a result, they generate those conditions promoting internal conflict.

These processes, as outlined in Figures 6 and 7, have occurred again

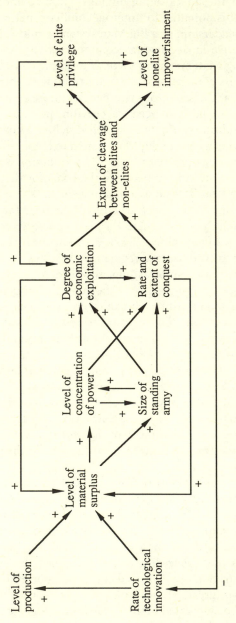

*Fig.* 7. The decline in the rate of technological innovation in excessively centralized and militarized states. A reconceptualization of Lenski and Lenski 1987: 174.

and again in the history of human societies, and not just for agrarian systems but for horticultural and Big Men gatherers and hunters as well. Thus, as resource extraction by elites expands, power tends to become more centralized and to impose a more restrictive cage on the population. Yet there are countervailing pressures to break out of this cage, or at least temporarily widen its bars or open its doors, until political centralization and surplus extraction reassert themselves. Although these processes have occurred in simpler horticultural and herding systems, they have been most pronounced in agrarian systems; and so, we should now examine the nature of agrarian societies, and their underlying dynamics of power, in more detail.

## Agrarian Social Organization

What distinguishes agrarian systems is the harnessing of animal power to plows and the consequent expansion of production (Curwen and Hatt 1961; Lenski and Lenski 1987). Yet as with all modal portrayals of societal types, there is considerable variation, which we will seek to capture in a distinction between "simple" and more "advanced" agrarian systems. Table 5 sets out the features of each form.[2]

Agrarian societies are generally much larger than horticultural societies, and settlements are bigger and more permanent, with some migration to market towns and cities as well as the core capital city (Sjoberg 1960; Hammond 1972; Eisenstadt and Shachar 1987). Simple agrarian systems can remain quite small, with perhaps only a few thousand people, but they can have as many as several million. More advanced systems usually range from a few million people to hundreds of millions. Cities can have up to 100,000 inhabitants in simple systems, compared with as many as one million in advanced ones, which will also have many more cities in the 100,000 range. Yet even with these larger urban centers, the vast majority of the population (usually over 90 percent) lives in rural areas, working land owned and controlled by elites. Agrarian systems tend to have a period of rapid growth, followed by a leveling off as the denser population succumbs to disease, war, and poverty. After particularly violent wars or virulent diseases, the population may even decline.

Most of the population in agrarian systems is arrayed in small villages and towns connected by extensive road networks to regional market cities and to the core capital city. Moreover, agrarian systems use considerably more land than horticultural systems in order to increase the pro-

---

[2] The text is drawn from the sources listed in Table 5.

## TABLE 5

### The Organizing Dimensions of Agrarian Societies

| Dimension | Description | |
|---|---|---|
| | Simple society | Advanced society |
| **1. DEMOGRAPHIC**<br>Population size | Wide range, from several thousand people to many millions | A few million people to several hundred million |
| Population movement | Some permanent settlements; some migration to central core city and "market towns" by unattached peasants and artisans; core cities can become as large as 100,000 inhabitants, but most peasants remain tied to local rulers and land controlled by local and regional elites | Many permanent settlements; considerable migration to core cities and market cities; cities can get as large as one million inhabitants, and many more cities of 100,000 than in simple systems, but, less than 10% of population typically resides in urban centers |
| Growth | Relatively high rates of population growth, with dramatically increasing population densities; war and disease may reduce population, but the long-term tendency is toward rapidly expanding population, placing extra demands for increased production, which may then level off | Some growth but high birth rates tempered by high death rates; some societies even experience a decline in population when death rates escalate (because of disease, crop failures, famine, and other disasters) |
| **2. SPATIAL**<br>Internal distribution | Villages and towns, with surrounding tracts of land for agricultural production; paths and roadways connecting villages and towns, especially market towns, to each other and to large core or central city where political and religious elites reside; at times, large economic projects, such as irrigation canals, undertaken by increasingly centralized state; large amounts of land used to sustain high levels of production, with ruling elites extracting economic surplus to sustain their wealth, privilege, and political control | Villages and towns, with surrounding agricultural tracts, connected to larger market towns/cities, in turn connected politically and economically to capital city, so that resources flow from rural villages to local districts and counties, thence to regional districts and the capital city; this flow of resources reflects one power of the state to control and regulate economic activity, but as empires expand, these linkages can become less viable, creating some autonomy for local villages and towns, and regional economic specialization can further complicate spatial patterns; but in all cases local elites and ruling elites extract most economic surplus; a growing separation of rural agricultural sector and urban commercial sectors is evident |
| External distribution | Warfare politically unites regions, at least for a time; empire-building becomes a prominent form of external contact as consolidated territories seek to conquer their neighbors; a considerable amount of trade and commerce with other "societies" is also evident | War and empire-building common, with increasing trade and commerce between territories within the empire or between nations/empires |

| 3. INSTITUTIONAL Economy: | | |
|---|---|---|
| Technology | Knowledge of herding, farming with animal-drawn plow, irrigation, fertilization, sailing, wheel and its uses on vehicles, orchards, husbandry, ceramics, metallurgy, writing, mathematical notations, and solar calendar; rate of innovation high, but tending to decline as political-economy begins to circumscribe activity in more advanced systems | In addition to technology of simple systems, knowledge of smelting and hardening iron mark a significant advance; other innovations include improved harnesses for horses, wood-turning lathe, auger, screws, printing, clocks, spinning and weaving, windmill and watermill technology |
| Capital | Plow, work animals, wood, ceramic, and sometimes iron tools; large facilities for storage and milling of grains; roads and often large-scale irrigation projects; and most significantly, increased use of money | In addition to capital of simpler systems, widespread use of metal tools marks a significant increase in capital formation; also, larger facilities for storage, transportation, and milling; more elaborate and extensive roads and irrigation projects; light "industry," made possible by new sources of power (water, wind); and most importantly, money becomes fully integrated into the economy |
| Labor | Dramatically increased division of labor as occupational trades expand; continued clear division of labor by age and sex; more merchants and other "trade specialties"; development of "free labor" and artisans who "sell" services in labor markets | Continuing increase in division of labor; peasantry increasingly constrained by slavery and serfdom, but also an increased pool of "free" or unattached laborers (as a result of losing their land or tenancy rights) available for hire, leading to sale of free labor in urban labor markets; the most prominent axes of differentiation are among merchants/traders and artisans, now typically pursuing between 100 and 200 different occupational specialties |
| Entrepreneurship | Kinship and village structures decline as major entrepreneurial mechanisms and are supplemented by new political and economic forms of entrepreneurship; political consolidation of territories creates hierarchies of authority and resource flow; market expansion generates new methods of stimulating production and distributing labor, goods, and services; and merchants, beginnings of banking and insuring, and early craft guilds become evident; but for a given individual, the first entrepreneurial structure is the family, increasingly less connected to larger kinship structures and dramatically more circumscribed by the state, but nonetheless a crucial unit organizing economic activity | Kinship and village as entrepreneurial mechanisms replaced in rural areas by servitude obligations to ruling elites; polity thus becomes a major entrepreneurial structure assuring the flow of resources from poor to rich, and from rural areas to urban centers; dramatic expansion of markets, along with money as a medium of exchange, increasing volume and velocity of goods and services exchanged across ever-larger amounts of territory (in fact, large networks of ties among merchants often develop across an empire, and certainly within a society or region of an empire); artisans and merchants increasingly organized into guilds that coordinate their activity and assure their privileges; law begins to regulate contracts and the enforcement of obligations |

*(Continued on next page)*

TABLE 5 (*continued*)

| Dimension | Description | |
|---|---|---|
| | Simple society | Advanced society |
| Land | Increased access to living resources with introduction of plow and irrigation, and expansion of agrarian production; declining resource depletion with better fertilization and irrigation; access to nonliving resources—metals and stone—increases significantly | Continued increase in access to resources with use of metal plow and other tools; new sources of energy—wind, water, and more efficiently harnessed animals—increase not only resource extraction but production; new technologies like smelting greatly expand access to inorganic resources, and development of weaving and spinning further expands resource use |
| **Kinship:** | | |
| Size and composition | Extended units still very evident but decline in frequency and embeddedness in larger kin structures; patrimonial family (male-dominated and including others, such as workers, beside kin) appears | Fewer extended units; extended and patrimonial families frequent among artisans and merchants; extended units still found among peasants, but patterns of political servitude disrupt kinship ties |
| Residence | Explicit rules begin to lose power, though offspring usually remain close to parents, or even in their household | Few explicit rules, but patterns of servitude in rural areas restrict mobility (though roving landless peasants are frequent); in urban areas, patrimonial households organize much economic activity |
| Activity | Clear division of labor by sex and age in all activities | Same as simple societies |
| Descent | Increasingly bilateral and truncated | Except for "royal" family, lineage less important, and increasingly bilateral and truncated; only royalty and nobility continue to use descent rules to a high degree |
| Authority | Male-dominated, and in patrimonial units, considerable male authoritarianism | Male-dominated, especially in patrimonial families |
| Marriage | Incest prohibited; rules of exogamy and endogamy decline, and dissolution allowed but economically difficult and rarely formal | Incest prohibited, except in a few cases for nobility; rules of exogamy and endogamy decline further; dissolution allowed but difficult and rarely formal |
| **Religion:** Beliefs | Clear conception of supernatural realm of beings, and at times, forces; relatively clear pantheon, hierarchically organized; explicit mythologies as well as values and moral | Clear separation of supernatural and natural, but pantheons decline in favor of "universal religions" proclaiming one god or force in the universe; mythology also declines |

| | | |
|---|---|---|
| | codes sanctioned by the supernatural and used to legitimate privilege of clergy and power of ruling elites | and is simplified; moral codes and values become explicit part of simplified religious doctrines; religious legitimation of elites still prominent, but religions seek to appeal to the "common person"; alongside spread of universal, monotheistic religions exist beliefs in magic and witchcraft tending to be localized in content |
| Rituals | Regular calendrical rituals, directed and led by full-time clergy; considerable control by clergy of economic production, either through ownership of property or, indirectly, through ritualized rights to economic surplus | Regular calendrical rituals, directed by full-time clergy; but rituals simplified and designed to appeal to mass audiences; clergy still major property holder, but rituals increasingly separated from economic and political spheres, being directed instead to a force/god that can improve life now and in hereafter |
| Cult structure | Clear structures, housed in elaborate temples of worship supporting full-time, bureaucratically organized clergy; explicit symbols, places, and times of worship evident; cults often control not only economic but also much social and political activity | Clear, bureaucratized structures in elaborate temples/churches; times and places of worship specified, and symbols simplified; cults still own property and exert political influence, but decreasingly so in the political arena; alongside large universal religions exist smaller cults with different beliefs and ritual, though these tend to adopt elements of dominant religion |
| Polity: Decision-making | Hereditary monarchy of king and other nobility organized into state bureaucracy composed of religious elites, military officials, and administrative personnel; generally, a feudal type of structure, in which local lords control peasantry and extract economic surplus, passing some on to king, though direct state taxation emerges as needs for revenue increase (usually as a result of war or large-scale capital projects, such as roads and waterways); almost always some overlap between state and religious bureaucracies | Hereditary monarchy, organized into coercive state bureaucracy; typically feudal, but increased control by monarch and centralized, professional army becomes evident; decision-making revolves around extraction of economic surplus, suppression of internal dissent, and mobilization for external threats; decision-making less influenced by religion as king, nobility, military, and state bureaucracy consolidate their control over territories and "citizens"; king and nobility own virtually all the land, which is used to generate privilege and coercive power to enforce decisions; some variation in degree of centralization of power and decision-making, depending on landed nobility's independence from monarch |

*(Continued on next page)*

TABLE 5 (*continued*)

| Dimension | Description | |
|---|---|---|
| | Simple society | Advanced society |
| Power-authority | Standing, professional armies, often supplemented by compulsory service by peasantry; clear taxation formulas, almost always tied to extraction of agricultural surplus; legitimation generally tied to religious symbols, giving religious elites considerable influence and power; no redistribution ethic, surplus being extracted in name of god and a king who is seen to have absolute right to administer society's affairs, both internally and externally | Standing, professional armies enforce claims of king and nobility; taxation emphasizes extraction of agricultural surplus, which is used to sustain privilege and coercive capacities; no redistributive ethic or effort to improve the lot of vast majority of people; power used to increase resource extraction; secular power and privilege legitimated by religious elites, but there is increasing tension between state and religion |
| Law: | | |
| Legal codes | Explicit legal codes, usually revealing clear differentiation between procedural and substantive law; codes can be written but are often tied to tradition and religion | Explicit codes and distinction between substantive and procedural law; codes mostly written and less tied to religious symbols; at times, religious codes stand alongside (and perhaps in contradiction to) state |
| Enforcement | Explicit enforcement agents, usurping most of traditional powers of kin and village leaders; restitution, imprisonment and/or servitude, and death all possible sanctions; explicit system of courts and full-time judges/administrators, though many courts composed of part-time personnel, especially at local level | Army and regional "police" enforce legal edicts; imprisonment and death increase as modes of punishment; explicit system of courts and full-time judges/administrators who evidence little independence from monarchy |
| Legislative bodies | Edicts from king and elite clergy create mixture (often in conflict) of religious and secular laws; at times, "councils" of nobility and elite clergy sit as legislative body; local councils increasingly circumscribed by centralized law-making | Edicts from king and, in less-centralized systems, councils of nobility are major legislative mechanisms; religious symbols and interests less involved in law-making and, at times, state and church councils constitute separate legislative bodies |
| Education | Explicit "schools" and/or tutelage for nobility, religious, and military elites; at times, schools for nonelites (high-ranking military, and state and religious bureaucrats); most education by apprenticeship within kinship or craft associations | Explicit schools for nobility, religious practitioners, military elites, and increasingly, various nonelites in military and state bureaucracy; most education still informal or by apprenticeship; in a few societies, a quasi-university structure emerges |
| Medicine | Clear medical specialists, especially for elites; little medical care for nonelites outside traditional family-administered folk practices | Clear medical specialists for a somewhat expanded clientele but still primarily for elites |

| | | |
|---|---|---|
| Science | Relatively little beyond military, medical, and astronomical (usually with religious implications) activities; but beginnings of secular concerns about the universe evident and, in a few cases, embodied in quasi-scientific structures (libraries, observatories, medical houses, military academies, and even religious structures) | Relatively little, though medicine, astronomy, and engineering activities are often housed in quasi-scientific structures; only in very advanced systems is "science" a distinguishable set of activities, usually housed in libraries, observatories, military academies, and emerging university structures |
| **4. STRATIFYING**<br>Resource distribution:<br>Material | Very high inequality; almost all material resources owned by nobility and church; some material accumulation possible by merchants, bankers/financiers, and craft specialists, but for vast majority (i.e., the peasantry) all surplus usurped by the state and religious elites | Very high inequality, similar to that in simple systems, but altered somewhat by monarch's increased power to extract surplus and expansion of new trading/merchant occupations permitting accumulation of wealth |
| Prestige | Very high inequality; king and his court, as well as religious and military elites, enjoy considerable prestige; high-level administrators and minor nobility enjoy some prestige; local trade specialists and artisans, as well as other skilled labor, can receive respect at village/town level | Very high inequality; elites in nobility, military, and religious cults enjoy high prestige; potential prestige for emerging literary elite; comparative little prestige accorded to successful artisans and merchants, except at local level; most members of society enjoy no prestige or honor |
| Power | High inequality; king buttressed by army possesses considerable coercive power, as well as administrative capacity to monitor, regulate, control, and extract resources | Very high inequality; king and army (as well as various "policing" agents) possess enormous coercive power and administrative control over all sectors of society |
| Class formation | Very clear cleavages, each with its own subculture; ruling class (including religious and military elites) clearly distinguished from rest of the population, which has virtually no say in political decisions (except during periodic revolts), urban minority vastly different from large rural majority, and there is a growing split between literate few and illiterate masses; additionally, there are highly salient class distinctions for various occupational specialists, especially for artisans, craft specialists, and merchants/traders | Very clear cleavages, similar to those in simple systems, with several modifications: the increased number of occupations allows for expansion of classes between the elites and peasants; there is increased capacity for some artisans, merchants, and even peasants to acquire wealth exceeding that possessed by some sectors of nobility; and the growing number of state bureaucrats, military personnel, and retainers for the nobility create additional classes, whose members can acquire wealth, power (or at least influence), and some prestige |
| Mobility | Little mobility, except for those with special military or economic skills | Little mobility, but expanding military, economic, and religious spheres provide more opportunities than in simple agrarian societies |

(*Continued on next page*)

TABLE 5 (*continued*)

| Dimension | Description | |
| --- | --- | --- |
| | Simple society | Advanced society |
| **5. CATEGORIC** | | |
| Age and sex | Young, old, and many intermediate distinctions; clear male-female distinctions in all activities | Same as simple societies |
| Ethnicity | Many distinctions, especially as conquest and trade expand | Increased number of distinctions with escalated warfare, empire-building, and migration across territorial and societal boundaries |
| Kinship | Descent rules decrease dramatically as integrating force in society | Descent virtually eliminated as integrating force in society; trend toward nuclear, quasi-extended, and patrimonial units |
| Economic | Numerous distinctions with respect to craft specialties and literary and merchant activity | Same as simple societies, except that number of distinctions increases with growth of occupational specialties |
| Religious | Clear distinctions of religious specialists and, at times, among various sects of worshipers | Emergence of universalistic religions and other religious movements can blur distinctions between lay and religious practitioners, though these are reasserted as particular cult structures come to dominate |
| Political | Clear distinctions between warriors and nonwarriors, nobility and nonnobility, religious and lay authority, local and central powers | Same as simple societies, except that number of distinctions increases as state grows and extends its power and authority |
| Educational | Clear distinction between literate and nonliterate, as well as religious and lay credentials | Literacy increases as a basis for categorization not only for the literate-nonliterate distinction but also for gradations of literary capacity |
| Spatial | Clear distinctions between urban and rural | Same as simple societies but even more pronounced |
| Class | Numerous classes, with major cleavages between ruling and nonruling, urban-rural, literate-nonliterate; class distinctions most numerous in urban areas, where artisans, craft specialists, religious practitioners, military personnel, merchants/traders, and state bureaucrats create and sustain distinctive subcultures separating them not only from each other but also from elites and peasants | Same as simple societies, except that number of intermediate distinctions increases with expansion of new positions in state, economy, and army |

| | | |
|---|---|---|
| 6. CORPORATE<br>Spatial units | Local villages of peasants, trading/market towns, and large cities politically and economically dominated by capital city; conquest produces new territorial and regional distinctions | Same as in simple societies, except that there is greater domination by capital city; and if empire is expanded, territorial and regional units become even more salient |
| Institutional units:<br>Kinship | Decline of unilineal descent reduces size and scope of kinship; nuclear units, often elaborated into quasi-extended or patrimonial units, increase and locate in an economic niche in the expanding division of labor | Same as in simple societies, with virtually complete erosion of descent as a major organizing mechanism |
| Economic | Many economic units differentiated from kinship, though nuclear and quasi-extended families still organize peasant, craft, artisan, and trading activities; guilds, merchant associations, and other distinctly economic units emerge and begin to proliferate | Same as in simple societies, but significant increase in number of occupational organizations |
| Political | State, army, and courts clearly differentiated from kinship, except for elite positions | State dominates and controls larger and more clearly differentiated army, courts, and administrative subunits |
| Religious | Cults, organized into bureaucratic structures, clearly differentiated from kinship, state, and economy; at times, competing sects emerge | Same as simple societies until religious movements begin displacing older religious sects, thereby reducing number of cults |
| Educational | Some explicit schools or academies for military, religious, and secular education; most education organized in guilds and family apprenticeship arrangements | Same as in simple societies, except for emergence of quasi-university structures in very advanced agrarian systems |
| Legal | Explicit courts, enforcement agents, and legislative bodies emerge, all of them dominated by state and heavily influenced by religion | Increased domination of courts, enforcement agents, and legislative bodies by state, and increased segregation of secular and religious law |
| Associational units | Economic, political, military, religious, and social clubs, groups, and "societies" emerge; status groups for urban and literate elites increasingly prominent | Increased number and diversity of associational units and increased number of status groups |

SOURCES: Murray 1949; Childe 1953; Kramer 1959; Eberhard 1959; Sjoberg 1960; Blum 1961; Curwen and Hatt 1961; Bloch 1961; McNeill 1963; *Cambridge* 1963; Wolley 1965; B. Moore 1966; Lenski 1966; Laslett and Wall 1972; Postan 1972; Garraty and Gay 1972; Hammond 1972; P. Anderson 1974; Tilly 1975; Hilton 1976; Bendix 1978; Moseley and Wallerstein 1978; Skocpol 1979; Wolf 1982; Giddens 1985; Evans et al. 1985; Mann 1986; Eisenstadt and Shachar 1987; Lenski and Lenski 1987: 164–208; Johnson and Earle 1987: 246–312.

duction of food so necessary to support the larger population and the growing privilege of elites. Indeed, resources tend to flow from rural villages to regional centers and market towns and ultimately the capital city as the state and its elites extract ever-greater amounts of surplus from peasants and the local nobility (Lenski and Lenski 1987: 184). Agrarian societies also occupy considerably more territory than typical horticultural systems, not just because of increased population and production but also because of war, conquest, and empire-building. As a result, considerable regional variation—culturally, ethnically, and economically—is evident within a society or an empire. Yet an "urban culture" tends to emerge across the society and its satellites in an empire as elites along with various artisan and merchant classes create network ties with their counterparts in different regions (Mann 1986).

Institutionally, dramatic transformations take place in the movement to an agrarian system. New technologies, heightened levels of capital formation, more complex divisions of labor, new entrepreneurial mechanisms, and increased access to resources greatly expand production, with the surplus being used to finance the privilege and power of elites (Lenski 1966). As production increases, new entrepreneurial mechanisms (markets, law, territorial specialization, guilds) and the ever-expanding and restrictive hierarchy of state power (local and regional elites connected to a monarch) replace kinship as the integrating and organizing mechanisms of society. Family structures—mostly nuclear but at times extended and/or patrimonial—still organize many portions of the labor force, such as peasants, artisans, and merchants, but unilineal descent and corporate units like lineages and clans recede as an important society-wide integrative mechanism (Weber 1916; Laslett and Wall 1972; Collins 1986: 267–321).

In their place is the expanding state, with a hereditary monarch at its apex and a variety of military and administrative positions in an ever-growing administrative and coercive bureaucracy. In centralized systems, most typical of advanced agrarian systems, the monarch uses the state bureaucracy and the coercive capacity of a professional army (and local enforcement capacities) to control territories, other elites, peasants, artisans, and merchants. The burden of financing the state, the army, and the privileges of the monarchy and nobility falls mainly on the peasantry, whose surplus is extracted by the state (usually directly from lands owned and controlled by the monarch, or indirectly, through taxes on other land-holding nobility), although the monarch often turns to artisans and merchants for additional revenue for military adventures, large-scale undertakings, and the like. To sustain such a heavy extraction, local nobility, regional bureaucrats, and other, intermediate-level officials are, in essence, given tax-collecting franchises, with the result that skimming and other forms of corruption escalate dramatically and force the monarch to borrow from wealthy merchants and other moneylenders and to find new ways to secure revenue (through new taxes as well as military conquest and plunder). In the end, the monarch and the state often find themselves in a financial crisis for many reasons: corruption in revenue collection; increased expenses to finance military campaigns; interest payments to wealthy moneylenders; decreased productivity by alienated or displaced peasants; protest and tax resistance by peasants, nobles, and even artisans and merchants, who tire of financing the monarch's military adventurism and privilege, requiring increased military and police expenditures for coercion and repression. The result can be what Jack Goldstone (1990) has termed "state breakdown," creating openings and opportunities in the cage of power.

In fact, there seems to be an inherent dialectic in the cage of power created in agrarian systems, which periodically centralize power, only to degenerate under protest and, on rare occasions, to collapse in outright revolution. In Figure 8, we have extended Goldstone's (1990) argument, which pertained only to the 1640–1840 period, to all agrarian societies.[3] The source of political crisis can be various, but for Goldstone, the growing size of the population is crucial,[4] for it begins to overburden the political economy of agrarian systems. As Figure 8 documents, constant external threat, war, rural protest, and elite dissatisfaction (over taxes, downward mobility, lack of patronage, and the like) aggravate the political and fiscal crises of the state and its monarch. Whether the society disintegrates, throwing power back to local nobility and regional leaders, or in rare cases into the hands of nonelites, depends on the values of the variables in the model portrayed in the figure and on the unique historical and empirical circumstances of the society in question. And while the cage of power always seems highly restrictive to the vast majority of people in agrarian societies, the composition and profile of its bars can change because of the inherent sources of instability in the centralization and consolidation of state power under a hereditary monarch. During these crises, some people can escape the cage for a time or even become part of its composition, but historically, the consolidation of power inevitably reasserted itself (perhaps with a different cast of characters) and began to impose itself on people's activities and options.

[3] Portions of Goldstone's argument can be found in many sources, including H. Spencer (1874–96); Weber ([1922] 1968: 901–1372; B. Moore 1966; Skocpol 1979; Collins 1986: 186–208.

[4] This will no doubt prove a controversial point, since it goes directly against the Marxist position on the sources of "crisis" in the state.

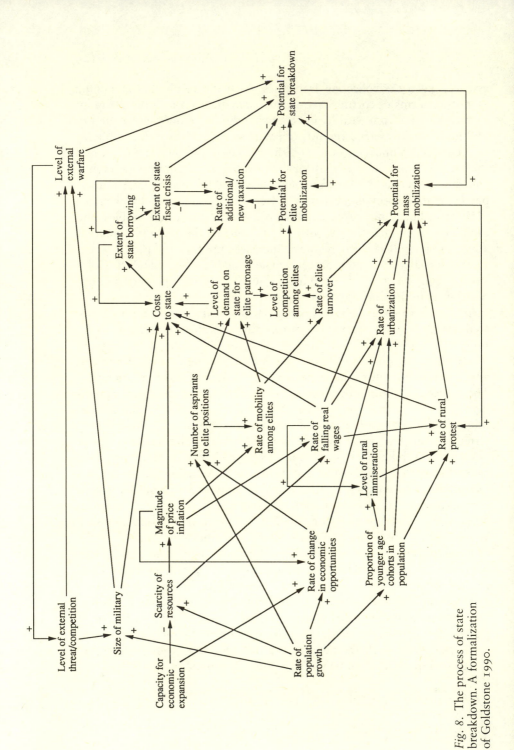

*Fig. 8.* The process of state breakdown. A formalization of Goldstone 1990.

The dynamics of power in a society are connected to intersocietal relations. As Figure 8 emphasizes, conditions of external threat and war increase costs to the state. If war has produced patterns of conquest and empire-building in agrarian systems, then the cage of power is extended to conquered peoples. Indeed, the pillage of conquered territories is one way that a society's fiscal and political crises can be delayed, at least for a while. But the existence of an empire, where one society coercively controls another, sets into motion a new set of power dynamics, which feeds back and influences the processes delineated in the figure.

Herbert Spencer (1874–96) was perhaps the first sociologist to emphasize the significance of war for the evolution of society. For him, war creates selection pressures for centralized political authority. In turn, increased political control escalates resentments as people resist the new restrictions on their freedom and the increased inequality that inevitably accompanies the concentration of power. As a result, the state must confront "internal enemies" and, in a counterproductive cycle, must consolidate even more power to control these internal threats, thereby raising resentments to a new level. Empire-building only serves to aggravate these tendencies, for as diverse populations are conquered, controlled, and exploited, additional sets of "internal enemies" are created. Eventually, these sources of resistance to state power overwhelm the state's capacity to sustain its coercive grip on its conquered territories and, at times, its own population. Consequently, the empire begins to implode back on itself, especially if it must divert resources to contain unrest at its home base.

Max Weber ([1922] 1968: 909–50) presents a similar line of argument in his contention that the legitimacy of the state is intimately connected to its capacity to maintain "prestige" in its external relations. Without legitimacy, the state has difficulty maintaining its capacity for internal domination. Sometimes states manufacture a sense of "threat"—both internally and externally—to sustain their legitimacy, for if a state can then "deal with" the threat, it increases its prestige and legitimacy. However, if threats—whether real or manufactured—are not effectively contained, then the state loses legitimacy and places itself in a vulnerable position.

Thus, the strength of the cage of power is connected to external relations with other societies; and an empire composed of diverse peoples makes a state vulnerable to a loss of legitimacy and, hence, its capacity to dominate and control its population. Randall Collins (1986: 186–208) has conceptualized the conditions that make empires vulnerable to collapse. For Collins, an empire's success is conditional on the extent to which the society possesses (1) a resource advantage over its neighbors (population size, access to natural resources, and productive capacity),

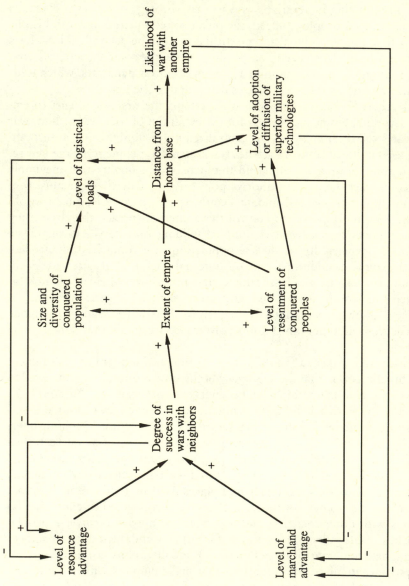

*Fig. 9.* Factors determining the success or failure of an empire. A formalization of Collins 1986.

(2) a marchland advantage (natural barriers on its rear flank and, as a consequence, enemies on only one border), (3) a large standing army, (4) a capacity to avoid a showdown war with another advancing empire, (5) an ability to keep its superior technologies from diffusing to its enemies, and (6) a capacity to sustain a marchland advantage as the empire grows. At some point, some or all of these conditions cannot be met and the empire overextends itself, taxing its logistical capacity to sustain an army in territories. As a result, the empire begins to collapse, breaking for a time the cage of power. Although this process occurs in advanced horticultural and early industrial systems, it reaches its zenith in agrarian societies. Figure 9 outlines some of the dynamics involved.

In sum, then, the key dynamics of agrarian systems revolve around the institution of the state and its capacity to impose control within its home territory and, if empire-building is involved, to sustain political authority over conquered territories. The institutionalization of power in the state is thus a double-edged sword: it gives some the right to control, coerce, and exploit others, but in so doing, it creates the seeds for its own destruction, at least until a new state can be formed, or an old one revived. Agrarian systems thus expand and contract, maintaining their stability for a time but ultimately falling victim to crises, revolt, and perhaps collapse.

Though the consolidation of power, as made possible by the expansion of production, is the most important change in the institutional structure of agrarian systems, there are other new institutional features in these societies. One major change is in the organization of religion. Such change is dependent on the political and economic infrastructure created by trade networks across large amounts of territory and common class interests and cultures of peoples with varying levels and types of resources within and among societies (Mann 1986). It essentially involves a series of religious revolts and movements from ecclesiastic cults and, then, their spread across large territories, probably because of the network structures created by the consolidation of power and the creation of homologous classes across large territories (J. Turner 1972). The most distinctive feature of these religions is their simplified pantheons. For example, Islam, Catholicism, and Judaism evidence clear tendencies toward monotheism. Older religions like Hinduism, by contrast, evidence a relatively ambiguous pantheon, as does its offshoot, Buddhism. Philosophical Hinduism (Wallace 1966: 94), with its all-encompassing supernatural being or force, the "One," is clearly monotheistic, but Sanskritic Hinduism maintains an elaborate pantheon of gods, including Siva, Krishna, Ram, Vishnu, and Lakshimi. The pantheon of Buddhism is similarly structured with the world being guided by a series of Buddhas (or "Enlightened

Ones"). Compared with traditional ecclesiastic religions, the mythology of these agrarian religions is also truncated. Robert Bellah (1964: 366) has called this the process of "de-mythologization," since few myths surround the creation of the all-powerful god and his court of relatives. Thus the elaborate accounts of the jealousies, conflicts, rivalries, and genealogies of gods and supernatural forces typical of religions in horticultural systems decline in agrarian systems.

As Bellah (1964: 367) has emphasized, in agrarian religions we see for the first time a stress on the possibility of understanding the fundamental nature of both natural and supernatural reality. Whereas in past religions, humans had simply been offered the chance to live in peace and harmony with the supernatural, Christianity and Islam, for example, provide for a life after death in a paradisical world. (There is also provision now for a place for the unworthy—hell, a poor reincarnation, and so forth.) Under these conditions, religious values become explicit, since it is conformity to these values that increases the possibility of salvation after death. These values become codified into a religious code spelling out appropriate behaviors for the members of a society (e.g., the Ten Commandments, the Noble Eightfold Path). What is significant about these religious codes is that they specify more than just stereotyped ritual behavior; they also place on people a set of diffuse obligations guiding everyday, nonritual conduct. Yet these codes often tend to emphasize worldly resignation and retreatism. In conforming to religious law in order to secure salvation, worshipers must turn away and withdraw from the natural world. To secure salvation requires one to be uncontaminated by natural events and to be "suspended in waiting" in this world.

In sum, then, the cosmology of religion is greatly altered in developing agrarian societies. It tends toward monotheism; it has a truncated pantheon and attendant mythology; and it contains substantive beliefs about the supernatural and salvation. Equally noticeable is the emergence of a codified value system controlling both ritual and nonritual behavior and encouraging a kind of worldly retreatism.

Ecclesiastic cults come to dominate over shamanic, communal, and individualistic cults in agrarian systems, although these simpler cults can still be found; and as in the case of Christianity, Islam, and Buddhism, a religious movement may arise that challenges existing ecclesiastic cults, and that eventually creates a new one in order to organize rituals (J. Turner 1972). These new cults in turn generate a new religious elite and bureaucratic structure that can become the basis for further revolts and religious movements (the best example, of course, is Protestantism as a revolt against Catholicism).

Although dominant ecclesiastic cults and the state maintain alliances, the two become increasingly separated as the state consolidates its control of territories. Nevertheless, the well-organized and financed church can remain a significant counter-source of ideological and, at times, economic power.

Other institutional structures also become more elaborated. Law develops explicit written codes and adjudicating agencies, and the expanded state formalizes enforcement through not only a standing army but various types of regional and local "police." Law enactment is still the prerogative of the monarch, but increasingly in advanced systems, councils of nobles have an influence on law-making (J. Turner 1974). Moreover, local government officials, councils, and nobility can be granted law-making rights, especially in the name of improved revenue collection and social control.

Formal education is still confined to the nobility and military and religious elites, although formal education and literacy begin to be extended to many nonelites, who will fill key positions in the state bureaucracy and military. Medicine also becomes an explicit occupational calling, involving a specified amount and type of formal education. Science is still recessive, but the increased number of civil projects and the growing wealth and leisure of the elite encourage the development of knowledge and the creation of specialized structures for conducting both intellectual and scientific inquiry. For the vast majority of the population, however, formal education, medicine, and science exert little influence on their daily lives.

Increasing productivity and concentrations of power inevitably influence stratifying dimensions. The distribution of resources becomes very unequal once power is used to extract as much material surplus as possible and a literate elite controls the allocation of honor and prestige (Lenski 1966; J. Turner 1984). The result is a hardened class structure in "an agrarian mold" (Lenski et al. 1991: 197), with elites and peasants ever more apart, both in their rate of contact and in their cultural characteristics. Between these extremes, however, the increased division of labor, coupled with expanded markets and new positions in the growing state bureaucracy and military, generates new intermediate classes with their own distinctive cultures and lifestyles. And for some, such as successful merchants and market brokers, considerable wealth can be accumulated and used to cultivate prestige (e.g., buying title) and power (e.g., lending money to elites). Moreover, some upward mobility from these intermediate classes becomes possible through the marriage of sons and daughters to elite families. Additionally, some enterprising peasants can become landholders and local rentiers.

Particularly significant are the creation of networks of ties and the cultivation of similar cultural characteristics among those in similar positions across the entire society, or even across the various societies of an empire. Elites in different regions converge, as do artisans and merchants, not only because of their structurally equivalent positions in the class system, but also because of direct and indirect social ties. The result is that there is perhaps more diversity within agrarian societies than between them. Merchants, artisans, nobles, military officers, and state bureaucrats from different societies come to have more in common with their counterparts than with those above or below them in the class system. This is, of course, another way to say that class boundaries are highly pronounced, but it also underscores the potential for extended intraclass relations within a society or across several societies in agrarian systems. For example, Michael Mann (1986) has argued that the spread of Christianity across the Roman Empire was made possible by the prior existence of extensive networks of trade and communication among artisans and merchants, and that the Romans were prompted to oppose Christianity not so much on religious grounds as out of fear that these networks would become solidified into a source of counter-power.

In a system with a hardening class structure, an expanding division of labor, a growing concentration of power and privilege, and a set of intraclass homologies transcending regions and societal borders, one would expect to find many categoric distinctions. Age and sex are, of course, universal distinctions and remain rigid in agrarian systems. Kinship categories—clans and lineages—decrease dramatically and are replaced by a larger number of occupational, political, educational, class, and regional distinctions. But despite the increased number and diversity of categoric distinctions, they do not signal a significant lessening of social constraints; on the contrary, they operate to provide additional means for triangulating and pigeonholing individuals in social niches.

In terms of corporate units, there is a greater diversity of spatial forms—small villages, local market towns, regional trading centers, large cities, and a capital city. Moreover, within larger cities, various "districts" come to have a corporate character of their own on the basis of the class position of their inhabitants. Institutionally, the most significant change in agrarian societies is the regression of kinship units back to the nuclear family and, on occasion, to extended and patrimonial units. In other spheres, the growth and differentiation of the economy and state create many new occupational, military, and state-centered units and subunits. Furthermore, the beginnings of a legal system with written and codified laws and the development of new educational, scientific, and medical structures work to increase the number and diversity of corporate units. Yet these units do not create high levels of cross-cutting memberships; instead, they tend to partition individuals from each other and reinforce the class system. Moreover, the increased number of associational units and networks operates to solidify status groups along urban-rural and regional lines, as well as along functional lines in the military, religious, economic, and administrative domains. Still, as the number and diversity of corporate units increase, there are always gaps and interstitial areas that enable people to escape the constraints of status groups.

## Conclusion

Once humans left nomadic hunting and gathering, they began to elaborate social structure, creating social cages. Power has been described as the "second cage" because it is not fully institutionalized before kinship becomes elaborated. But as a population grows, as social densities increase, as internal and external conflict escalates, as capital investments for increased productivity become necessary, and as problems of coordination become acute, power is mobilized and structured—at first in Big Men and chiefs, later in paramount chiefs, and finally in kings and the state. Few of these processes, we argue, can be explained by sociobiology, because they are primarily the result of cultural and social dynamics. Coevolutionary approaches can, perhaps, explain these processes in terms of selection among the cultural codes in a meme pool, but they would miss many of the complex, dynamic processes outlined in the various models presented in Figures 6–9. And neither sociobiology nor coevolution would, we feel, fully capture the tension between the construction of the second cage and humans' primate legacy.

Agrarian systems thus represent a qualitative change not just in their productive technologies but in the separation of kinship from the state. Kinship becomes less of a cage, only to be replaced by the monarchy and its consolidation of power in the military and the state administrative bureaucracy.

The exploitive and coercive nature of the monarchy and nobility in agrarian systems often imposes a terrible burden on the peasant masses, constraining their options, discouraging entrepreneurship, and extracting the spoils of their labor. And it confines and channels the energies of new occupational specialties. Yet the very scale and diversity of agrarian systems make the cage of power a little less confining than the cage of kinship in horticultural systems. Moreover, revolt and the inevitable collapse of empires and regimes create opportunities and options for individuals. And most significantly, new and expanded economic forces—markets, merchants, financial entrepreneurs, and diverse specialties—provide additional opportunities for people to escape constraint, or at least mitigate its effects.

Still, agrarian systems are the most tyrannical and stratified of all societal types in human history, imposing barriers and hardship on all but a few. The periodic revolts and uprisings in both rural and urban areas, and even at times by elites themselves, signal that the cage of power is precariously maintained. For individualistic primates, whose most "natural" state is hunting and gathering, state power and crushing stratification are hardly compatible with humans' basic genetic tendencies. Hence, it is not surprising that, when possible, members of agrarian systems have traditionally revolted, migrated, and otherwise sought to escape the sociocultural cage of state power. And it could be expected that they would embrace and sponsor new social constructions, allowing for more mobility and choice.

Industrialization represented one such new social construction, for despite the obvious exploitation and abuse so well documented and trumpeted by Marx, Engels, and Marxists in general, capitalism allowed people to escape the first two cages in human evolution, at least up to a point. Of course, it created new restrictions, but none as oppressive as those in agrarian systems, except for the unfortunate merging of industrialism and totalitarianism in some parts of the world. Yet even then, it is not clear if the constraint is any worse than in agrarian systems; but as events of the early 1990's have now made very clear, people will challenge highly restrictive cages of power, given the slightest opening, and even in the face of the massive coercive power of a totalitarian state.

Thus, contrary to Max Weber's great agonizing over the "iron cage" of rational-legal authority, and critical theorists' general concerns about domination, industrialization produces a far less constraining cage than traditional agrarianism. And post-industrialization perhaps creates even more potentialities for lessening the constraints of power. It is to such considerations that we now turn.

# 7

# BREAKING OUT OF

# THE SOCIAL CAGE:

## Industrial Societies

Reading a passage from Friedrich Engels's *Conditions of the Working Class in England* (1845) is a sobering reminder of the horrors of early capitalist industrialization:

Heaps of refuse, offal and sickening filth are everywhere interspread with pools of stagnant liquid. The atmosphere is polluted by the stench and is darkened by the thick smoke of a dozen factory chimneys. A horde of ragged women and children swarm about the streets and they are just as dirty as the pigs which wallow happily on the heaps of garbage and in the pools of filth. . . . The inhabitants live in dilapidated cottages, the windows of which are broken and patched with oilskin. The doors and door posts are broken and rotten. The creatures who inhabit these dwellings and even their dark, wet cellars, and who live confined amidst all this filth and foul air—which cannot be dissipated because of the surrounding lofty buildings—must surely have sunk to the lowest level of humanity (1958: 71).

For Engels, as for many who have commented on early industrialization, it was past imagining that these people had, at least in part, broken out of a cage of any kind. Indeed, had they been thinking in such terms, they would surely have argued that industrial peoples had traded one cage for a worse one—unsafe factories where they worked long hours for little money and squalid cities where their lives were punctuated with filth, disease, and desperation. And such conditions have often reproduced themselves in the contemporary world, for the shanty towns and slums of the industrializing societies of the Third World reveal similar conditions, perhaps even worse than those of industrializing England.

Why, then, would people leave the cage of power for something that might be even worse—control and constraint by factories, urban slums, and crushing poverty? Part of the answer is that they typically do not have a choice, for once industrialization is initiated, it begins to destroy the feudal and quasi-feudal system that encloses peasants, forcing them to leave rural poverty in search of jobs in urban industrial areas. What typically awaited these migrants in the past, and even today in many societies, was more poverty and new forms of constraint—labor markets with an oversupply of labor, dangerous and unpleasant factories where workers subordinated themselves to machines, and slum housing in unhealthy and menacing neighborhoods. Yet while people are often miserable in early industrial societies, they have a certain freedom, autonomy, and capacity for individuality not present in traditional agrarian systems. And as industrialization continues, the opportunities increase, especially in relation to those available in agrarian systems. Thus, although life may not be pleasant outside the cages of kinship and power in earlier types of societies, an industrial system (especially a capitalist industrial system) allows more autonomy and individualism as it develops, expanding the division of labor, creating markets for everything, providing free schooling and education, allowing for political participation in an increasingly democratic polity, and working to raise the standard of living for everyone, even the poor (relative to the poverty of peasants).

Of course, once humans left hunting and gathering, they could not escape sociocultural constraints. Thus, unlike the cage of kinship, the cage of power does not wither away; indeed, as government democratizes, it ironically gets bigger and potentially even more powerful. Still, the industrialized state is less confining, and coupled with rights of citizenship and the vote, its power is held at bay and not used in the wholly exploitive way of agrarian systems. And along with an ever-expanding number of work settings as well as markets for virtually all goods and services, people can regain some of their lost capacities for choice and individuality. Industrial systems, then, though they do not allow the autonomy, freedom, and equality of hunting and gathering systems, are more in accordance with humans' basic hominoid heritage than either horticultural or agrarian societies. Moreover, as these systems move toward a post-industrial profile, mostly as the result of the internal dynamics of capitalism itself but also partly in response to basic human needs for individualism and freedom from constraint, the structure and culture of society may become even more compatible with our primate heritage. Post-industrialization is no utopia, for all the contemporary problems of industrial societies remain, but such systems are still far better than their predecessors, not just because of their affluence but, equally important, because of their capacity to free people from much physical drudgery and to give them wide arrays of options and opportunities and more say in how they run their lives.

How, then, does industrialization partially break the cage of power? Historically, it could be argued, industrialization was a chance event, for agrarian systems appear to be locked into endless cycles of expansion, consolidation of power, exploitive use of power, and collapse or at least retrenchment. But in fact there were cumulative processes at work in agrarian systems that set the stage for the transformation of even these seemingly stagnant societies. One such process was the slow accumulation of technologies. If the rate of innovation in agrarian societies tends to decline as power and exploitation escalate (see Fig. 7), these systems were nonetheless responsible for important advances in metallurgy, shipbuilding, agriculture (rotation of crops, irrigation, fertilization, etc.), milling, mining, navigating, road construction, carriage making, printing and the capacity to disseminate information, the selective breeding of animals, simple machines and the use of nonanimal power such as water, and so on (McNeill 1963; Singer 1954–56; Lenski et al. 1991; Clough and Cole 1941; Wallerstein 1974). This kind of slowly developing fund of knowledge was to build on itself, encouraging further changes. Consider the following chain of events, for example. Improvements in shipbuilding and navigation led to the discovery of the New World, which in turn created a flow of silver and gold to Europe, which encouraged the use of money, which expanded markets, which stimulated new kinds of production and rapid inflation, which decreased the wealth of the landed aristocracy (whose wealth was less liquid), which redefined traditional relationships and distributions of wealth and power, which subsequently forced the landed aristocracy to adopt more efficient techniques in agriculture, which led to the displacement of peasants off the land and their migration to urban areas, which added a new and politically volatile mix to centers of power and commerce, and so on. Moreover, each of these changes set into motion other chains of subtle but fundamental transformations.

Another crucial process was the gradual secularization of beliefs, especially in Europe. The Protestant Reformation, whether a chance event, or the inevitable by-product of gradual technological changes, or a revolt against abusive ecclesiastical hierarchies, certainly encouraged a more secular, "this world" orientation, or what Max Weber (1904–5) termed "worldly asceticism." Thus, the secularization of beliefs, as it disrupted the ideological hegemony of the established church, reinforced the transformation of the political economy.

Still another critical force was the cycles of consolidating power and revolt, for these tended to encourage, albeit haltingly and sporadically, various cumulative transformations, including laws and courts to mitigate conflicts, extensions of citizenship rights, increased record keeping, literacy among administrators of the state bureaucracy, experiments with new organizational forms (if only to allow the state to collect more taxes or field an army), and dependence on nonelites for loans to finance privi-

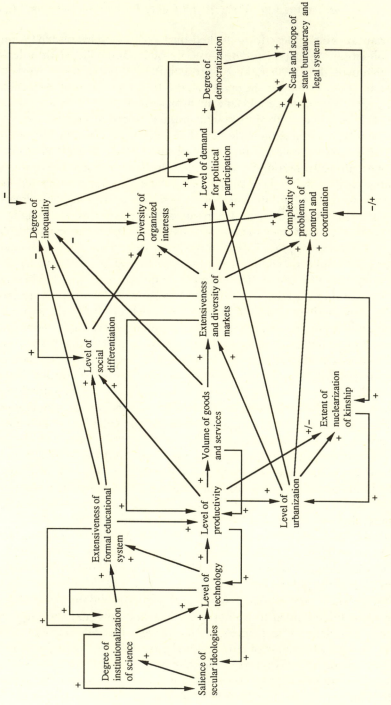

*Fig. 10.* The dynamics of industrialization

lege and foreign adventures, thereby encouraging and freeing the enterprise of merchants and brokers.

Thus, agrarian systems are not wholly stagnant. They contain the forces for their own transformation, although these may not lead to dramatic alterations. But once these cumulative changes begin to transform the means of production, as they did in England in the late eighteenth and early nineteenth centuries, they inevitably spread and accelerate change in other societies. Since there are many interesting descriptions of the changes occurring during the Industrial Revolution, we do not need to recapitulate the details here. Rather, we will focus on the processes that allowed people to break out of the second cage, as highlighted in Figure 10.

Let us begin by reviewing some of the key causal chains. One chain is economic, revolving around the reinforcing effects (direct, indirect, reverse, and feedback causal chains) among (1) technology and secular ideologies, (2) advances in technology with respect to the harnessing of inanimate power (at first water, then fuels) to machines and the expansion of production through new organizational forms like the factory system, and (3) the increased production of goods (both consumer goods and capital goods like machines that are reinserted back into the process of production) and the expansion and diversification of markets as the principal mechanism for the distribution of resources. A crucial aspect of the model in Figure 10 is the set of positive reverse causal chains. For these economic processes are mutually reinforcing, and as a result, they become difficult to arrest once they are initiated.

Other causal chains flow out of these economic dynamics. The bottom portion of the model outlines the final breakdown of the first social cage, kinship. Mobility, urbanization, and non-kinship employment in factories and businesses generate pressures for the nuclearization of the family. Some of this change has already occurred in agrarian systems, as we outlined in Chapter 6, but industrialization completes the process, especially with respect to patrimonial family structures. For now the family becomes a consumption unit, buying its goods and services in markets and selling its labor in markets. In the agricultural sector and in various ethnic enclaves, the remnants of extended family units (and even patrimonial structures) remain, but the younger members of these families are often pulled out of the remnants of the cage of kinship by the market system.

At the far left of Figure 10 there is another important causal chain, revolving around the secularization of ideologies and beliefs, the expansion of technology, and the institutionalization of science. This chain interfaces with one that initiates and sustains the expansion of a formal education system. Literacy is required in many jobs as production expands and as new markets create new kinds of "white collar" work, and as a result, a state-funded mass educational system replaces the narrow, often private, and elite-oriented system of agrarian societies. These processes also encourage the creation of a system of higher education, especially as science becomes an important technological force and as market differentiation generates vast complexes of professions and other skilled jobs. Once established, the educational system feeds back and encourages routine science, liaisons between pure science and applied technology, and the use of educational credentials for the sorting of skill levels and spheres in the labor market (indeed, credential inflation often ensues).

Another basic causal process revolves around the transformation of the stratification system. The dramatic increase in productivity so expands the volume of goods and services that their distribution becomes less of a zero-sum game, in which elites use their power to grab virtually all of the available privilege. They can now afford to share more of the material pie because the pie is so much bigger and, equally significant, nonelites become a political force that cannot be ignored or easily repressed. Coupled with the expansion of labor and service markets, the dramatic differentiation in the labor force, the extension of education (and marketable credentials) to more and more members of the population, and the democratization of the state, there is a significant decrease in the level of inequality with respect to material wealth, prestige, and power. Moreover, these same processes create pressures for greater equality between males and females, as well as among various ethnic subpopulations. For all this, considerable inequality remains and constitutes a source of chronic tension and conflict in industrial systems.

A final set of causal processes is political and involves the breakdown of the oppressive cage of power typical of agrarian systems. Urbanization, as stimulated by the factory system and the expansion of business, creates the reality or potential for urban volatility, which, in turn, operates to press the state to increase nonelite participation. Similarly, the expansion of markets and the creation of so many new economic sectors and interests force the state to respond to new demands for political participation. The differentiation of the labor force into various sectors and industries both reflects productive and market differentiation and feeds back to reinforce the pressures for political participation, especially as sectors of the labor force become economically and politically organized (unions and political parties, for example). All these emerging interests are fueled by inequality: those who have less want more; those who have privilege wish to preserve it. The end result of these conflicts is threefold: to open the doors of political participation, to develop channels for representing diverse interests (political parties and elected decision-makers), and to create procedures for adjudicating differences (laws, courts, and legislative bodies). Political democratization thus increases, at least in the long run.

Ironically, as we have noted, political democratization also increases the size and scale of the state. As each diverse interest pushes for the government to "do something" about its needs, new laws and agencies are created. Moreover, the problems of coordination (of diverse activities) and control (of not only activities but increased rates of deviance) are inevitable as industrial systems break down traditional sources of control, urbanize, and become more and more socially diverse. To cope with these problems, especially under conditions of increased political participation, the state expands its law-making, adjudicating, and coercing functions and extends its administrative reach into ever more arenas. As this occurs, state workers, agencies, and bureaus become, themselves, one of the most influential interests in the political process, creating a whole new set of political demands (the −/+ on the feedback arrows from "Scale and scope of state bureaucracy" to "Complexity of problems of control and coordination" is intended to emphasize that the state initially works to resolve these problems but as it adds agencies to this end, they create still more problems, triggering a new spurt of agency-building to resolve the new round of problems).

Democratization itself also produces new interests because it holds out the prospects for "doing something" about certain conditions—such as increasing equality (by sex, ethnicity, age, class, etc.), environmental sensitivity and regulation, and the curbs on potentially harmful activities. The result is that the legal system and state expand and, at the same time, encourage further mobilization of interests.

This kind of "rationalization" of law, expressed in the growth of rational-legal bureaucracies (in the state as well as in the economy), is what gave Max Weber such concern about the "iron cage of bureaucracy." But he dramatically overestimated the extent to which such "rational-legal" bureaucracies could regulate and control humans. In fact, as Georg Simmel (1902, 1907) emphasized, the existence of markets and the widespread use of money give individuals options and choices not available in nonmonetary market systems: the one generates many niches and opportunities, and the other enables people to buy and sell in accordance with their preferences. And because bureaucratic structures recruit workers in markets and remunerate them with money, they provide their employees with options—where to work and how to spend money—and only constrain and restrict activities for an agreed-on number of hours (the workday).[1] Moreover, as social differentiation increases in society, bureaucracies themselves become highly specialized, creating large inter-

---

[1] Luhmann (1982: 71–89) makes a similar point, emphasizing the "entrance/exit" rules of organizations that delimit the range of people's obligations toward those structures.

stitial gaps in their power to regulate social life, especially when so much activity is connected by open markets.

Perhaps the old Eastern Bloc countries came close to Weber's pessimistic projections, but Simmel's argument more accurately reflects what eventually occurs: fluidity and mobility between and within ever more specialized bureaucratic structures operating in increasingly complex markets fueled by money and speculation. True, money and markets create a kind of quantification and commodification of social relations, as well as crass commercialism and materialism, but even these drawbacks do not cage humans in the same way as kinship in horticultural systems and power in agrarian systems do. Both Marx and Weber went astray, then, when they saw capitalist forms of industrialization as somehow taking away from humans' basic nature. In actual fact, the processes outlined in Figure 10 allow people more freedom, autonomy, and choice than either horticultural or agrarian systems; and for this reason, they are more concordant with our primate legacy. This is why, we suspect, that for all the initial hardships and chronic problems of industrial systems, people still prefer them. It is early academic sociologists who worried about their dehumanizing effects; the majority of people outside the Ivory Tower actually flourished when measured by the living conditions of the agrarian era; for the illiterate and poor peasant of yesterday has been transformed into the relatively informed and affluent consumer of today.

Or more accurately, this is the case in parts of the contemporary world. For while industrial systems have the power to displace older agrarian systems, just as those systems displaced horticulture, a number of forces often prevents full-scale industrialization and the realization of these transforming effects. Overpopulation frequently requires people to maintain old patterns of agrarian dependence, while creating political instability unconducive to industrial development. A lack of indigenous resources and capital also works against industrialization for many populations. And established patterns of dependence on, and exploitation by, more advanced industrial systems has often stymied indigenous development, or at least made it uneven. Thus, industrialization has not completely transformed human societies; and dramatic differences in the level of development around the world will no doubt persist well into the future, sustaining patterns of societal stratification and tension at the global level.

## Industrial and Post-Industrial Social Organization

The details of our description of an industrial societal type are outlined in Table 6. We have distinguished between industrial and post-industrial systems. Below, we will offer an even briefer capsule summary of the table than before, since we are all familiar with the nature of the society in which we reside.[2]

Demographically, industrial and post-industrial societies vary enormously in size—from a few million people to hundreds of millions—but small or large, they all tend toward lowered birthrates and a stabilized population. Migration and the typically higher birthrates of immigrants from less industrial systems are as much responsible for population growth as the birthrate of long-term inhabitants. And despite some tendencies for dispersal outside urban-suburban areas, 70 percent to 90 percent of the population typically resides in urban areas, with a corresponding decrease in the number and modal size of small towns in rural areas. Spatially, all industrial systems have complex and extensive systems of transportation and communication, subsidized and usually regulated by the state. These transportation and media systems transform certain patterns of social relations. For example, mass media increases individuals' awareness of other groups and cultures; instantaneous communications create interpersonal and corporate networks across larger amounts of space; and access to fast and efficient transportation encourages mobility and the maintenance of diverse network ties.

Externally, warfare is frequent, and the threat of war ever-present; and though empire-building occurs during industrialization, the logistical loads on a high-technology military make political empires difficult to sustain—as the recent collapse of the Russian empire attests. Economic empires, consisting of market domination in certain industries, become more typical, but these too are difficult to sustain in a world capitalist system in which governments and their corporate allies compete with one another. During post-industrialization, the often exploitive use of poorer societies' resources—both material and human—continues, especially as dominant societies engage in economic competition. But the long-term effect of this relationship is to connect societies—both rich and poor—in a world system. Militarily, full-scale war becomes increasingly unlikely among the major powers because of the destructive capacity of nuclear technology and its coupling with increased information-processing capacities. As a result, with post-industrialization, wars tend to be regional and fought among less-industrialized societies with histories of antagonism; at times such wars may become "proxy wars" where dominant powers can fight without fear of direct confrontation. Increasingly, as military technology is diffused to all societies, guerilla warfare escalates in frequency and destructiveness, but it is typically contained by the in-

[2] Elements of this summary have been taken from Lenski et al. 1991; J. Turner 1972, 1984; R. Heilbroner 1985; H. Davis and Scase 1985; Chirot 1986; Beaud 1983.

## TABLE 6
### The Organizing Dimensions of Industrial Societies

| Dimension | Description | |
|---|---|---|
| | Industrial society | Post-industrial society |
| **1. DEMOGRAPHIC** | | |
| Population size | Wide range, from a few million people to 300 million | Same as industrial societies |
| Population movement | Rapid urbanization, with over 70–90% of population living in urban areas | Continued urbanization, with some tendencies for creating exurban areas |
| Growth | Rapid initial growth as medical technologies reduce death rate, but eventually slowing or stabilizing; much of the population growth, when evident, owes to in-migration from other societies, especially less industrialized ones | Stable population, and in some cases, actual or potential decline; migration increasingly accounts for growth or stabilization of population |
| **2. SPATIAL** | | |
| Internal distribution | Large urban and suburban areas connected by extensive network of roads, rails, and air traffic; decline of rural population and small towns; decline in small family farms in favor of large private or state-owned farming operations; massive public works projects to provide transportation, communication, and productive resources | Same as industrial societies, but with increasing reliance on communications resources and air transportation; mass media and instantaneous communication create larger networks of weak and indirect ties, as well as new patterns of vicarious identification with non-membership groups and categories; continued decline in rural population, small agricultural towns, and family farms; maintaining transportation and productive infrastructure begins to pose financial burdens on population |
| External distribution | Warfare frequent but of shorter duration than in agrarian societies because military technology and weaponry are vastly more destructive; empire-building during initial phases of industrialization, but empires eventually collapse; vast amounts of external trade and commerce, creating economic alliances among societies; political alliances typically reflect outcomes of war and economic trade; high levels of economic exploitation of nonindustrial nations, creating patterns of world stratification | Warfare frequent, but with the great destructive power of military technologies, wars tend to be short, to be confined to less-developed territories, to be battles by proxy of major military powers or regional conflicts among ethnic/religious populations, and to use high technology conventional weapons; wars no longer lead to empire-building, but in fact are often part of the collapse of an existing empire; guerrilla warfare and terrorism increase as military tactics in regional conflicts |
| **3. INSTITUTIONAL** | | |
| Economy: Technology | Harnessing of inanimate sources of energy to machines creates search for more efficient fuels (resulting in heavy re- | Same as industrial societies, except for increasing emphasis on developing ways to make new materials (especially syn- |

148

| | | |
|---|---|---|
| | liance on fossil fuels, supplemented by water-generated electricity, nuclear power, and for limited application, solar energy) leads to mechanization of all productive sectors and generates both new social technologies—the factory system, assembly line, and corporation—and new productive technologies, especially with respect to new materials (metals and synthetics), new machines (machine tools, robotics), new modes of transportation (trains, ships, cars, airplanes), and new capacities to store, process, and send information; technological innovation becomes institutionalized in the educational system, scientific establishment, secularized values and beliefs, economic/political competition, research and development by corporations and government, and laws (i.e., patents) | thetic products), to use information in the production process (robotics, computers, communication networks), and to reduce time and cost of transportation; institutionalization of innovation proceeds, increasingly driven by world-level economic competition |
| Capital | Capital formation and accumulation increase dramatically, with money used to buy and construct tools, machines, factories, and large-scale infrastructural projects (revolving around transportation, energy, and communication); capital may be heavily concentrated in either the private sector or the state; new mechanisms—bond, stock, and money markets—are used to concentrate capital coming from ever-more diverse sources: taxes, pension funds, mutual funds, individuals, and corporations | Same as industrial societies, except that capital formation and accumulation increase and become more and more a global process involving multinational corporations, foreign governments, and private investing consortiums |
| Labor | Division of labor becoming dramatically more differentiated and complex, while revolving less around primary industries (farming, mining and other basic producer sectors) and more around secondary industries (mills, factories, construction) and tertiary industries (services, such as retailing, banking, insuring, education, health care, police, social welfare, government, and managing); women increase their nonhousehold economic roles; and self-employment decreases as a proportion of work force; labor increasingly allocated to economic positions by a labor market guided by expertise as determined by educational credentials | Division of labor increases in complexity, along with marked shift from secondary to tertiary industries as machines coupled with information-processing computers increasingly perform many routine activities in the secondary sector; women continue to increase as proportion of nonhousehold work force, and self-employment continues to decline; educational credentials and labor markets increase as criteria for allocating workers to economic positions |

(Continued on next page)

TABLE 6 (*continued*)

| Dimension | Description | |
| --- | --- | --- |
| | Industrial society | Post-industrial society |
| Entrepreneurship | Household and family lose virtually all their integrative functions, except for the relatively few remaining family-run businesses; markets, corporations, law, and state become principal entrepreneurial structures, with law and state predominating in some systems, and corporations in others | Same as industrial societies, except that there are more differentiated and varied markets (labor, money, commodities, bonds, precious metals, etc.), larger corporations, more extensive bodies of law, and increased state regulation of markets and corporations; increasing use of markets, combined with state regulation, evident in all postindustrial systems; world-level economic integration by global markets, world-level banking, international economic alliances (partnerships, joint ventures, stock purchases, and government-to-government cooperative agreements) become increasingly evident |
| Land | Dramatic increase in access to all natural resources; problems of resource depletion become acute in both the renewable (forests, land, water, air, etc.) and the nonrenewal domain (minerals, oil, coal, etc.), as does problem of pollution, by the agricultural as well as the industrial sector; high rates of consumption and disposal escalate these problems | Same as industrial societies, with increasing concern over resource depletion provoking sociopolitical movements to "protect" and "husband" environment |
| Kinship: Size and composition | Extended kinship virtually disappears except for various ethnic migrants/businesses and for some portions of agricultural sector; decrease in birth rates reduces family size to nuclear units of parents and 2–3 offspring | Same as industrial societies, except modal family size decreases and number of childless families increases |
| Residence | Neolocal, with freedom to move in accordance with labor-market opportunities; multiple-family residence typically only of poor underclass, ethnic migrants, and portions of agricultural sector | Same as industrial societies |
| Activity | Increasingly ambiguous division of labor by sex and age as women enter nonhousehold labor force and children become integrated in peer cultures | Same as industrial societies, with considerable ambiguity over division of labor by sex and age; incipient trend toward increased egalitarianism by sex and, to a lesser extent, by age; also, increased activity by all family members outside family |

| | | |
|---|---|---|
| Descent | Unilateral descent virtually disappears in favor of a truncated, bilateral system | Same as industrial societies |
| Authority | Still male-dominated but with less clarity and decisiveness | Still male-dominated but with considerable ambiguity and with trend toward egalitarian or, at least, sharing of authority between males and females |
| Marriage | Incest prohibited; no explicit rules of exogamy or endogamy; dissolution allowed and increasingly easy to secure; rising rates of divorce and dissolution initially but tending to level off | Same as industrial societies, except divorce rates increase again with no signs so far of leveling off |
| Religion: Beliefs | Clear separation of supernatural and natural, domination by universal religions proclaiming one god and/or force in their sparse pantheons, very little mythology, and explicit codes of ethics and systems of values; new secular ideologies legitimating economic activity ("capitalism," "socialism," "communism"), political activity ("democracy," "republicanism," "nationalism," "socialism," and "communism"), and social activity ("humanism," "equality," "freedom") emerge, to sap religions of their legitimating functions and to prompt, in many societies, a separation/partitioning of religion and state | Same as industrial societies, with more emphasis on non-religious beliefs and ideologies |
| Rituals | Some calendrical rituals, certain of which lose their religious significance (e.g., Christmas gift giving); private rituals are also encouraged; mass media increasingly a vehicle for observing and expressing religious sentiments | Same as industrial societies, except that religious rituals often supplemented/supplanted by secular rituals (e.g., "meditation," "daily workouts," "weekly therapy"); mass media increasingly important as means for ritual enactment |
| Cult structures | Bureaucratized structures in variety of temples/churches (from large and grand to simple); times and places of worship specified but less regularly followed and/or enforced; little political influence, except through capacity to mold public opinion; some trends for consolidation of cults, counteracted in some systems by new, splinter cults; in democratic systems, cults may become political interest group/party lobbying for particular legislative programs | Same as industrial societies, except that new national cult structures are created through mass media, particularly TV (in those societies allowing private TV), and cults increasingly involved in political lobbying and party activity |

(Continued on next page)

TABLE 6 (*continued*)

| Dimension | Description | |
|---|---|---|
| | Industrial society | Post-industrial society |
| **Polity:** | | |
| Decision-making | Disappearance of monarchy, except as symbolic force; clear tendency toward democracy and party system, with decision-makers elected by citizenry and constituted in legislature; varying degrees of decision-making power in elected heads of state bureaucracy, with decentralized systems (such as the Western democracies) tending to concentrate power in president/prime minister, and with highly centralized systems decentralizing decision-making; citizenship becomes universal right, as does vote for decision-makers; decision-making increasingly lodged in varying mixes of elected leaders, elected members of legislative bodies, and career bureaucrats of constantly expanding state, which in all systems increases its functions and activities | Same as industrial societies, except for clear increase in representative democracy, along with varying trends toward centralization of decision-making and expansion of state functions |
| Power-authority | Large, high-technology standing army and police; complex taxation formulas extending to all sectors of society, with varying degrees of emphasis on redistribution of wealth and income, but in all systems material inequality decreases, partly as result of dramatically expanded production and economic opportunity (a bigger pie for all to eat) and partly as result of redistributive policies; legitimation almost exclusively based on secular law and nationalism | Same as industrial societies, with increased complexity of taxation system, emphasis on redistribution, and legitimation through secular ideologies |
| **Law:** | | |
| Legal codes | Vast bodies of written law (substantive, procedural, criminal, administrative) wholly secular; laws increasingly codified but dramatically proliferate to regulate ever more spheres and types of social activity, though often circumscribed by a constitution | Same as industrial societies, except that administrative law becomes more prominent and the body of law increases dramatically; some efforts to create bodies of international law to regulate increasing levels of global transactions |

| | | |
|---|---|---|
| Enforcement | State monopoly on coercive power through various types and levels of police, along with a military capable of reinforcing those forces in emergencies; imprisonment, executions (in a few societies), and increasing system of rehabilitative and/or restitutive structures to manage crime and deviance; complex system of national, regional, and local courts for adjudicating both criminal and civil disputes | Same as industrial societies |
| Legislative bodies | Elected legislatures at national and regional levels; church now completely excluded from law-making; high or supreme courts often perform legislative functions in deciding "constitutional issues" | Same as industrial societies |
| Education | Mandatory, formal, state-financed, and administered primary and secondary schools for all citizens; state-financed system of universities based on entrance requirements; both supplemented at times by private institutions | Same as industrial societies, except that university system expands its enrollments and research functions |
| Medicine | Full medical coverage, financed through various combinations of taxes and fees, for most of citizenry; fully professional medical practitioners becoming significant drain on tax revenues and consuming large portion of the total GNP | Same as industrial societies |
| Science | Fully institutionalized in research universities and/or academies of science, in research and development units of state and private corporations, in systems of government financing and support, and in systems of beliefs emphasizing the importance of innovation and secular knowledge | Same as industrial societies |
| 4. STRATIFYING<br>Resource distribution:<br>Material | Decreased inequality compared with agrarian systems as result of governmental tax-redistributive policies, increased productivity (making distribution less of a zero-sum game), and episodes of political-economic-social conflict between privileged and nonprivileged sectors, but still considerable material inequality | Same as industrial societies |

(Continued on next page)

TABLE 6 (*continued*)

| Dimension | Description | |
|---|---|---|
| | Industrial society | Post-industrial society |
| Prestige | High inequality, based on educational credentials, income, power, and autonomy from supervision, but much greater proportion of population can secure some symbols and markers of prestige | Same as industrial societies |
| Power | High inequality, although dramatically mitigated by expansion of citizenship rights, legal protections, and state administrative bureaucracy, as well as of electoral politics, political parties, and capacity to organize interest groups (primarily in Western democracies, but also in old Soviet bloc countries); political and economic elites still hold disproportionate amounts of power, much of it informal and hidden from public view | Same as industrial societies |
| Class formation | Nobility as a class virtually disappears, although continuing in some systems as symbols and in some cases as holders of considerable wealth; very clear modal differences in behavior, culture, and income, and sources of power and prestige among elites, high education/salaried professionals, small business entrepreneurs, white collar workers, blue collar workers, and the poor; but considerable income overlap among members of different classes; higher rates (compared with agrarian systems) of mobility (both individual and structural) also work against maintenance of hard class barriers; the few continuing cultural differences between rural and urban mitigated by smallness of rural population, with ethnic and urban-suburban differences becoming more salient than rural-urban distinctions | Same as industrial societies, except that cultural capital (in the form of educational credentials) becomes more salient for making class distinctions |
| Mobility | Rapid increase in mobility from rural farm to urban industrial positions; increase in white collar and business opportunities creates relatively high rates of mobility among nonelite classes, though expanding industrial base provides mobility to elite classes | Further increase in mobility, with educational credentials a sorting mechanism; most mobility "structural," reflecting shift from labor intensity in manufacturing to white-collar services; mobility tends to be confined to movement within "middle classes," though movement to and from elites also occurs |

## 5. CATEGORIC

| | | |
|---|---|---|
| Age | Young, old, and many intermediate distinctions; "youth culture" highly prominent | Same as industrial societies, except that mass media becomes more important in communicating essentials of age (and all other types of categories) |
| Sex | Clear male-female distinctions, but increasing ambiguity and tension over their salience for family, social, religious, economic, and political activities | Same as industrial societies, except that ambiguity and tension over salience increase and begin to be resolved toward less distinctiveness in all major activities |
| Ethnic | Still highly salient and often point of tension and conflict | Same as industrial societies |
| Kinship | Categories based on unilineal descent eliminated; only salient categories are married-unmarried, with or without children, divorced/separated, and working-nonworking mother | Same as industrial societies |
| Economic | Numerous distinctions, but tending to collapse into several basic types revolving around manual-nonmanual and professional-nonprofessional (as dictated by educational credentials) | Same as industrial societies |
| Religious | Membership in cult structure still somewhat salient, but religious-nonreligious distinction becomes more important | Same as industrial societies |
| Political | Party affiliation of citizens somewhat salient, as are various types of occupational positions in the dramatically expanded state bureaucracy | Same as industrial societies |
| Educational | Educational credentials increasingly salient basis for classifying individuals | Same as industrial societies, except even more so as "mental labor" becomes an increasingly valued ability |
| Spatial | Urban-suburban, especially if associated with race/ethnicity and social class; areas, neighborhoods, districts in urban and suburban areas become highly salient; rural-urban/suburban distinctions continue but less critical because of small proportion living in rural areas | Same as industrial societies |
| Class | Numerous distinctions by nature of occupation, collapsing into several basic types as determined by income, education, manual vs. nonmanual labor | Same as industrial societies |

(Continued on next page)

155

TABLE 6 (continued)

| Dimension | Description | |
| --- | --- | --- |
| | Industrial society | Post-industrial society |
| 6. CORPORATE<br>Spatial units | Geopolitical boundaries of nation increase in salience, as do various politico-economic alliances or confederations; within nations, capital city, regions, key cities, suburbs, and towns are important organizational units | Same as industrial societies, except that cities and towns in urban-suburban conglomerations begin to assume corporate character |
| Institutional units: | | |
| Kinship | Nuclear family units only significant corporate unit | Same as industrial societies |
| Economic | Wide varieties of corporations, small businesses, unions, trade associations, and professional associations dominant | Same as industrial societies |
| Political | Key divisions of state, courts, political parties, specialized interest groups, and reified (as a corporate unit) "public opinion" dominant | Same as industrial societies |
| Religious | Varieties of bureaucratic cult structures; some systems have just a few cults, others (such as the U.S.) many different types (in terms of size, bureaucracy, stability) | Same as industrial societies |
| Education | Many new distinctions by school district, school level, public vs. private, and prestige | Same as industrial societies |
| Legal | Explicit courts, enforcement units, legislative bodies, legal professions, legal corporations, incarceration structures, and restitutive units | Same as industrial societies, with legal corporations and professions increasingly salient |
| Associational units | Enormous increase in number, type, and diversity of both voluntary and involuntary organizations; status groups less salient and prominent, except among high level elites | Same as industrial societies, except that mass media create large numbers of "imagined communities" or reference groupings with which individuals identify |

creasing economic and political liaisons among mature industrial and post-industrial systems.

Institutionally, the defining feature of industrial societies is the dramatic transformations in the economy—primarily the harnessing of inanimate power to machines. Later, with post-industrialization, information-processing capacities allow for the replacement of much labor with machines. The result of these technological advances is to alter the nature of society as vast quantities of goods are produced, increasing the need for markets and services. With money and capital markets, the process of capital formation becomes highly dynamic, usually involving a combination of state funding and regulation, private investment by individuals and collective investors (corporations and pooled funds), and, increasingly, transnational investments in other economies and world markets. Labor becomes highly differentiated, increasingly skilled and nonmanual, and subject to the dynamics of a global labor market. Entrepreneurship is taken out of kinship, except for small businesses, and is now performed by national and multinational corporations, regulated by the state and legal system, while operating in national and global markets. The vast expansion of productivity is the result and, at the same time, the cause of increased access to resources, not only in the society involved but also in other, dependent societies. Serious problems of depletion in nonrenewable resources emerge, and the disruption of the environment begins to pose an economic and political dilemma, especially in systems moving toward post-industrialism.

Kinship in industrial and post-industrial systems completes its odyssey back to its original nuclear profile in hunting and gathering societies. Smaller, nucleated families tend to become more mobile, egalitarian, and unstable, creating dilemmas in some systems over the socialization of the young. Religion remains well institutionalized but typically partitioned from political, economic, and most social activity. Moreover, it must now compete in a market for leisure time with many other activities dominated by secular ideologies and beliefs. Yet, while membership in cult structures declines with industrialization, it tends to level off and remain stable, so that a majority of the population usually adheres to religious beliefs and values and performs key rituals.

As noted earlier, the state is transformed with industrialization, becoming more democratic and larger. Even in less democratic industrial systems, the state is large because of the need to exert social control and coordinate economic activity (particularly in the absence of free and open markets); but over the long run, as world markets become increasingly important in sustaining a society's economic growth and prosperity, these larger and often repressive states move in the direction of more representative democracy, freer markets, and increased participation in the world economic system. As participation in the open market or subunits of it expands, the increased freedom on which market participation relies and the increased factionalization of interests on the basis of market location operate to encourage the organization of interests in political parties or blocs, which in turn help sustain democratization. And democratic systems always reveal a large state, as diverse interests push for "programs" to meet their needs, and as the problems of open markets (lack of coordination in addition to consumer abuse, worker exploitation, corruption and collusion among market leaders, environmental problems, and the like) escalate to a point requiring governmental regulation. Further, war or even the threat of it creates pressures for central control to meet perceived or manufactured military needs. Much governmental regulation occurs through the acceleration of legislative activity and the expansion of legal codes, courts, and enforcement agencies. For increasingly, the legal system becomes the mediator of social relations between the state and the public, as well as between individuals; and as the law assumes these burdens, there is a dramatic increase in the size, scale, and complexity of legal codes, courts, and enforcement agencies.

Along with the changes in the economy, state, and legal system, there is an expansion of the mass public education system to provide the skilled personnel needed for these institutional complexes. Moreover, as the technology and knowledge needed to sustain institutional activities increase, higher education, government institutes of science (in many but not all systems), research granting agencies, and research adjuncts of corporations all expand and organize scientific inquiry. The exact combination of these structures varies enormously, but the procedures of science become embedded in educational, governmental, and economic structures. Along with these changes, medicine becomes a dominant institutional complex, accounting for a significant portion of total GNP and consuming a large share of the state's budget.

Turning to stratification, we find a decrease in the level of inequality in the distribution of power (through the democratization of the state), material wealth (through increased productivity, state redistribution policies, and reliance on skilled/professional wage earners), and prestige (through the escalated importance of educational credentials, coupled with the increased capacity for more individuals to accumulate wealth and power in a political democracy and an open-market economy). As a result of the decrease in inequality, and coupled with the increasing importance of knowledge and information skills, class-formation processes become complex. There are distinctions among (1) the unskilled, unemployed poor, (2) unskilled industrial workers, (3) small farmers, (4) skilled craft workers, (5) relatively unskilled nonmanual workers, (6) skilled nonmanual workers, (7) local small business owners/managers, (8) professional elites, (9) large-scale owners/managers of businesses, (10) national corporate, governmental, and military elites, and (11) old, inherited monied elites. Depending on the society, various class distinctions are highlighted or are recessive. For example, all these distinctions are relevant for the United States, but in the Soviet Union of old, many of them were of little or no importance—for example, (9) and (11).

The crucial point is that class formation persists in industrial and postindustrial systems, but the number of classes increases, and the boundaries between them decrease with rising rates of social mobility. And rates of mobility remain relatively high because of a combination of structural forces (e.g., economic expansion and contraction, the export of unskilled or routine industrial jobs to foreign countries, the mechanization of routine jobs, the growth of service industries) and demographic forces (e.g., migration patterns and differential fertility rates). Moreover, with democratization, there are episodic social movements to reduce inequalities associated with categoric distinctions—particularly sex and ethnicity.

The number of categoric units increases with the expansion and differentiation of institutional structures and, to a lesser extent, with the increasing number of loosely bounded classes. Probably the most significant changes revolve around the redefinition of sex, ethnicity, and kinship. Although sex remains a basic distinction, there are pressures for equal participation in key roles (particularly family and economic) and for the equal distribution of resources (prestige, material, and political) not only in these roles but also in those that still denote sexual differences. Ethnicity becomes a focal point of conflict as a result of past and present patterns of conquest and migration, and there are contradictory pressures to sustain ethnic identity and to equalize the opportunities for ethnic groups and the distribution of resources. Kinship declines even more as a basic categoric distinction, only to be replaced by another criterion, educational attainment. Class distinctions proliferate but lose some of their salience, although such distinctions as manual and nonmanual, high and low educational attainment, and high and low income/wealth remain highly relevant. Regional distinctions still obtain, and they become particularly important if associated with ethnicity, class formation, or cities, suburbs, and towns of a particular economic and/or cultural orientation.

Alongside these categoric distinctions are a myriad of corporate units. Again, kinship is generally viable only at the nuclear level—a far cry from its scope in horticultural systems, where kinship constituted the first cage. The greatest proliferation of corporate units is in the economy, for each axis and dimension of differentiation produces vast clusters of them. Politically, democratization increases the number of organized interests, political parties (or factions in a party), and divisions within the state. Religion also retains a wide variety of cult structures, but their salience and power decrease somewhat with the general trend toward the secularization of beliefs and the proliferation of non-kin corporate units. The expansion of the educational system introduces many new corporate units—from schools, levels within schools, school systems, various interest groups concerned with educational issues, and subunits of the state charged with administering national educational policies. Similarly, just as education expands in response to its increased functions, so the legal system's corporate units proliferate at every level—legislative (party, interest groups, factions, etc.), judiciary (courts, the professionalization of attorneys, the organization of magistrates), and enforcement (police forces and advocacy organizations, prisons, jails). Other growing institutional complexes, such as medicine, leisure activity, and the media, also generate a myriad of corporate units, organizing an enormous amount of each individual's time. Finally, the number of associational units increases, especially in market-oriented and highly democratic systems. Most of these are voluntary in nature, although status groups remain, especially among elites and even among the professions. Moreover, the existence of mass media allows for what Craig Calhoun (1991) has termed "imagined communities," or people's sense that they are members of corporate units portrayed in the media. These are not status groups, or even loose networks, but they influence people's actions and their sense of identity. Although the full effects of such vicarious "memberships" are difficult to discern, there is no question that they greatly extend and expand individuals' symbolic involvement in different types of groups.

## A Note on Post-Modernity

Some scholars (e.g., Lyotard 1984) consider changes in post-industrial societies so fundamental as to constitute a new stage of human organization—"post-modernity." Just what "post-modernity" involves seems to vary somewhat, depending on who is making the portrayal (Touraine 1988), but four themes seem to run through all accounts: (1) the increase in plurality, heterogeneity, and diversity of societies has reached such a high level that there is a "decentering" and an inability to integrate the whole; (2) the increase in differentiation is accompanied by a de-differentiation of culture, with the result that there are fewer clear distinctions among science, art, literature, and daily life, as well as fewer clear standards and criteria by which to make distinctions; (3) the growing diversity, coupled with the merging of cultured spheres, increases the distrust of rationality; and (4) the distrust of rationality, along with the decline in clear standards or criteria for evaluation and distinction, increases the sense that all knowledge is relative, and that objective reality is somewhat illusory.

These themes are popular in intellectual discourse on post-industrialization, but they may be exaggerations created by intellectuals looking for new ideas and for ways to discuss the effects of several basic changes in post-industrial systems, namely: (1) the dramatic increase in markets for distributing both material and cultural products, thereby increasing people's access to signs and symbols of differentiation and distinction; (2) the use of money and other generalized media (e.g., educational credentials, knowledge of rules, authority) in social relations, enabling people to participate in many new and diverse social situations; (3) the increase in the proportion of indirect social relations and networks over direct face-to-face relations; (4) the apparent decline in highly scripted (normatively and routinized) roles and the corresponding expansion in the number of roles requiring flexibility, skill, and adaptability; (5) the seeming decline in hierarchical corporate units (such as corporations) toward more horizontal, network structures; and (6) the dramatic increase in the speed and scale of communications and, to a lesser extent, transportation, both of which escalate the velocity, extent, and nature of many social relations.

From our viewpoint, these changes are extensions of those evident during industrialization and, hence, are still "modern." The differentiation of positions and roles, mobility, the use of generalized media like money, increased communications, the diffusion of mass culture, and the expansion of secondary over primary relations are all part of initial industrialization and do not require, we believe, a new label like "post-modernity." Moreover, both the imputed hierarchy and rationality of "modern" structures and the portrayal of modern organizations and societies as fluid, flexible, horizontal, and decentered are probably overdrawn by postmodernists. The creation of "imagined communities" by the mass media, the new "post-entrepreneurial" corporation (Kanter 1989), and the decline of hierarchy and corresponding rise of flexible networks and roles (Hage and Powers 1991) are, in all likelihood, trends of the future, but it is hard to see them as radically new "post-modern" creations.

In any case, whether modern or post-modern, the changes associated with post-industrial systems are more compatible with humans' biological nature than those occurring in earlier ones. Post-modern scholars are often as biased as their nineteenth-century counterparts were in their implicit assumption that changes promoting autonomy, fluidity, flexibility, mobility, weak and transient ties, choices, and options are somehow problematic for humans, requiring great intellectual agonizing, debate, and discourse over the pathologies of the modern world. Our view is that humans will adjust rather easily to a system comparatively well attuned to their ape ancestry.

## Conclusion

Industrialization has often been a brutal, ruthless process, destroying old forms of social control and forcing the exploited masses to endure such hardships as the factory system. But in its brutality, industrialization allows people to tear down at least some of the cage of power. The state, of course, does not "wither away," as Lenin envisaged. Quite the contrary. But it also becomes more democratic and responsive to a broader array of interests. And as productivity, markets, education, science, medicine, and law all increase in size, scale, and prominence, inequality is actually reduced for the first time in humans' evolution since the agrarian era (Lenski et al. 1991: 296). Moreover, large and highly differentiated structures, operating in monied markets, provide options and choices never available in agrarian systems. For all the early sociologists' deep concern with "the loss of community," in truth ordinary people embrace the chance to live and participate in a system relatively well attuned to their primate heritage. Thus, despite all the abuses and indignities that industrial society fosters on humans, it has allowed them to tear down, at least partially, the cages of their confinement. And if post-industrialism has indeed ushered in a new "post-modern" stage of evolution, it should further reduce the humans' sociocultural cages. Too often, these transformations breaking the cage of human confinement have been viewed as problematic by modernists and post-modernists alike. We argue just the opposite: these new structures are far less problematic for a big-brained hominoid than is often assumed. Indeed, modernists and post-modernists often appear to believe that humans are a monkey, requiring embeddedness in tightly woven social structures. They are not: humans are an evolved ape, a primate that has little trouble with weak tie relations, loose and fluid communities, mobility, and fluctuating social structures.

And finally, as was the case for agrarian systems, these dynamics of industrial societies cannot be explained by simple reductionist appeals to the genic level, as many sociobiologists contend. They can be examined from a coevolutionary approach, it is true, but would such an approach add new insights by analyzing the dynamics of industrialization in terms of isomorphisms to biological selection? Moreover, both sociobiology and more recent coevolutionary approaches cannot, we feel, fully capture the biological bases for trying to tear down the cage of power.

# 8

THE OVERLY SOCIAL

CONCEPTION OF

HUMANS AND SOCIETY

# How Social Are Humans?

Many years ago, Dennis Wrong (1961) attacked Parsonian functionalism for its "overly socialized conception of man and society." Parsons
was criticized for viewing actors as socialized in ways that fulfill society's need for value consensus, role-playing skills, and motivational
tendencies to conform to values and normative requirements of status
positions. There is an element of truth in this indictment, although, like
most of the severest attacks on Parsons, it is overdrawn and somewhat
unfair.

In a sense, this book makes a similar criticism of sociology in general
but pushes the focus of the attack one step further: sociologists presume
humans to be far more social than they really are, at least from a biological point of view. For "sociality" is more the result of socialization
than biology. Thus, Wrong's attack on the particulars of Parsonian functionalism may have been correct, but our view is that sociologists may
have an undersocialized conception of humans, at least in the sense of
assuming that basic needs for social bonding and group involvement are
primarily biological.

True, few sociologists come right out and say so, but their theories all
tend to reflect an implicit presumption that humans are inherently (read:
biologically) *social*. Indeed, the great agonizing by early sociologists over
such pathological conditions as alienation, egoism, and loss of community rested on the assumption that humans were highly social creatures
driven by powerful needs for embeddedness in group structures. More
modern theories—for all their concern in the post-Parsonian era over inequality, power, coercion, and the like—retain this presumption of high

sociality, whether this is conceptualized as a need for ontological security and trust (Giddens 1984), for positive emotional energy in encounters (Collins 1984, 1988), for maintaining an identity (Stryker 1980), for self-anchorage in roles (R. Turner 1978), for communicative action (Habermas 1984), for sustaining even an illusory sense of facticity (Garfinkel 1967), for being attracted to nonmaterial exchanges (Homans 1961; Blau 1964), for maintaining social bonds (Scheff 1990), and so on and so forth. None of these theorists explicitly makes a biological argument, but we think they do so tacitly. It is difficult to know, of course, the relative proportions of biology and socialization in producing humans' preference to live in groups, but our view is that sociologists have not adequately thought through the questions revolving around biology, evolutionary processes, and patterns of social organization.

In making this claim, our intent has not been to set up a "straw man" to knock down. But one conclusion from our analysis is that as big-brained hominoids, we are by nature somewhat individualistic, prone to free spatial mobility,[1] and resistant to hierarchies and rigid group structures, especially as compared with our more distant cousins, the monkeys. Selection pressures for group organization obviously increased when hominids—*Australopithecus*, *Homo habilis*, *Homo erectus*, and *Homo sapiens*—adapted to an open ecology, but these hominids brought with them the biological characteristics of apes, which had sacrificed strong grouping (and perhaps bonding) tendencies as they were pushed to the arboreal extremes, allowing better adapted monkeys to proliferate and take over the vacated niches.

Survival depended on many accommodations of pre-hominids to the wide-ranging environment of the African savanna. Bipedalism was the first major adaptation of early hominid anatomy, a crucial adaptation that laid the groundwork for the restructuring of the vocal tract and the modulation of a variety of phonetic sounds. There were, no doubt, selection pressures for the increased organization of bipedal hominids, but whether these went a lot further than present-day chimpanzees and gorillas is hard to know. Our reconstruction of the Last Common Ancestor in Chapter 2 would suggest that, at best, the first hominid groupings were

---

[1] That is, humans prefer to be self-directed in their movement through space, walking about either alone or joining or leaving temporary clusters at will, much like their chimpanzee relatives. For example, when humans walk in company, most large parties break up into smaller, more flexible clusters of two, three, or at most five people. This desire for autonomy and freedom may help explain why humans resist car-pooling: it forces a rigid synchronization of each person's schedule. Mass transit (train, trolley, bus, or plane) is less confining, for though it too requires adhering to a schedule, it offers time options and allows for self-movement in space. But where the car is used for transportation, a single driver will probably remain the most popular pattern because it provides the greatest flexibility and independence of movement.

loose-knit and fluid. The fact that modern human hunters and gatherers remain individualistic and mobile adds further credence to the view that early hominid species retained the ape legacy of self-reliance, autonomy, and individualism.

Further, given the complex neuroanatomy of anthropoids in general and apes in particular, small but significant alterations in the primate brain could produce culturally directed social organization. In this way, natural selection would not have to restructure apes' neuroanatomy back to a more monkeylike pattern—a process so complex that it would in all likelihood have led to the extinction of savanna-dwelling apes. Fortunately for us, selection could produce changes compatible with ape neuroanatomy that would increase social organization through culture and, as a result, would increase the fitness of hominids. As Chapter 3 documented, the pressures of an open habitat favored in early hominids the freeing of the vocal-auditory channel from the limbic cortex, putting it largely under control of the neocortex. Once this change occurred, the neurological foundation for language and culture was complete. The dramatic increase in the size of the neocortex in *Homo habilis* and then *Homo erectus* gives us a time yardstick for *when* selection for increased social organization in terms of culture began to operate. We believe that in order to overcome millions of years of ape evolution in the arboreal niche for low sociality and fluid structure, natural selection had to favor subtle extensions of cognitive changes that were already occurring in the neuroanatomy of early hominids adapting to an open-range habitat. Thus, laid over the tendencies for the individualism, or relatively low degrees of sociality of most apes, were cultural processes—language, speech, and socially constructed bonds—producing more cohesive patterns of social organization.

The glimpses of our distant societal past that we get from those hunters and gatherers who managed to survive into this century are our best looking glass into how our hominoid ancestry was accommodated to increased levels of social organization in cultural terms. What we see in this more proximate and, no doubt, somewhat distorted mirror are patterns of fluid and loose structure, in which individuals in food-collecting societies retain considerable autonomy and freedom. Such structuring is only modestly more constraining than that among our closest ape relatives. Since human social evolution has involved the elaboration of structure and constraint, it has also involved increasing the tension between our biological legacy and our sociocultural constructions.

This kind of biosocial argument does not need the extreme assumptions of sociobiology, which, if anything, errs in the opposite direction of positing an "underly social" conception of humans, where even altruism is selfishness in the name of genic fitness. The big error of sociobiology when applied to humans is to overemphasize selection at the genic level and underemphasize the operation of cultural processes. When such processes are underemphasized, it becomes necessary to explain culture and social structure in terms of genes, with the result that, much as in the extreme utilitarianism it emulates, there is "an invisible hand of order" imposed by the miraculous ability of totally selfish and maximizing genes to explain sociocultural constructions. Few of the concepts specific to sociobiology—except what is borrowed from the synthetic theory of evolution—are needed to explain the characteristics of humans or society. There is a simpler way to incorporate biology into sociological analysis, perhaps less technically elegant but we think more accurate. One conclusion from our simple alternative to much sociobiology is to view human social structure as contradicting, rather than reflecting, humans' biological propensities. And it is for this reason that we resurrected the old metaphor of "the social cage." Sociocultural evolution has involved creating cages that, to varying degrees, have violated humans' basic biological tendencies.

Similarly, we do not believe that more recent coevolutionary arguments can fully incorporate our view of the relation between culture and social organization, on the one hand, and human biology on the other. One could, of course, analyze the sociocultural changes that have caged humans from a coevolutionary approach. Indeed, we are positing a new kind of coevolutionary analysis, but without the assumption that cultural and biological evolution operates in terms of isomorphic processes. Perhaps it is possible to rephrase our argument in coevolutionary terms—memes, meme pools, allomemes, holomemes, selection, and the like—but it is not clear that such an effort would improve on the simple description we have offered. For by simply describing primate evolution and, then, following the course of sociocultural evolution, we can gain much insight into the biology of human organization without adding the debatable theoretical assumptions of many coevolutionary approaches.

## How Caged Are Humans?

We have viewed social evolution as a caging process because it has involved enclosing and repressing humans' most basic (let us use the word) "instincts" for individualism, autonomy, and freedom. With big brains, culture, and socialization, humans can accommodate themselves to confinement, but not without a fundamental tension. Horticultural systems, structured as they are through the elaboration of kinship bonds, are the most restrictive; and the tension in these systems is all too obvious: constant war, feuds, violent explosions, and desperate rituals to keep a lid on the tension. Agrarian systems impose a second cage, much more exploitive and vicious but somewhat less restrictive. And industrial societies, for all their problems so clearly articulated by Marx, Weber, Durkheim, and numbers of Marxists and post-modernists, impose even fewer restrictions on humans' basic instincts. Indeed, much of the "loss of community" that has so worried both early and contemporary sociologists, we believe, is based on highly romanticized or incomplete portrayals of sociocultural cages of earlier societal types. Industrialization and post-industrialization in fact allow people more choice, freedom, autonomy, and mobility than either horticultural or agrarian systems. True, these societies are far from ideal places, especially when compared with what Marshall Sahlins (1968a) calls the "original affluent society" of hunting and gathering, but they are far closer to an accommodation of human biology to sociocultural constraints than either horticultural or agrarian societies. Humans have thus begun to dismantle the cage, perhaps as much as is going to be possible for now in large and crowded societies.

Yet curiously, much of sociology involves a critique of industrial society. How can this be so in light of the fact that such a society is more liberating than its predecessors? Part of the answer resides in the exploitive nature of early industrial capitalism—as Marx so powerfully documented and as contemporary Marxists, who still hold to Marx's collectivist utopia, continue to assert. Another part is a historically based naïveté, or at least selective interpretation, of horticultural and agrarian systems. Marx's intellectual companion Friedrich Engels (1845), for example, portrays past societies with a romanticism that stands in stark contrast to his realistic and brutal description of early industrialism in Manchester, England. Or, to take another example, Jurgen Habermas (1962) portrays "the public sphere" of cafes, conversation, and discourse of pre-industrial systems with an equal romanticism that is then juxtaposed to a picture of domination and colonization by economic and political forces in more contemporary societies. To illustrate further, many early American sociologists, looking at the obvious problems of urban-industrial America, also tended to juxtapose a rather romanticized view of communal, small-town life with the impersonality of the modern metropolis.

Still another part of the explanation of why sociologists remain critical of modern society lies in the misinterpretation of modern industrial systems as creating Max Weber's "iron cage of bureaucracy" and other constraints that control, regulate, and depersonalize social life. Further confusing matters, and juxtaposed to this dreary Weberian scenario, is post-modernism, where just the opposite condition of no constraint and integration is portrayed. And, finally, the answer lies in part in a bias toward collectivism and against individualism in contemporary social theory. Marx and Marxists certainly viewed collectivism as more basic to human needs than the individualism evident in market-driven systems. Similarly, Durkheim (1902) advocated another form of collectivism, based on common ideas representing society and institutionalized rituals directed toward such symbolic representations of society.

In fact, if we look back at the early sociologists, only Herbert Spencer (1852, 1874–96) and Georg Simmel (1907) emphasized some of the more positive and liberating aspects of highly differentiated industrial systems driven by market forces. As a result, Spencer was vilified first by Durkheim (1893), then by Parsons (1937), and finally for all practical purposes forgotten. Simmel has stood up better, perhaps because he was less influential in his time, and now enjoys a new respect as one of the first post-modernists stressing the fragmented (and also free and open) nature of modern society (Frisby 1985). But the stigmatization of Spencer should warn us about the collectivist bias of much sociology, which still makes its living by studying the problematic aspects of modern society, and which is often contemptuous of thinking that points to the beneficial aspects of industrial capitalism.

We mention this situation only to highlight the reasons why many sociologists—save for the post-modernists—view life in industrial systems as a new kind of cage. But it is not. We are, as a species, far less caged than we have been for several thousand years. Who could deny, of course, the many miseries associated with inequality, concentrations of power, fluctuating and at times exploitive labor markets, individual pathologies, and abuses of corporations in industrial systems? We certainly do not, but there is a perversion in much sociological analysis, based on a combination of idealized representations of nonindustrial systems, portrayals of human nature as social and therefore collectivist, and a desire to do something (or at least to talk about doing something) about the problems and pathologies of big and differentiated societies. The result of these biases, we argue, is a failure to (1) recognize fully the extent to which such systems are more compatible with our primate legacy than horticultural and agrarian societies and (2) appreciate the implications of this primate legacy for social policy.

## Some Implications and a Final Comment

There are two major policy conclusions from our analysis. One is that humans are not collectivists; indeed, at a biological level, we would not be all that social were it not for the effects of socialization into culture (it is, perhaps, a good thing that humans are "oversocialized"). The other is that, for all the obvious problems of industrial societies, many critics, especially the Marxists, would impose yet another cage—whether that of the police state or, if the state really would "wither away," that of repressive and constraining "consensus" and "will of the people." In either case, a big-brained hominoid would seek escape.

But escape to what? Our answer is to a system allowing for more choice, freedom, autonomy, and individualism. Industrial capitalism is certainly not ideal in this regard, particularly when set against romanticized portrayals of the past or even accurate descriptions of the few remaining hunters and gatherers, but given our primate legacy, it is certainly more compatible with human nature than most of the alternatives proposed by critics.

We do not wish to sound like apologists for "The System"; and in truth, we share most of the ideological biases of sociologists. But our review of the "evidence," as best it can be summarized in a short book on human evolution, suggests that a society which allows choice and restricts inequality and power is more compatible with human nature than the ones it succeeded (always excepting the "first" society), as that nature evolved in the primate order over the last 60 million years. The task of the critic is not to preach utopias based on a misinterpretation of this biological heritage or to extol the virtues of social constructions that would recage humans; rather, the goal should be to recreate, under the obvious limitations and inevitable constraints of large populations and sociocultural differentiation, a system that enables people to stay out of highly restrictive and oppressive cages.

What would such a system look like? It would be politically democratic; it would give people choices in open and free markets; it would let them maintain a sense of personal identity; it would reduce inequalities; and it would hold back both the cage of extended kinship (and by extension, the repressiveness of "community") and the cage of power. Some of these ideal tenets are contradictory, however. For example, to reduce inequality requires concentrations of power (to tax and redistribute); to prevent the abuse, exploitation, and fraud of open markets would similarly concentrate regulatory power and, in so doing, limit options and choices. Thus, the reality of organizing large, differentiated populations prevents a return to anything approaching the "affluence" of hunters and gatherers. At best, humans can construct a cage of power—so essential to maintaining freedoms, choices, and individuality, while reducing inequalities, abuses, and exploitation—that is democratic and, itself, less exploitive and restrictive than its predecessor in preindustrial societies.

It has become somewhat chic to be cynical about modern societies—

either as a critic or as an essayist on post-modernism or some other trendy line of cafe-thinking. These critiques are, we feel, based on an assumption that humans do not want this system. But if we will only consider this issue objectively, it is clearly the case that humans do want an open, fluid, and individualistic system; and our job as social scientists is to understand the dynamics of such a system and, if policy should be our goal, to use that understanding to allow these big-brained primates to live in a social cage with widely spaced bars and an open door.

# BIBLIOGRAPHY

# BIBLIOGRAPHY

Abravanel, E. 1968. *The Development of Inter Sensory Patterning with Regard to Selected Spatial Dimensions.* University of Chicago Monographs of the Society for Research in Child Development 33, no. 2: 1–52.

————. 1971. "Active Detection of Solid Shape Information by Touch and Vision." *Perception and Psychophysics* 9: 327–28.

Adams, Mark. 1979. "From 'Gene Fund' to 'Gene Pool': On the Evolution of Evolutionary Language." *Studies in the History of Biology* 3: 241–85.

Alexander, R. D. 1974. "The Evolution of Social Behaviours." *Annual Review of Ecological Systems* 5: 325–83.

————. 1987. *The Biology of Moral Systems.* New York: Aldine De Gruyter.

Allen, Garland. 1969. "Hugo de Vries and the Reception of the 'Mutation Theory.'" *Journal of the History of Biology* 2: 55–85.

Allman, John, and Evelynn McGuinness. 1988. "Visual Cortex in Primates." In Steklis and Erwin 1988.

Altenmüller, Eckart, Richard Jung, Thomas Winker, and Bernhard Landwehrmeyer. 1989. "Premotor Programming and Cortical Processing in the Cerebral Cortex." *Brain Behavior and Evolution* 33: 141–46.

Amaral, D. G., and A. J. Price. 1984. "Amygdalo-Cortical Prosections in the Monkey (Macaca fasciularis)." *Journal of Comparative Neurology* 230: 465–94.

Andelman, Sandy. 1986. "Ecological and Social Determinants of Cercopithecine Mating Patterns." In D. Rubenstein and R. Wrangham, eds., *Ecological Aspects of Social Evolution.* Princeton, N.J.: Princeton Univ. Press.

Andersen, R. A., C. Asanuma, G. Essick, and R. M. Siegel. 1990. "Corticocortical Connections of Anatomically and Physiologically Defined Subdivisions Within the Interior Parietal Lobule." *Journal of Comparative Neurology* 296: 65–113.

Anderson, Connie. 1986. "Predation and Primate Evolution." *Primates* 27: 15–39.

Anderson, Perry. 1974. *Passages from Antiquity to Feudalism*. London: New Left Books.

Andrews, Peter. 1981. "Species Diversity and Diet in Monkeys and Apes During the Miocene." In C. B. Stringer, ed., *Aspects of Human Evolution*. London: Taylor and Francis.

Andrews, Peter, and Lawrence Martin. 1987. "Cladistic Relationships of Extant and Fossil Hominoids." *Journal of Human Evolution* 16: 101–18.

Ardrey, Robert. 1966. *The Territorial Imperative*. New York: Atheneum.

Arensburg, B., L. A. Schepartz, A. M. Tillier, B. Vandermeersch, and Y. Rak. 1990. "A Reappraisal of the Anatomical Basis for Speech in Middle Palaeolithic Hominids." *American Journal of Physical Anthropology* 83: 137–46.

Baldwin, John D., and Janice I. Baldwin. 1981. *Beyond Sociobiology*. New York: Elsevier.

Barlow, H. B. 1983. "Intelligence, Guesswork and Language." *Nature* 304: 207–9.

Barry, Herbert, Irving Child, and Margaret Bacon. 1959. "Relation of Child Training to Subsistence Economy." *American Anthropologist* 61: table 2.

Bartholomew, G. A., and J. P. Birdsell. 1953. "Ecology and the Proto-Hominids." *American Anthropologist* 55: 481–98.

Bar-Yosef, Ofer, and Mordochai Kislev. 1989. "Early Farming Communities in the Jordan Valley." In D. Harris and G. Hullman, eds., *Foraging and Farming: The Evolution of Plant Exploitation*. London: Unwin Hyman.

Bates, Daniel, and Fred Plog. 1991. *Human Adaptive Strategies*. New York: McGraw-Hill.

Batic, Nidia, and Pier Gabassi. 1987. "Visual Dominance in Olfactory Memory." *Perceptual and Motor Skills* 65: 88–90.

Beaud, Michel. 1983. *A History of Capitalism, 1500–1980*. New York: Monthly Review Press.

Bellah, Robert. 1964. "Religious Evolution." *American Sociological Review* 9: 358–74.

Bellugi, Ursula, Howard Poizner, and Edward Klima. 1989. "Language, Modality and the Brain." *Trends in Neuroscience* 12: 380–88.

Bender, Barbara. 1975. *Farming in Prehistory*. London: Baker.

Bendix, Reinhard. 1978. *Kings or People: Power and the Mandate to Rule*. Berkeley: Univ. of California Press.

Bennett, J. H. 1983. *Natural Selection, Heredity and Eugenics*. Oxford: Clarendon.

Bicchieri, M. G., ed. 1972. *Hunters and Gatherers Today*. New York: Holt, Rinehart and Winston.

Binford, L. 1968. "Post-Pleistocene Adaptations." In S. R. Binford and L. R. Binford, eds., *New Perspectives in Archaeology*. Chicago: Aldine.

Black, C. M., J. S. McDougal, B. L. Evatt, and C. B. Reimer. 1991. "Human Markers for $IgC_2$ and $IgC_4$ Appear to Be on the Same Molecule in the Chimpanzee." *Immunology* 72: 94–98.

Blau, Peter M. 1964. *Exchange and Power in Social Life*. New York: Wiley.

————. 1977. *Inequality and Heterogeneity: A Primitive Theory of Social Structure*. New York: Free Press.

Bloch, Marc. 1962. *Feudal Society*. Trans. L. A. Manyon. Chicago: Univ. of Chicago Press.

Blum, Jerome. 1961. *Lord and Peasant in Russia from the Ninth to the Nineteenth Century*. Princeton, N.J.: Princeton Univ. Press.

Blumler, Mark, and Roger Byrne. 1991. "The Ecological Genetics of Domestication and the Origins of Agriculture." *Current Anthropology* 32: 23–54.

Boas, Franz. 1921. *Ethnology of the Kwakiutl*. Washington, D.C.: Smithsonian Institution Press.

Boaz, Noel T. 1983. "Morphological Trends and Phyletic Relationships from Middle Miocene Hominoids to Late Pliocene Hominids." In Ciochon and Corruccini 1983.

————. 1988. "Status of Australopithecus Aforensis." *Yearbook of Physical Anthropology* 31: 85–113.

Bodley, John. 1975. *Victims of Progress*. Menlo Park, Calif.: Cummings.

Boserup, Ester. 1965. *The Conditions of Agricultural Growth: The Economics of Agrarian Change Under Population Pressure*. Chicago: Aldine.

Boulding, Kenneth. 1978. *Ecodynamics: A New Theory of Societal Evolution*. Newbury Park, Calif.: Sage.

Bower, T. G. R., J. M. Broughton, and M. K. Moore. 1970. "The Coordination of Visual and Tactual Input in Infants." *Perception and Psychophysics* 8: 51–53.

Boyd, Robert, and P. J. Richerson. 1976. "A Simple Dual Inheritance Model of Conflict Between Social and Biological Evolution." *Zygon* 11: 254–62.

————. 1985. *Culture and the Evolutionary Process*. Chicago: Univ. of Chicago Press.

Boyden, Stephen. 1987. *Western Civilization in Biological Perspective*. Oxford: Clarendon Press.

Brain, Lord. 1965. "Perception: A Trialogue." *Brain* 88: 697–708.

Braitenberg, V. 1977. *On the Texture of Brains*. Berlin: Springer.

Bryant, P. E., P. Jones, V. Claxton, and G. M. Perkins. 1972. "Recognition of Shapes Across Modalities by Infants." *Nature* 240: 303–4.

Byrne, R. 1987. "Climatic Change and the Origins of Agriculture." In L. Manzanilla, ed., *Studies in the Neolithic and Urban Revolutions*. British Archaeological Reports International Series 349.

Calhoun, Craig. 1991. "Imagined Communities, Indirect Relationships, and Postmodernism." In C. Calhoun, ed., *Social Theory in a Changing Society*. New York: Russell Sage.

*The Cambridge Economic History of Europe*. 1963. London: Cambridge Univ. Press.

Campbell, Bernard. 1985a. *Human Evolution*. 3d ed. Chicago: Aldine de Gruyter.

————. 1985b. *Humankind Emerging*. Boston: Little, Brown.

Campbell, C. B. G. 1969. "The Visual System of Insectivores and Primates." *Annual of the New York Academy of Science* 167: 338.

Campbell, F., and L. Maffer. 1976. "Contrast and Spatial Frequency." In Held and Richards 1976.

Carneiro, Robert L. 1967. "On the Relationship Between Size of Population and Complexity of Social Organization." *Southwestern Journal of Anthropology* 23: 234–43.

———. 1970. "A Theory of the Origin of the State." *Science* 169: 733–38.

Carneiro, Robert L., and S. F. Tobias. 1963. "The Application of Scale Analysis to the Study of Evolution." *Transactions of the New York Academy of Science*, series 2, 26: 196–207.

Carpenter, Ray. 1942. "Societies of Monkeys and Apes." In *Biological Symposia*, vol. 8: 177–204.

Cartmill, M. 1974. "Rethinking Primate Origins." *Science* 184: 436–43.

Cashdan, S. 1968. "Visual and Haptic Form Discrimination Under Conditions of Successive Stimulation." *Journal of Experimental Psychology* 76: 215–18.

Cavalli-Sforza, L. L., and M. W. Feldman. 1981. *Cultural Transmission and Evolution*. Princeton, N.J.: Princeton Univ. Press.

Cavallo, John, and Robert Blumenschine. 1989. "Tree-Stored Leopard Kills: Expanding the Hominid Scavenging Niche." *Journal of Human Evolution* 18: 393–99.

Chagnon, Napoleon A. 1983. *Yanomamö: The Fierce People*. 3d ed. New York: Holt, Rinehart and Winston.

Chang, Kwang-chih. 1963. *The Archeology of Ancient China*. New Haven, Conn.: Yale Univ. Press.

Charles-Dominique, Pierre. 1977. *Ecology and Behaviour of Nocturnal Primates*. New York: Columbia Univ. Press.

Cheney, Dorothy, and Robert Seyfarth. 1990. *How Monkeys See the World*. Chicago: Univ. of Chicago Press.

Cheney, Dorothy, Robert Seyfarth, and Barbara Smuts. 1986. "Social Relationships and Social Cognition in Non-Human Primates." *Science* 234: 1361–66.

Childe, V. Gordon. 1930. *The Bronze Age*. London: Cambridge Univ. Press.

———. 1951. *Man Makes His Way*. New York: Mentor Books.

———. 1952. *New Light on the Most Ancient East*. London: Routledge and Kegan Paul.

———. 1953. *Man Makes Himself*. New York: Mentor Books.

———. 1960. "The New Stone Age." In H. Shapiro, ed., *Man, Culture and Society*. New York: Oxford Galaxy.

———. 1964. *What Happened in History*. Baltimore: Penguin.

Chirot, Daniel. 1986. *Social Change in the Modern Era*. Orlando, Fla.: Harcourt Brace Jovanovich.

Chivers, David. 1974. "The Siamang in Malaya." In *Contributions to Primatology*, vol. 40. New York: S. Karger.

———. 1984. "Feeding and Ranging in Gibbons: A Summary." In H. Prevschoft, D. Chivers, W. Brockelman, and N. Creel, eds., *The Lesser Apes*. Edinburgh: Edinburgh Univ. Press.

Chomsky, Noam. 1975. *Reflections on Language*. New York: Pantheon.

————. 1980. "Rules and Representations." *The Behavioral and Brain Sciences* 3: 1–15.

Ciochon, R. L. 1987. "Cladistics and the Ancestry of Modern Apes and Humans." In Ciochon and Fleagle 1987.

Ciochon, R. L., and R. Corruccini, eds. 1983. *New Interpretations of Ape and Human Ancestry*. New York: Plenum.

Ciochon, R. L. and J. Fleagle, eds. 1987. *Primate Evolution and Human Origins*. New York: Aldine de Gruyter.

Ciochon, R. L., D. E. Savage, T. Tint, and T. Maw. 1985. "Anthropoid Origins in Asia? New Discovery of Amphipittecus from the Eocene of Burma." *Science* 229: 756–59.

Claessen, H., and P. Skalnick, eds. 1978. *The Early State*. The Hague: Mouton.

Clark, Grahame, and Stuart Piggott. 1965. *Prehistoric Societies*. New York: Knopf.

Clark, J. G. D. 1952. *Prehistoric Europe: The Economic Basis*. London: Methuen.

Cloe, C. S., R. B. Welch, R. M. Gilford, and J. F. Juola. 1975. "The Ventriloquist Effect: Visual Dominance or Response Bias?" *Perception and Psychophysics* 18: 55–60.

Clough, S. B., and C. W. Cole. 1941. *Economic History of Europe*. Boston: Heath.

Clutton-Brock, T. H. 1974. "Primate Social Organization and Ecology." *Nature* 250: 539–42.

Clutton-Brock, T. H., and P. Harvey. 1977. "Primate Ecology and Social Organization." *Journal of the London Zoological Society* 183: 1–39.

Cobb, Stanley. 1965. "Brain Size." *Archives of Neurology* 12: 46–52.

Cohen, Joel. 1975. "The Size and Demographic Composition of Social Groups of Wild Orang-utans." *Animal Behaviour* 23: 543–50.

Cohen, Mark. 1977. *The Food Crisis in Prehistory: Overpopulation and the Origins of Agriculture*. New Haven, Conn.: Yale Univ. Press.

Cohen, Ronald, and Elman Service, eds. 1977. *Origins of the State*. Philadelphia: Institute for the Study of Human Issues.

Coimbra-Filho, Adelman, and Russell Mittermeier. 1981. *Ecology and Behavior of Neotropical Primates*. Vol. 1. Rio de Janeiro: Academia Bras, Leira de Ciencias.

Colavita, F. B. 1974. "Human Sensory Dominance." *Perception and Psychophysics* 16: 499–512.

Coleman, James. 1990. "Summary of Epigenic and Experimental Contributions Underlying Formation of Sensory Systems in Mammals." In James Coleman, ed., *Development of Sensory Systems in Mammals*. New York: Wiley and Sons.

Collins, Randall. 1984. "The Role of Emotion in Social Structure." In K. R. Scherer and P. Ekman, eds., *Approaches to Emotion*. Hillsdale, N.J.: Erlbaum.

————. 1986. *Weberian Sociological Theory*. Cambridge, Eng.: Cambridge Univ. Press.

————. 1988. *Theoretical Sociology*. San Diego, Calif.: Harcourt Brace Jovanovich.

Comte, Auguste. [1830] 1896. *Course of Positive Philosophy.* London: Bell and Sons.

Conroy, Glenn. 1990. *Primate Evolution.* New York: Norton.

Cook, Norman. 1986. *The Brain Code.* London: Methuen.

Coon, Carleton S. 1971. *The Hunting Peoples.* Boston: Little, Brown.

Corruccini, R. S., and R. L. Ciochon. 1983. "Overview of Ape and Human Ancestry: Phyletic Relationships of Miocene and Later Hominoidea." In Ciochon and Corruccini 1983.

Corruccini, Robert, Russell Ciochon, and Henry McHenry. 1975. "Osteometric Shape Relationships in the Wrist Joint of Some Anthropoids." *Folia Primatologica* 24: 250–74.

Covert, Herbert. 1986. "Biology of Early Cenozoic Primates." In Daris Swindler and J. Erwin, eds., *Systematics, Evolution, and Anatomy,* vol. 1. New York: Alan Liss.

Craik, K. W. 1943. *The Nature of Explanation.* London: Cambridge Univ. Press.

Crelin, E. S. 1987. *The Human Vocal Tract Anatomy: Function, Development and Evolution.* New York: Vantage Press.

Critchley, MacDonald. 1969. *The Parietal Lobes.* New York: Hafner.

Cronin, J. E. 1983. "Apes, Humans, and Molecular Clocks: A Reappraisal." In Ciochon and Corruccini 1983.

Crow, James. 1987. "Population Genetics History: A Personal View." *Annual Review of Genetics* 21: 1–22.

Curwen, Cecil, and Gudmund Hatt. 1961. *Plough and Pasture: The Early History of Farming.* New York: Collier.

Daly, Martin, and Margo Wilson. 1984. "A Sociobiological Analysis of Human Infanticide." In G. Hausfater and S. Blaffer, eds., *Infanticide: Comparative and Evolutionary Perspectives.* New York: Aldine.

Damas, David. 1969. "Characteristics of Central Eskimo Band Structure." In *Band Societies: Proceedings of the Conference on Band Organization, Ottawa, 30 August to 2 September 1965.* National Museum of Canada, Bulletin no. 228.

Damasio, Antonio, and Norman Geschwind. 1984. "The Neural Basis of Language." *Annual Review of Neuroscience* 7: 127–47.

Darwin, Charles. [1854] 1958. *On the Origin of Species.* New York: New American Library.

Davenport, R. K., C. M. Rogers, and I. S. Russell. 1973. "Cross-Modal Perception in Apes." *Neuropsychologica* 11: 21–28.

Davis, Howard, and Richard Scase. 1985. *Western Capitalism and State Socialism: An Introduction.* Oxford: Basil Blackwell.

Davis, L. B., and B. O. K. Reeves. 1990. *Hunters of the Recent Past.* London: Unwin Hyman.

Dawkins, Richard. 1976. *The Selfish Gene.* Oxford: Oxford Univ. Press.

Demarest, William. 1977. "Incest Avoidance Among Human and Nonhuman Primates." In S. Chevalier-Skolnikoff and F. Poirier, eds., *Primate Bio-Social Development: Biological, Social, and Ecological Determinants.* New York: Garland.

Dennert, Eberhart. 1904. *At the Deathbed of Darwinism*. Trans. E. B. O'Hara and John Peschges. Burlington, Iowa: German Literary Board.

De Valois, Russell, and Gerald Jacobs. 1971. "Vision." In Allan Schrier and Fred Slottnitz, eds., *Behavior of Non-Human Primates*. New York: Academic Press.

DeVore, I. 1964. "The Evolution of Social Life." In S. Tax, ed., *Horizons in Anthropology*. Chicago: Univ. of Chicago Press.

De Vries, Hugo. 1901–3. *Die Mutations Theorie*. 2 vols. Leipzig: Von Veit.

Diamond, A. S. 1951. *The Evolution of Law and Order*. London: Watts.

Dickemann, M. 1985. "Human Sociobiology: The First Decade." *New Scientist* 108: 38–42.

Dixson, A. F. 1981. *The Natural History of the Gorilla*. New York: Columbia Univ. Press.

Dobzhansky, Theodosius. 1950. "Mendelian Populations and Their Evolution." *American Naturalist* 14: 401–18.

Dowdeswell, W. H. 1960. *The Mechanism of Evolution*. New York: Harper and Row.

Doyle, G. A., and R. O. Martin. 1979. *The Study of Prosimian Behavior*. New York: Academic Press.

Draper, Patricia. 1975. "!Kung Women: Contrasts in Sexual Egalitarianism in Foraging and Sedentary Contexts." In R. Reiter, ed., *Toward an Anthropology of Women*. New York: Monthly Review Press.

Duchin, Linda. 1990. "The Evolution of Articulate Speech: Comparative Anatomy of the Oral Cavity in Pan and Homo." *Journal of Human Evolution* 19: 687–97.

Dunaif-Hattis, Janet. 1984. *Doubling the Brain: On the Evolution of Brain Lateralization and Its Implications for Language*. New York: Peter Long.

Durham, William H. 1990. "Advances in Evolutionary Culture Theory." *Annual Review of Anthropology* 19: 187–210.

———. 1991. *Coevolution: Genes, Culture, and Human Diversity*. Stanford, Calif.: Stanford Univ. Press.

Durkheim, Emile. [1893] 1933. *The Division of Labor in Society*. New York: Free Press.

———. [1897] 1951. *Suicide*. New York: Free Press.

———. [1902] 1933. "Preface to the Second Edition." *The Division of Labor in Society*. 2d ed. New York: Macmillan.

———. [1912] 1954. *The Elementary Forms of Religious Life*. New York: Macmillan.

Earle, Timothy, ed. 1984. *On the Evolution of Complex Societies*. Malibu, Calif.: Undena.

Earle, Timothy, and J. Ericson, eds. 1977. *Exchange Systems in Prehistory*. New York: Academic Press.

Eberhard, Wolfram. 1960. *A History of China*. 2d ed. Berkeley: Univ. of California Press.

Eibl-Eibesfeldt, Irenöus. 1991. "On Subsistence and Social Relations in the Kalahaic." *Current Anthropology* 32: 55–57.

Eisenberg, J. F. 1977. "The Evolution of the Reproductive Unit in the Class Mammalia." In J. S. Rosenblatt and B. R. Komisaruk, eds., *Reproductive Behavior and Evolution*. New York: Plenum.

Eisenberg, J. F., N. A. Muckenhirn, and R. Rudran. 1972. "The Relations Between Ecology and Social Structure in Primates." *Science* 176: 863–74.

Eisenman, Leonard. 1978. "Vocal Communication in Primates." In Charles Noback, ed., *Sensory Systems of Primates*. New York: Plenum.

Eisenstadt, S. N., and A. Shachar. 1987. *Society, Culture and Urbanization*. Newbury Park, Calif.: Sage.

Elkin, A. P. 1954. *The Australian Aborigines*. 3d ed. Sydney: Angus and Robertson.

Ellefson, S. O. 1974. "A Natural History of White-Handed Gibbons in the Malaysian Peninsula." In D. Rumbaugh, ed., *Gibbon and Siamang*, vol. 3. Basel: Karger.

Ember, Carol. 1978. "Myths About Hunters-Gatherers." *Ethnology* 17: 439–48.

Ember, Carol, Melvin Ember, and Burton Pasternak. 1974. "On the Development of Unilineal Descent." *Journal of Anthropological Research* 30: 69–94.

Ember, Melvin, and Carol Ember. 1971. "The Conditions Favoring Matrilocal Versus Patrilocal Residence." *American Anthropologist* 73: 571–94.

Engels, Friedrich. [1845] 1958. *The Condition of the Working Class in England*. Trans. W. O. Henderson and W. H. Chaloner. Stanford, Calif.: Stanford Univ. Press.

Ettlinger, G. 1973. "The Transfer of Information Between Sense-Modalities: A Neuropsychological Review." In H. P. Zeppel, ed., *Memory and Transfer of Information*. New York: Plenum.

———. 1977. "Cross-Modal Equivalence in Non-Human Primates." In A. M. Schriver, ed., *Behavioral Primatology*, vol. 1. Hillsdale, N.J.: Erlbaum.

Evans, Peter, Dietrich Rueschemeyer, and Theda Skocpol, eds. 1985. *Bringing the State Back In*. New York: Cambridge Univ. Press.

Evans-Pritchard, E. 1940. *The Nuer*. Oxford: Oxford Univ. Press.

Falk, Dean. 1978. "Cerebral Asymmetry in Old World Monkeys." *Acta Anatomica* 101: 334–39.

———. 1983. "Cerebral Cortices of East African Early Hominids." *Science* 222: 1072–74.

———. 1986. "Endocranial Casts and Their Significance for Primate Brain Evolution." In Daris Swindler and J. Erwin, eds., *Comparative Primate Biology*, vol. 1. New York: Alan Liss.

———. 1989. "Ape-Like Endocast of 'Ape-Man' Taung." *American Journal of Physical Anthropology* 80: 335–39.

Falk, Dean, J. Cheverud, M. W. Vanner, and C. G. Conroy. 1986. "Advanced Computer Graphics Technology Reveals Cortical Asymmetry in Endocasts of Rhesus Monkeys." *Folia Primatologica* 46: 98–103.

Falk, Dean, Charles Hildebolt, and Michael Vannier. 1989. "Reassessment of the Taung Early Hominid from a Neurological Perspective." *Journal of Human Evolution* 18: 485–92.

Fay, Michael, Marcellin Agnagna, Jim Moore, and Ruffin Oko. 1989. "Gorillas (Gorilla gorilla gorilla) in the Likouala Swamp Forests of North Central

Congo: Preliminary Data on Populations and Ecology." *International Journal of Primatology* 10: 477–95.

Fedigan, L. M. 1982. *Primate Paradigms: Sex Roles and Social Bonds.* St. Albans, Vt.: Eden Press Women's Pubns.

Fisher, R. A. 1930. *The Genetical Theory of Natural Selection.* Oxford: Clarendon.

Flannery, Kent V. 1973. "The Origins of Agriculture." *Annual Review of Anthropology* 2: 271–310.

———. 1986. "The Research Problem." In K. V. Flannery, ed., *Guilá Naquitz: Archaic Foraging and Early Agriculture in Oaxaca, Mexico.* Orlando, Fla.: Academic Press.

Fleagle, John. 1978. "Size Distributions of Living and Fossil Primate Faunas." *Paleobiology* 4: 67–76.

———. 1988. *Primate Adaptation and Evolution.* New York: Academic Press.

Foley, Robert. 1984. *Hominid Evolution and Community Ecology.* London: Academic Press.

———. 1987a. *Another Unique Species.* New York: Longman Scientific and Technical.

———. 1987b. "Hominid Species and Stone-Tool Assemblages: How Are They Related?" *Antiquity* 61: 380–92.

Foley, Robert A., and P. C. Lee. 1989. "Finite Social Space, Evolutionary Pathways, and Reconstructing Hominid Behavior." *Science* 243: 901–6.

Forbes, James, and James King. 1982. "Vision: The Dominant Sense Modality." In J. Forbes and J. King, eds., *Primate Behavior.* New York: Academic Press.

Fossey, D. 1972. *Living with Mountain Gorillas.* Washington, D.C.: National Geographic Society.

———. 1976. "The Behaviour of the Mountain Gorilla." Ph.D. diss., Univ. of Cambridge.

———. 1983. *Gorillas in the Mist.* Boston: Houghton Mifflin.

Fox, Robin. 1967. *Kinship and Marriage.* Baltimore, Md.: Penguin.

Freeman, Linton. 1976. *A Bibliography of Social Networks.* Monticello, Ill.: Council of Planning Librarians.

Freeman, Linton, Douglas White, and A. Kimball Romney. 1989. *Research Methods in Social Network Analysis.* Fairfax, Va.: George Mason Univ. Press.

Freeman, Linton C., and Robert F. Winch. 1957. "Societal Complexity: An Empirical Test of a Typology of Societies." *American Journal of Sociology* 62: 461–66.

Freides, David. 1974. "Human Information Processing and Sense Modality: Cross-Modal Functions, Information Complexity, Memory, and Deficit." *Psychological Bulletin* 81, no. 5: 284–310.

Fried, Morton H. 1967. *The Evolution of Political Society.* New York: Random House.

Friedman, William. 1959. *Law in a Changing Society.* Berkeley: Univ. of California Press.

Frisby, David. 1985. *Fragments of Modernity.* New York: Blackwell.

Furuichi, Takeshi. 1989. "Social Interactions and the Life History of Female Pan paniscus in Wamba, Zaire." *International Journal of Primatology* 10: 173–97.

Gabassi, P. G., and N. Batic. 1987. "Interference Processes in Visual and Olfactory Stimulations." *Perceptual and Motor Skills* 65: 79–82.

Gabow, Stephen. 1977. "Population Structure and the Rate of Hominid Evolution." *Journal of Human Evolution* 6: 643–65.

Gaeng, Paul. 1971. *Introduction to the Principles of Language*. New York: Harper and Row.

Galaburda, Albert. 1984. "Anatomical Asymmetries." In Norman Geschwind and Albert Galaburda, eds., *Cerebral Dominance*. Cambridge, Mass.: Harvard Univ. Press.

Galdikas, Biruti. 1985. "Adult Male Sociality and Reproductive Tactics Among Orangutans of Tanjung Puting." *Folia Primatologica* 45: 9–24.

———. 1988. "Orangutan Diet, Range, and Activity at Tanjung Puting, Central Borneo." *International Journal of Primatology* 9: 1–35.

Gans, Carl. 1986. "The Sensory World of Animals." In R. J. Hoage and Larry Goldman, eds., *Animal Intelligence: The Evolution of the Brain and the Nature of Animal Intelligence*. Washington, D.C.: Smithsonian Institution Press.

Gardner, R., B. Gardner, and T. Cantfort. 1989. *Teaching Sign Language to Chimpanzees*. Albany: State Univ. of New York Press.

Garfinkel, Harold. 1967. *Studies in Ethnomethodology*. Englewood Cliffs, N.J.: Prentice Hall.

Garraty, John A., and Peter Gay, eds. 1972. *The Columbia History of the World*. New York: Harper and Row.

Geschwind, Norman. 1965. "Disconnection Syndromes in Animals and Man." *Brain* 88: 237–85.

———. 1985. "Implications for Evolution, Genetics and Clinical Syndromes." In Stanley Glick, ed., *Cerebral Lateralization in Non-Human Species*. New York: Academic Press.

Geschwind, Norman, and Antonio Damasio. 1984. "The Neural Basis of Language." *Annual Review of Neuroscience* 7: 127–47.

Gibbs, James, ed. 1965. *Peoples of Africa*. New York: Holt.

Giddens, Anthony. 1984. *The Constitution of Society*. Berkeley: Univ. of California Press.

———. 1985. *The Nation State and Violence*. Berkeley: Univ. of California Press.

Gidley, J. W. 1919. "Significance of the Divergence of the First Digit in the Primitive Mammalian Foot." *Journal of the Washington Academy of Science* 9: 273–80.

Gingerich, Philip. 1990. "African Dawn for Primates." *Nature* 346: 411.

Gittens, S. P. 1908. "Territorial Behavior in the Agile Gibbon." *International Journal of Primatology* 1: 381–99.

Goldman, I. 1970. *Ancient Polynesian Society*. Chicago: Univ. of Chicago Press.

Goldschmidt, Walter. 1959. *Man's Way: A Preface to Understanding Human Society*. New York: Holt, Rinehart and Winston.

Goldstone, Jack. 1990. *Revolution and Rebellion in the Early Modern World, 1640–1840*. Berkeley: Univ. of California Press.

Goodale, Jane. 1959. "The Tiwi Women of Melville Island." Ph.D. diss., Univ. of Pennsylvania.

Goodall, Jane. 1986. *The Chimpanzees of Gombe: Patterns of Behavior*. Cambridge, Mass.: Harvard Univ. Press.

Goodall, Jane, and David Hamburg. 1975. "Chimpanzee Behaviour as a Model for the Behaviour of Early Man." In D. Hamburg and K. H. Brodie, eds., *American Handbook of Psychiatry*, vol. 6. New York: Basic Books.

Goodall-Lawick, Jane. 1975. "The Behavior of the Chimpanzee." In G. Kurth and I. Eibl-Eibesfeldt, eds., *Hominisation and Behavior*. Stuttgart: Gustav Fischer Verlag.

Goode, William J. 1951. *Religion Among the Primitives*. New York: Free Press.

Goodman, M., D. A. Tagle, D. H. A. Fitch, W. Bailey, J. Czelusnak, B. F. Koop, P. Benson, and J. L. Slightom. 1990. "Primate Evolution at the DNA Level and a Classification of Hominids." *Journal of Molecular Evolution* 30: 260–66.

Gordon, R. T. 1914. *The Khasis*. London: Macmillan.

Gouzoules, S. 1984. "Primate Mating Systems, Kin Associations, and Cooperative Behavior: Evidence for Kin Recognition." *Yearbook Physical Anthropology* 27: 99–134.

Graburn, Nelson, ed. 1971. *Readings in Kinship and Social Structure*. New York: Harper and Row.

Granovetter, Mark. 1973. "The Strength of Weak Ties." *American Journal of Sociology* 78: 1360–80.

———. 1985. "Economic Action and the Problem of Embeddedness." *American Journal of Sociology* 91: 481–510.

Greenwood, P. J. 1980. "Mating Systems, Philopatry, and Dispersal in Birds and Mammals." *Animal Behavior* 28: 1140–62.

Gregory, W. K. 1916. "Studies of the Evolution of the Primates." *Bulletin of the American Museum of Natural History* 35: 239–355.

Grine, Frederick. 1988. *Evolutionary History of the "Robust" Australopithecines*. New York: Aldine de Gruyter.

Groves, Colin. 1984. "A New Look at the Taxonomy of the Gibbons." In H. Prevschoft, D. Chivers, W. Brockelman, and N. Creel, eds., *The Lesser Apes: Evolutionary and Behavioural Biology*. Edinburgh: Edinburgh Univ. Press.

Gurvitch, George. 1953. *Sociology of Law*. London: Routledge and Kegan Paul.

Haas, Jonathan. 1982. *The Evolution of the Prehistoric State*. New York: Columbia Univ. Press.

Haberly, Lewis. 1990. "Olfactory Cortex." In Gordon Shepherd, ed., *The Synaptic Organization of the Brain*. Oxford: Oxford Univ. Press.

Habermas, Jurgen. 1962. *Struckturwandel de Offentlicheit*. Neuwied: Lochterhand.

———. 1979. *Communication and the Evolution of Society*. London: Heinemann.

———. 1984. *The Theory of Communicative Action*. Vol. 1. Boston: Beacon.

Hage, Jerald, and Charles Powers. 1992. *Symbolic Roles and Fluid Networks: A Theoretical Treatise on the Transformation of Mind, Self, and Interaction in Post-Industrial Society*. Newbury Park, Calif.: Sage.

Hall, K. R. L. 1967. "Social Interactions of the Adult Male and Adult Females of a Patas Monkey Group." In S. Altmann, ed., *Social Communication Among Primates*. Chicago: Univ. of Chicago Press.

Halperin, S. O. 1979. "Temporary Association Patterns in Free-Ranging Chimpanzees: An Assessment of Individual Grouping Preferences." In Hamburg and McCown 1979.

Hamburg, D., and E. McCown, eds. 1979. *The Great Apes*. Menlo Park, Calif.: Benjamin-Cummings.

Hamilton, William D. 1963. "The Evolution of Altruistic Behavior." *American Naturalist* 97: 354–56.

———. 1971. "Geometry for the Selfish Herd." *Journal of Theoretical Biology* 33: 295–311.

———. 1982. "Baboon Sleeping Site Preferences and Relationships to Primate Grouping Patterns." *American Journal of Primatology* 3: 41–53.

Hammond, Mason. 1972. *The City in the Ancient World*. Cambridge, Mass.: Harvard Univ. Press.

Harcourt, A. 1977. "Social Relationships of Wild Mountain Gorillas." Ph.D. diss., Univ. of Cambridge.

———. 1978. "Strategies of Emigration and Transfer by Primates, with Particular Reference to Gorillas." *Zeitschrift für Tierpsychologie* 48: 401–20.

———. 1979a. "The Social Relations and Group Structure of Wild Mountain Gorillas." In Hamburg and McCown 1979.

———. 1979b. "Social Relationships Among Adult Female Mountain Gorillas." *Animal Behavior* 27: 251–64.

———. 1979c. "Social Relationships Between Adult Male and Female Gorillas in the Wild." *Animal Behavior* 27: 325–42.

Harcourt, A., K. Stewart, and D. Fossey. 1976. "Male Emigration and Female Transfer in Wild Mountain Gorilla." *Nature* 263: 226–27.

———. 1981. "Gorilla Reproduction in the Wild." In Charles Graham, ed., *Reproductive Biology of the Great Apes*. New York: Academic Press.

Harlan, J. R. 1975. *Crops and Man*. Madison, Wis.: American Society of Agronomy.

Harris, D. R. 1977. "Alternative Pathways Toward Agriculture." In C. A. Reed, ed., *Origins of Agriculture*. The Hague: Mouton.

Harris, J. W. K. 1983. "Cultural Beginnings: Plio-Pleistocene Archaeological Occurrences from the Afar, Ethiopia." *African Archaeological Review* 1: 3–31.

Harris, Marvin. 1978. *Cannibals and Kings: The Origins of Cultures*. New York: Vintage.

Harrison, Terry. 1989. "New Postcranial Remains of Miocene of Kenya." *Journal of Human Evolution* 18: 3–54.

Hart, C. W. M., Arnold Pilling, and Jane Goodale. 1988. *The Tiwi of North Australia*. Chicago: Holt, Rinehart and Winston.

Hass, Mary. 1966. "Historical Linguistics and the Genetic Relationship of Languages." *Current Trends in Linguistics* 3: 113–53.

Hawkes, Jacquetta. 1965. *Prehistory: UNESCO History of Mankind*, vol. 1, pt. 1. New York: Mentor.

Hawley, Amos. 1950. *Human Ecology*. New York: Ronald Press.

———. 1986. *Human Ecology: A Theoretical Essay*. Chicago: Univ. of Chicago Press.

Hayaki, H. 1988. "Association Partners of Young Chimpanzees in the Mahale Mountains National Park, Tanzania." *Primates* 29: 147–61.

Hayasaka, K., T. Gojobori, and S. Horai. 1988. "Molecular Phylogeny and Evolution of Primate Mitochondrial DNA." *Molecular Biology and Evolution* 5: 626–44.

Hayden, B. 1981. "Subsistence and Ecological Adaptations of Modern Hunter/Gatherers." In R. Harding and G. Teleki, eds., *Omnivorous Primates*. New York: Columbia Univ. Press.

Heffner, Henry, and Rickye Heffner. 1990. "Role of Primate Auditory Cortex in Hearing." In William Stebbins and Mark Berkley, eds., *Comparative Perception*, vol. 7. New York: Wiley and Sons.

Heider, Karl. 1970. *The Dugum Dani: A Papuan Culture in the Highlands of West New Guinea*. New York: Wenner-Gren Foundation.

Heilbroner, Peter, and Ralph Holloway. 1989. "Anatomical Brain Asymmetry in Monkeys: Frontal, Temporoparietal and Limbic Cortex in Macaca." *American Journal of Physical Anthropology* 80: 203–11.

Heilbroner, Robert L. 1985. *The Making of Economic Society*. 7th ed. Englewood Cliffs, N.J.: Prentice Hall.

Held, Richard, and Whitman Richards, eds. 1976. *Recent Progress in Perception*. San Francisco: Freeman.

Hennig, W. 1966. *Phylogenetic Systematics*. Urbana: Univ. of Illinois Press.

Hershkovitz, Philip. 1977. *Living New World Monkeys (Platyrrhini)*, vol. 1. Chicago: Univ. of Chicago Press.

Herskovits, M. J. 1938. *Dahomey*. Locust Valley, N.Y.: Augustin.

Hewes, Gordon. 1973. "Primate Communication and the Gestural Origin of Language." *Current Anthropology* 14, no. 1–2: 5–11.

———. 1975. *Language Origins: A Bibliography*. 2 vols. The Hague: Mouton.

Hiatt, B. 1961–62. "Local Organization Among the Australian Aborigines." *Oceania* 32: 267–86.

———. 1966. "The Lost Horde." *Oceania* 37: 81–92.

Hill, Jane. 1972. "On the Evolutionary Foundations of Language." *American Anthropologist* 74: 308–15.

Hill, W. C. Osman. 1972. *Evolutionary Biology of the Primates*. New York: Academic Press.

Hilton, Rodney, ed. 1976. *The Transition from Feudalism to Capitalism*. London: New Left Books.

Hinde, Robert A. 1979. "The Nature of Social Structure." In Hamburg and McCown 1979.

———. 1983. *Primate Social Relationships*. Oxford: Blackwells.

Hodos, William. 1986. "The Evolution of the Brain and the Nature of Animal Intelligence." In R. J. Hoage and Larry Goldman, eds., *Animal Intelligence: Insights into the Animal Mind*. Washington, D.C.: Smithsonian Institution Press.

Hoebel, E. A. 1954. *The Law of Primitive Man*. New York: Atheneum.

Hoenigswald, H. 1950. "The Principal Step in Comparative Grammar." *Language* 26: 357–64.

———. 1960. *Language Change and Linguistic Reconstruction*. Chicago: Univ. of Chicago Press.

Holloway, Ralph W. 1968. "The Evolution of the Primate Brain: Some Aspects of Quantitative Relations." *Brain Research* 7: 121–72.

———. 1970. "New Endocranial Values for the Australopithecines." *Nature* 227: 179–200.

———. 1978. "The Relevance of Endocasts for Studying Primate Brain Evolution." In Charles Noback, ed., *Sensory Systems of Primates*. New York: Plenum.

Holly, B. Smith. 1990. "The Cost of a Large Brain." *Behavioral and Brain Sciences* 13: 365–66.

Holmberg, Allan. 1950. *Nomads of the Long Bow: The Siriono of Eastern Bolivia*. Institute for Anthropology, no. 10. Washington, D.C.: Smithsonian Institution Press.

Homans, George C. 1961. *Social Behavior: Its Elementary Forms*. New York: Harcourt.

Horel, James. 1988. "Limbic Neocortical Interrelations." In Horst Steklis and J. Erwin, eds., *Neurosciences*, vol. 4. New York: Alan Liss.

Horgan, J. 1988. "The Violent Yanomamö: Science and Citizens." *Scientific American* 255: 17–18.

Hose, Charles, and William McDougall. 1912. *The Pagan Tribes of Borneo*. London: Macmillan.

Howard, I. P. 1973. "Orientation and Motion in Space." In Edward Carterette and Morton Friedman, eds., *Handbook of Perception*. New York: Academic Press.

Howell, Nancy. 1988. "Understanding Simple Social Structure: Kinship Units and Ties." In Wellman and Berkowitz 1988.

Hultkrantz, Ake, and Ornulf Vorren. 1982. *The Hunters*. Oslo: Universitetsforlaget.

Hunt, Kevin. 1991. "Positional Behavior in the Hominoidea." *International Journal of Primatology* 12: 95–118.

Isaac, Glynn. 1978. "The Archaeological Evidence for the Activities of Early African Hominids." In Clifford Jolly, ed., *Early Hominids of Africa*. London: Duckworth.

———. 1989. *The Archaeology of Human Origins*. New York: Cambridge Univ. Press.

Isaac, Glynn, and Elizabeth McCown. 1975. *Human Origins. Lovis Leakey and the East African Evidence*. Menlo Park, Calif.: Benjamin-Cummings.

Isaacson, Robert. 1982. *The Limbic System*. New York: Plenum.

James, Steven. 1989. "Hominid Use of Fire in the Lower and Middle Pleistocene." *Current Anthropology* 30: 1–26.

Jarvis, M. J., and G. Ettlinger. 1977. "Cross-Modal Recognition in Chimpanzees and Monkeys." *Neuropsychologia* 15: 499–506.

Jeffers, Robert, and Ilse Lehiste. 1979. *Principles and Methods for Historical Linguistics*. Cambridge, Mass.: MIT Press.

Jenkins, F. A., Jr. 1987. "Tree Shrew Locomotion and the Origins of Primate Arborealism." In Ciochon and Fleagle 1987.

Jerison, Harry. 1973. *Evolution of the Brain and Intelligence*. New York: Academic Press.

Johannson, Gunnar. 1976. "Visual Motor Perception." In Held and Richards 1976.

Johanson, D. C. 1980. "Early African Hominid Phylogenesis: A Re-Evaluation." In L. K. Konigsson, ed., *Current Argument on Early Man*. Oxford: Pergamon Press.

Johanson, D. C., and T. D. White. 1979. "A Systematic Assessment of Early African Hominids." *Science* 203: 321–30.

Johnson, Allen W., and Timothy Earle. 1987. *The Evolution of Human Societies: From Foraging Group to Agrarian State*. Stanford, Calif.: Stanford Univ. Press.

Jolly, Alison. 1985. *The Evolution of Primate Behavior*. New York: Macmillan.

Jolly, Clifford. 1970. "The Seed-Eaters: A New Model of Hominid Differentiation Based on a Baboon Analogy." *Man* 5: 5–26.

Jones, Bill. 1981. "The Developmental Significance of Cross-Modal Matching." In Richard Walk and Herbert Pick, Jr., eds., *Intersensory Perception and Sensory Integration*. New York: Plenum.

Jones, Clyde, and Jorge Sabater Pi. 1971. *Comparative Ecology of Gorilla gorilla (Savage and Wyman) and Pan troglodytes (Blumenbach) in Rio Muni, West Africa*. New York: S. Karger.

Jones, Mari. 1976. "Time, Our Lost Perception: Towards a New Theory of Perception, Attention and Memory." *Psychological Review* 83, no. 5: 323–55.

Julesz, Bela. 1976. "Experiments in the Visual Perception of Texture." In Held and Richards 1976.

Jürgens, U. 1974. "Elicitability of Vocalization from the Cortical Larynx Area." *Brain Research* 81: 564–66.

Kaas, Jon, and T. P. Pons. 1988. "The Somatosensory System of Primates." In Steklis and Erwin 1988.

Kabo, Vladimir. 1985. "The Origins of the Food-Producing Economy." *Current Anthropology* 26: 601–16.

Kanter, Rosabeth Moss. 1989. *When Giants Learn to Dance: Mastering the Challenges of Strategy, Management and Careers in the 1990's*. New York: Simon and Schuster.

Kass, John. 1987. "The Organization and Evolution of Neocortex." In Stephen Wise, ed., *Higher Brain Functions*. New York: Wiley and Sons.

Kay, R. F., and E.L. Simons. 1987. "The Ecology of Oligocene African Anthropoidea." In Ciochon and Fleagle 1987.

Keesing, Robert. 1975. *Kin Groups and Social Structure*. New York: Holt, Rinehart and Winston.

Kehoe, Thomas. 1990. "Corralling: Evidence from Upper Paleolithic Cave Art." In L. Davis and B. Reeves, eds., *Hunters of the Recent Past*. London: Unwin Hyman.

Khanna, Shyam, and Juergen Tonndorf. 1978. "Physical and Physiological Principles Controlling Auditory Sensitivity in Primates." In Charles Noback, ed., *Sensory Systems of Primates*. New York: Plenum.

King, M., and A. Wilson. 1975. "Evolution at Two Levels in Humans and Chimpanzees." *Science* 188: 107–16.

Kinzey, Warren, ed. 1987. *The Evolution of Human Behavior: Primate Models*. Albany: State Univ. of New York Press.

Kirch, P. 1980. "Polynesian Prehistory: Cultural Adaptation in Island Ecosystems." *American Scientist* 68: 39–48.

———. 1984. *The Evolution of Polynesian Chiefdoms*. Cambridge, Eng.: Cambridge Univ. Press.

Kolata, Gina. 1974. "!Kung Hunter-Gatherers: Feminism, Diet and Birth." *Science* 185: 932–34.

Kortlandt, Adriaan. 1972. *New Perspectives on Ape and Human Evolution*. Amsterdam: Univ. of Amsterdam Press.

Kramer, Samuel Noah. 1959. *It Happened at Sumer*. Garden City, N.Y.: Doubleday.

Lackner, J. R. 1973. "Visual Rearrangement Affects Auditory Localization." *Neuropsychologia* 11: 29–32.

Laitman, Jeffrey. 1985. "Evolution of the Hominid Upper Respiratory Tract: The Fossil Evidence." In Phillip Tobias, ed., *Hominid Evolution: Past, Present and Future*. New York: Alan Liss.

Lancaster, Jane. 1968. "On the Evolution of Tool-Using Behavior." *American Anthropologist* 70: 56–66.

Landtman, Gunnar. 1927. *The Kiwi Papuans of British Guinea*. London: Macmillan.

Laslett, Peter, and Richard Wall. 1972. *Household and Family in Past Times*. Cambridge, Eng.: Cambridge Univ. Press.

Latimer, Bruce, and C. Owen Lovejoy. 1990. "Metatarsophalangeal Joints of Australopithecus afarensis." *American Journal of Physical Anthropology* 83: 13–23.

Lavelle, C. L. B., R. P. Shellis, and D. F. Poole. 1977. *Evolutionary Changes to the Primate Skull and Dentition*. Springfield, Ill.: Charles C. Thomas.

Leach, E. R. 1954. *Political Systems of Highland Burma*. Boston: Beacon.

Leakey, M., and R. Hay. 1979. "Pliocene Footprints in Laetoli Beds at Laetoli Northern Tanzania." *Nature* 278: 317–28.

Leakey, M. D. 1971. *Olduvai Gorge: Excavations in Beds I and II, 1960–1963*. Cambridge, Eng.: Cambridge Univ. Press.

Leakey, M. G., R. E. Leakey, J. T. Richtsmeier, E. L. Simons, and A. C. Walker. 1991. "Similarities in Aegyptopithecus and Afropithecus Facial Morphology." *Folia Primatologica* 56: 65–85.

Leakey, Richard. 1989. "Recent Fossil Finds from East Africa." In John Durant, ed., *Human Origins*. Oxford: Clarendon Press.

Lee, Richard B. 1968. "What Hunters Do for a Living, or How to Make Out on Scarce Resources." In Lee and DeVore 1968.

———. 1972. "The !Kung Bushmen of Botswana." In Bicchieri 1972.

————. 1979. *The !Kung San.* Cambridge, Eng.: Cambridge Univ. Press.

Lee, Richard, and Irven DeVore, eds. 1968. *Man the Hunter.* Chicago: Aline.

————, eds. 1976. *Kalahari Hunter-Gatherers.* Cambridge, Eng.: Cambridge Univ. Press.

Le Grand, Yves. 1975. "History of Research on Seeing." In Edward Carterette and Morton Friedman, eds., *Handbook of Perception*, vol. 5. New York: Academic Press.

Leighton, Donna. 1987. "Gibbons: Territoriality and Monogamy." In Smuts et al. 1987.

LeMay, Marjorie. 1985. "Asymmetries of the Brains and Skulls of Non-Human Primates." In Stanley Glick, ed., *Cerebral Lateralization in Non-Human Primates.* New York: Academic Press.

LeMay, Marjorie, and Norman Geschwind. 1975. "Hemispheric Differences in the Brains of Great Apes." *Behavior and Evolution* 11: 48–52.

Lenneberg, Eric. 1971. "Of Language, Knowledge, Apes and Brains." *Journal of Psycholinguistic Research* 1: 1–29.

Lenski, Gerhard. 1966. *Power and Privilege.* New York: McGraw-Hill.

Lenski, Gerhard, and Jean Lenski. 1987. *Human Societies.* 5th ed. New York: McGraw-Hill.

Lenski, Gerhard, Jean Lenski, and Patrick Nolan. 1991. *Human Societies.* 6th ed. New York: McGraw-Hill.

Lévi-Strauss, C. 1969. *The Elementary Structures of Kinship.* Boston: Beacon.

Lewin, R. 1988. "A Revolution of Ideas in Agricultural Origins." *Science* 240: 984–86.

Lewis, O. J. 1974. "The Wrist Articulations of the Anthropoidea." In Farish Jenkins, Jr., ed., *Primate Locomotion.* New York: Academic Press.

Lieberman, P. 1984. *The Biology and Evolution of Language.* Cambridge, Mass.: Harvard Univ. Press.

Linden, Eugene. 1986. *Silent Partners.* New York: Times Books.

Lloyd, D. 1964. *The Idea of Law.* Baltimore, Md.: Penguin.

Lopreato, Joseph. 1984. *Human Nature and Biocultural Evolution.* Boston: Allen and Unwin.

Lorenz, Konrad. 1960. *On Aggression.* New York: Harcourt Brace Jovanovich.

Lovejoy, C. Owen. 1981. "The Origin of Man." *Science* 211: 341–50.

Lovilot, A., K. Tagifzouti, H. Simon, and M. Le Moal. 1989. "Limbic System, Basal Ganglia and Dopaminergic Neurons." *Brain Behavior and Evolution* 33: 157–61.

Lowie, Robert H. 1948. *Primitive Religion.* New York: Boni and Liveright.

Lucas, P. W., R. T. Corlett, and D. A. Luke. 1985. "Plio-Pleistocene Hominid Diets: An Approach Combining Masticatory and Ecological Analysis." *Journal of Human Evolution* 14: 187–202.

Luhmann, Niklas. 1982. *The Differentiation of Society.* Trans. S. Holmes and C. Larmore. New York: Columbia Univ. Press.

Lumsden, C. J., and E. O. Wilson. 1981. *Genes, Mind and Culture.* Cambridge, Mass.: Harvard Univ. Press.

———. 1985. "The Relation Between Biological and Cultural Evolution." *Journal of Social and Biological Structures* 8: 343–59.

Lyotard, J.-F. 1984. *The Post Modern Condition.* Minneapolis: Univ. of Minnesota Press.

Maas, P. 1958. *Textual Criticism.* Oxford: Oxford Univ. Press.

MacKinnon, John. 1971. "The Orang-utan in Sabah Today." *Oryx* 11: 141–91.

MacKinnon, J. R., and K. S. MacKinnon. 1984. "Territoriality, Monogamy, and Song in Gibbons and Tarsiers." In H. Prevschoft, D. Chivers, W. Brockelman, and N. Creel, eds., *The Lesser Apes.* Edinburgh: Edinburgh Univ. Press.

MacLean, P. 1978. "A Mind of Three Minds: Educating the Triune Brain." In Jeanne Chall and Allan Mirsky, eds., *Seventy-Seventh Yearbook of the National Society for the Study of Education.* Chicago: Univ. of Chicago Press.

———. 1982. "On the Origin and Progressive Evolution of the Triune Brain." In Este Armstrong and Dean Falk, eds., *Primate Brain Evolution.* New York: Plenum.

———. 1990. *The Triune Brain in Evolution.* New York: Plenum.

MacNeish, R. 1964. "Ancient Mesoamerican Civilization." *Science* 143: 531–37.

Maglio, V., and H. B. S. Cooke. 1978. *Evolution of African Mammals.* Cambridge, Mass.: Harvard Univ. Press.

Mair, Lucy. 1962. *Primitive Government.* Baltimore, Md.: Penguin.

Malinowski, Bronislaw. 1922. *Argonauts of the Western Pacific.* New York: Dutton.

———. [1925] 1955. *Magic, Science, and Religion.* Garden City, N.Y.: Doubleday.

Malone, David. 1987. "Mechanisms of Hominoid Dispersal in Miocene East Africa." *Journal of Human Evolution* 16: 469–81.

Malthus, Thomas R. 1798. *An Essay on the Principle of Population as It Affects the Future Improvement of Society.* London: Oxford Univ. Press.

Mankowitsch, Hans. 1988. "Introducing Information Processing by the Brain." In H. Mankowitsch, ed., *Information Processing by the Brain.* Toronto: Hans Huber.

Mann, Michael. 1986. *The Social Sources of Power,* vol. 1: *A History of Power from the Beginning to A.D. 1760.* Cambridge, Eng.: Cambridge Univ. Press.

Marler, Peter. 1965. "Communication in Monkeys and Apes." In Irven DeVore, ed., *Primate Behavior.* New York: Holt, Rinehart and Winston.

Martin, John, and Donald Stewart. 1982. "A Demographic Basis for Patrilineal Hordes." *American Anthropologist* 84: 79–96.

Martin, Lawrence. 1986. "Relationships Among Extant and Extinct Great Apes and Humans." In B. Wood, L. Martin, and P. Andrews, eds., *Major Topics in Primate and Human Evolution.* Cambridge, Eng.: Cambridge Univ. Press.

Martin, R. D. 1990a. *Primate Origins and Evolution: A Phylogenetic Reconstruction.* London: Chapman and Hall.

———. 1990b. "Some Relatives Take a Dive." *Nature* 345: 291–92.

Maryanski, Alexandra. 1986. "African Ape Social Structure: A Comparative Analysis." Ph.D. diss., Univ. of California, Irvine.

———. 1987. "African Ape Social Structure: Is There Strength in Weak Ties?" *Social Networks* 9: 191–215.

———. 1992. "The Last Ancestor: An Ecological Network Model on the Origins of Human Sociality." *Advances in Human Ecology* 2: 1–32.

Maryanski, Alexandra, and Jonathan H. Turner. 1991. "Biological Functionalism." In J. Turner, ed., *The Structure of Sociological Theory*, 5th ed. Belmont, Calif.: Wadsworth.

Masterton, Bruce, and Irving Diamond. 1973. "Hearing: Central Neural Mechanisms." In Edward Carterette and Morton Friedman, eds., *Handbook of Perception*, vol. 3. New York: Academic Press.

Matsuzawa, Tetsuro. 1990. "Form Perception and Visual Acuity in a Chimpanzee." *Folia Primatologica* 55: 24–32.

Maynard-Smith, J. 1974. "The Theory of Games and the Evolution of Animal Conflicts." *Journal of Theoretical Biology* 47: 209–21.

———. 1978. "Optimization Theory in Evolution." *Annual Review of Ecological Systems* 9: 31–56.

———. 1982. *Evolution and the Theory of Games*. London: Cambridge Univ. Press.

Mayr, E. 1963. *Animal Species and Evolution*. Cambridge, Mass.: Harvard Univ. Press.

McCorriston, Joy, and Frank Hole. 1991. "The Ecology of Seasonal Stress and the Origins of Agriculture in the Near East." *American Anthropologist* 93: 46–69.

McGeer, Patrick, Sir John Eccles, and Edith McGeer. 1987. *Molecular Neurobiology of the Mammalian Brain*. New York: Plenum.

McGinnis, P. R. 1979. "Patterns of Sexual Behavior in a Community of Free-Living Chimpanzees." Ph.D. diss., Univ. of Cambridge.

McGrew, W. C. 1981. "The Female Chimpanzee as a Human Evolutionary Prototype." In F. Dahlberg, ed., *Woman the Gatherer*. New Haven, Conn.: Yale Univ. Press.

McNeill, William. 1963. *The Rise of the West*. Chicago: Univ. of Chicago Press.

Meggitt, M. J. 1962. *Desert People: A Study of Walbiri Aborigines of Central Australia*. Sydney: Angus and Robertson.

Mellaart, James. 1965. *Earliest Civilizations of the Near East*. London: Thames and Hudson.

Melnick, Don, and Mary Pearl. 1987. "Cercopithecines in Multimale Groups: Genetic Diversity and Population Structure." In Smuts et al. 1987.

Mendel, Gregor. 1865. "Versuche über pflanzen-nybriden." *Verhandlungen des Naturforschenden Vereines in Brünn* 10: 28–62.

Menzel, E. W. 1971. "Communication About the Environment in a Group of Young Chimpanzees." *Folia Primatologica* 15: 220–32.

Mesulam, M. M. 1983. "The Functional Anatomy and Hemispheric Specialization for Directed Attention." *Trends in Neurosciences* 6: 384–87.

Miller, George. 1972. "Linguistic Communication as a Biological Process." In J. W. S. Pringle, ed., *Biology and the Human Sciences*. Oxford: Clarendon.

Mogenson, Gordon. 1977. *The Neurobiology of Behavior: An Introduction*. New York: Wiley and Sons.

Moore, Barrington, Jr. 1966. *Social Origins of Dictatorship and Democracy.* Boston: Beacon.

Moore, Jim. 1984. "Female Transfer in Primates." *International Journal of Primatology* 5: 537–89.

Morris, Desmond. 1967. *The Naked Ape: A Zoologist's Study of the Human Animal.* New York: McGraw-Hill.

Moseley, K. P., and Immanuel Wallerstein. 1978. "Precapitalist Social Structures." *Annual Review of Sociology* 4: 259–90.

Moynihan, Martin. 1976. *The New World Primates.* Princeton, N.J.: Princeton Univ. Press.

Müller, F. Max. 1871. *Lectures on the Science of Language.* Vol. 1. London: Longmans, Green.

Muncer, S. J., D. Malone, and G. Ettlinger. 1982. "Language in a Monkey." *Perceptual and Motor Skills* 54: 1179–82.

Murdock, George Peter. 1949. *Social Structure.* New York: Macmillan.

———. 1959. *Africa: Its Peoples and Their Cultural History.* New York: McGraw-Hill.

———. 1967. *Ethnographical Atlas.* Pittsburgh: Univ. of Pittsburgh Press.

Murra, J. 1980. *The Economic Organization of the Inka State.* Greenwich, Conn.: JAI Press.

Murray, Margaret. 1949. *The Splendor That Was Egypt.* London: Sidgwick and Jackson.

Myers, Ronald. 1978. "Comparative Neurology of Vocalization and Speech: Proof of a Dichotomy." In S. L. Washburn and E. McCown, eds., *Human Evolution: Biosocial Perspectives.* Menlo Park, Calif.: Benjamin-Cummings.

Napier, John. 1963. "Brachiation and Brachiators." In John Napier and N. A. Barnicot, eds., *The Primates*, vol. 10. London: Symposia of the Zoological Society of London.

Naier, J. R., and P. H. Napier. 1985. *The Natural History of the Primates.* Cambridge, Mass.: MIT Press.

Napier, J. R., and A. C. Walker. 1987. "Vertical Clinging and Leaping: A Newly Recognized Category of Locomotor Behavior of Primates." In Ciochon and Fleagle 1987.

Nebes, Robert. 1977. "Man's So-Called Minor Hemisphere." In M. C. Wittrock, ed., *The Human Brain.* Englewood Cliffs, N.J.: Prentice Hall.

Newman, John. 1988. "Primate Hearing Mechanisms." In Steklis and Erwin 1988.

Nishida, Toshisada. 1979. "The Social Structure of Chimpanzees of the Mahale Mountains." In Hamburg and McCown 1979.

———. 1990. "A Quarter Century of Research in the Mahale Mountains." In T. Nishida, ed., *The Chimpanzees of the Mahale Mountains.* Tokyo, Japan: Univ. of Tokyo Press.

Nishida, Toshisada, and Mariko Hiraiwa-Hasegawa. 1987. "Chimpanzees and Bonabas: Cooperative Relationships Among Males." In Smuts et al. 1987.

Noback, Charles. 1982. "Neurobiological Aspects in the Phylogenetic Acquisition of Speech." In Este Armstrong and Dean Falk, eds., *Primate Brain Evolution.* New York: Plenum.

Noback, Charles, and Lois Laemle. 1970. "Structural and Functional Aspects of the Visual Pathways of Primates." In Noback and Montagna 1970.

Noback, Charles, and N. Maskowitz. 1963. "The Primate Nervous System: Functional and Structural Aspects in Phylogeny." In J. Buettner-Janosch, ed., *Evolutionary and Genetic Biology of Primates*, vol. 1. New York: Academic Press.

Noback, Charles, and William Montagna, eds. 1970. *The Primate Brain*. New York: Appleton-Century-Crofts.

Norbeck, E. 1961. *Religion in Primitive Society*. New York: Harper and Row.

O'Connor, W., and B. Hermelin. 1981. "Coding Strategies of Normal and Handicapped Children." In Richard Walk and Herbert Pick, Jr., eds., *Intersensory Perception and Sensory Integration*. New York: Plenum.

O'Dea, Thomas F. 1970. *Sociology and the Study of Religion*. New York: Basic Books.

Ogle, Kenneth. 1962a. "Objective and Subjective Space." In Hugh Davison, ed., *The Eye*. New York: Academic Press.

———. 1962b. "Spatial Localization Through Binocular Vision." In Hugh Davison, ed., *The Eye*. New York: Academic Press.

O'Keefe, John, and Lynn Nadel. 1978. *The Hippocampus as a Cognitive Map*. Oxford: Clarendon Press.

O'Leary, Dennis. 1989. "Do Cortical Areas Emerge from a Neocortex?" *Trends in Neuroscience* 12, no. 10: 400–406.

Olsen, Sandra. 1989. "Solutre: A Theoretical Approach to the Reconstruction of Upper Paleolithic Hunting Strategies." *Journal of Human Evolution* 18: 295–327.

Oxnard, C. E. 1963. "Locomotor Adaptations in the Primates." In John Napier and N. A. Barnicot, eds., *The Primates*, vol. 10. London: Symposia of the Zoological Society of London.

Pandya, Deepak, Benjamin Seltzer, and Helen Barbas. 1988. "Input-Output Organization of the Primate Cerebral Cortex." In Steklis and Erwin 1988.

Parsons, Talcott. 1937. *The Structure of Social Action*. New York: McGraw-Hill.

———. 1966. *Societies: Evolutionary and Comparative Perspectives*. Englewood Cliffs, N.J.: Prentice Hall.

Passingham, R. E. 1982. *The Human Primate*. Oxford: Freeman.

———. 1985. "Rates of Development in Mammals Including Man." *Brain Behavior and Evolution* 26: 167–75.

Pasternak, Burton. 1976. *Introduction to Kinship and Social Organization*. Englewood Cliffs, N.J.: Prentice Hall.

Peck, H. L., D. H. Warren, and J. C. Hay. 1969. "Sensory Conflict in Judgements of Spatial Direction." *Perception and Psychophysics* 6: 203–5.

Phillips, C. G., S. Zeki, and H. B. Barlow. 1984. "Localization of Function in the Cerebral Cortex." *Brain* 107: 328–61.

Pilbeam, David. 1984. "The Descent of Hominoids and Hominids." *Scientific American* 250: 84–96.

Platnick, Norman, and H. Don Cameron. 1977. "Cladistic Methods in Textual, Linguistic, and Phylogenetic Analysis." *Systematic Zoology* 26: 380–85.

Platt, B. P., and D. H. Warren. 1972. "Auditory Localization: The Importance of Eye Movements and a Textured Visual Environment." *Perception and Psychophysics* 12: 245–48.

Poirier, Frank. 1987. *Understanding Human Evolution*. Englewood Cliffs, N.J.: Prentice Hall.

Poizner, Howard, Ursula Bellugi, and Edward Klima. 1990. "Biological Foundations of Language." *Annual Review of Neuroscience* 13: 283–307.

Posner, Michael, Mary Jo Nissen, and Raymond Klein. 1976. "Visual Dominance: An Information-Processing Account of Its Origins and Significance." *Psychological Review* 83: 157–71.

Postan, Michael. 1972. *The Medieval Economy and Society*. Berkeley: Univ. of California Press.

Provine, William. 1978. "The Role of Mathematical Population Geneticists in the Evolutionary Synthesis of the 1930's and 1940's." *Studies in the History of Biology* 2: 167–92.

Pusey, A. E. 1980. "Inbreeding Avoidance in Chimpanzees." *Animal Behavior* 28: 543–52.

Pusey, A. E., and C. Packer. 1987. "Dispersal and Philopatry." In Smuts et al. 1987.

Radcliffe-Brown, A. R. 1914. *The Andaman Islanders*. New York: Free Press.

———. 1930. "The Social Organization of Australian Tribes." *Oceania* 2: 34–63, 206–46, 322–41, 426–56.

———. 1952. *Structure and Function in Primitive Society*. New York: Free Press.

———. 1971. "On Rules of Descent and Interkin Behavior." In Graburn 1971.

Radinsky, L. B. 1968. "A New Approach to Mammalian Cranial Capacity Illustrated by Examples of Prosimian Primates." *Journal of Morphology* 124: 167–80.

———. 1970. "The Fossil Evidence of Prosimian Brain Evolution." In Noback and Montagna 1970.

———. 1974. "The Fossil Evidence of Anthropoid Brain Evolution." *American Journal of Physical Anthropology* 41: 15–28.

———. 1975. "Primate Brain Evolution." *American Scientist* 63: 656–63.

———. 1977. "Early Primate Brains: Facts and Fiction." *Journal of Human Evolution* 6: 79–86.

———. 1979. *The Fossil Record of Primate Brain Evolution*. New York: American Museum of Natural History.

———. 1982. "Some Cautionary Notes on Making Inferences About Relative Brain Size." In Este Armstrong and Dean Falk, eds., *Primate Brain Evolution*. New York: Plenum.

Rak, Yoel. 1983. *The Australopithecine Face*. New York: Academic Press.

Rakic, P. 1988. "Specification of Cerebral Cortical Areas." *Science* 241: 170–76.

Rapporteur, M. P., J. Allman, C. Blakemore, J. M. Gueuel, J. H. Kass, M. M. Merzenich, P. Rakic, W. Singer, G. S. Stent, H. von der Loos, and T. N. Wiesel. 1988. "Group Report: Principles of Cortical Self-Organization." In P. Rakic and W. Singer, eds., *Neurobiology of Neocortex*. New York: Wiley and Sons.

Rearden, Ann, Huan Phan, Shinichi Kuda, and Minoru Fubuda. 1990. "Evolution of the Glycophorin Gene Family in the Hominoid Primates." *Biochemical Genetics* 28: 209–21.

Reeve, Gilmour, Lesia Mackey, and Gene Fober. 1986. "Visual Dominance in the Cross-Modal Kinesthetic to Kinesthetic Plus Visual Feedback Condition." *Perceptual and Motor Skills* 62: 243–52.

Relethford, John. 1990. *The Human Species*. London: Mayfield.

Rensch, Bernhard. 1956. "Increases of Learning Capacity with Increase of Brain Size." *The American Naturalist* 90 (March–April): 81–95.

———. 1967. "The Evolution of Brain Achievements." In Theodosur Dabzhansky, ed., *Evolutionary Biology*, vol. 1. New York: Appleton-Century-Crofts.

Reynolds, Vernon. 1966. "Open Groups and Hominid Evolution." *Man* 3: 209–23.

Rhine, R. J., P. Boland, and L. Lodwick. 1985. "Progressions of Adult Male Chocma Baboons (Papio ursinus) in the Moremi Wild Life Reserve." *International Journal of Primatology* 6: 116–22.

Riches, David. 1982. *Northern Nomadic Hunter-Gatherers*. London: Academic Press.

Rick, J. 1978. *Prehistoric Hunters of the High Andes*. New York: Academic Press.

Rightmire, G. Philip. 1988. "Homo erectus and Later Middle Pleistocene Humans." *Annual Review of Anthropology* 17: 239–59.

———. 1990. *The Evolution of Homo erectus*. New York: Cambridge Univ. Press.

Rijksen, Herman. 1975. "Social Structure in a Wild Orangutan Population in Sumatra." In S. Kondo, M. Kawai, and A. E. Hara, eds., *Contemporary Primatology*. Basel: Karger.

Robson, J. G. 1975. "Receptive Fields: Neural Representation of the Spatial and Intensive Attributes of the Visual Image." In Morton Friedman, ed., *Handbook of Perception*, vol. 5. New York: Academic Press.

Rock, Irvin. 1966. *The Nature of Perceptual Adaptation*. New York: Basic Books.

Rodieck, R. W. 1988. "The Primate Retina." In Steklis and Erwin 1988.

Rodman, Peter. 1973. "Population Composition and Adaptive Organization Among Orang-utans of the Kutai Reserve." In R. P. Michael and J. H. Crook, eds., *Comparative Ecology and Behaviour of Primates*. London: Academic Press.

Rodman, Peter, and John Mitani. 1987. "Orangutans: Sexual Dimorphism in a Solitary Species." In Smuts et al. 1987.

Romer, A. S. 1972. *The Vertebrate Body*. Philadelphia: Saunders.

Roonwal, M. L., and S. M. Mohnot. 1977. *Primates of South Asia*. Cambridge, Mass.: Harvard Univ. Press.

Rose, K. D., and J. G. Fleagle. 1987. "The Second Radiation-Prosimians." In Ciochon and Fleagle 1987.

Rose, M. D. 1987. "Miocene Hominoid Postcranial Morphology: Monkey-Like, Ape-Like, Neither, or Both?" In Ciochon and Fleagle 1987.

Rosenberg, Alexander. 1981. *Sociobiology and the Preemption of Social Science.* Baltimore: Johns Hopkins Univ. Press.

Roth, H. Ling. 1890. *The Aborigines of Tasmania.* London: Kegan, Paul, Trench, and Trubner.

Rudel, R. G., and H. L. Teuber. 1964. "Cross-Modal Transfer of Shape Discrimination by Children." *Neuropsychologia* 2: 1–8.

Rudnick, M., V. Martin, and G. Sterritt. 1972. "On the Relative Difficulty of Auditory and Visual, Temporal and Spatial, Integrative and Nonintegrative Sequential Pattern Comparisons." *Psychonomic Science* 27: 207–9.

Rumbaugh, Duane, and E. Sue Savage-Rumbaugh. 1990. "Chimpanzees: Competencies for Language and Numbers." In William Stebbins and Mark Berkley, eds., *Comparative Perception*, vol. 2. New York: Wiley and Sons.

Sade, D. S. 1968. "Inhibition of Son-Mother Matings Among Free-Ranging Rhesus Monkeys." *Science and Psychoanalysis* 12: 18–38.

Sahlins, Marshall. 1958. *Social Stratification in Polynesia.* Seattle: Univ. of Washington Press.

———. 1963. "Poor Man, Rich Man, Big Man, Chief: Political Types in Melanesia and Polynesia." *Comparative Studies in Society and History* 5: 285–303.

———. 1968a. "Notes on the Original Affluent Society." In Lee and DeVore 1968.

———. 1968b. *Tribesmen.* Englewood Cliffs, N.J.: Prentice Hall.

———. 1972. *Stone Age Economics.* Chicago: Aldine.

Sanders, William T. 1972. "Population, Agricultural History, and Societal Evolution in Mesoamerica." In B. Spooner, ed., *Population Growth: Anthropological Implications.* Cambridge, Mass.: MIT Press.

Sanderson, Stephen K. 1988. *Macrosociology.* New York: Harper Collins.

Sanides, Friedrich. 1970. "Functional Architecture of Motor and Sensory Cortices in Primates in the Light of a New Concept of Neocortex Evolution." In Noback and Montagna 1970.

Sapir, Edward. 1933. "Language." In *Encyclopaedia of the Social Sciences.* New York: Macmillan.

Savage, D., and D. Russell. 1983. *Mammalian Paleofaunas of the World.* Reading, Mass.: Addison-Wesley.

Savage-Rumbaugh, E. Sue, ed. 1986. *Ape Language.* New York: Columbia Univ. Press.

Savage-Rumbaugh, E. Sue, Duane Rumbaugh, William Hopkins, Jeannine Murphy, Elizabeth Rubert, and J. Philip Shaw. 1986. "Ape-Language Research Beyond Nim." In Savage-Rumbaugh 1986.

Savage-Rumbaugh, E. Sue, Duane Rumbaugh, and Kelly McDonald. 1985. "Language Learning in Two Species of Apes." *Neuroscience and Biobehavioral Reviews* 9: 653–65.

Schaller, G. 1962. "The Ecology and Behavior of the Mountain Gorilla." Ph.D. diss., Univ. of Wisconsin.

Schapera, I. 1956. *Government and Politics in Tribal Societies.* London: Watts.

Scheff, Thomas. 1990. *Microsociology.* Chicago: Univ. of Chicago Press.

Schlegel, Alice. 1972. *Male Dominance and Female Autonomy.* New Haven, Conn.: HRAF Press.

Schneider, David, and Kathleen Gough, eds. 1961. *Matrilineal Kinship*. Berkeley: Univ. of California Press.

Schrive, Carmel, ed. 1984. *Past and Present in Hunter Gatherer Studies*. Orlando, Fla.: Academic Press.

Schwartz, Richard D., and James C. Miller. 1964. "Legal Evolution and Societal Complexity." *American Journal of Sociology* 70: 159–69.

Sebeok, T., and J. Umiker-Sebeok. 1979. "Performing Animals: Secrets of the Trade." *Psychology Today* 13: 778–91.

Servas, Philip, and Michael Peters. 1990. "A Clear Left Hemisphere Advantage for Visuo-Spatially Based Verbal Categorization." *Neuropsychologia* 28: 1251–60.

Service, Elman. 1962. *Primitive Social Organization: An Evolutionary Perspective*. New York: Random House.

———. 1966. *The Hunters*. Englewood Cliffs, N.J.: Prentice Hall.

———. 1975. *Origins of the State and Civilizations: The Process of Cultural Evolution*. New York: Norton.

Shapiro, Judith. 1972. "Sex Roles and Social Structure Among the Yanomamö Indians of Northern Brazil." Ph.D. diss., Columbia Univ.

Shepherd, Gordon. 1988. *Neurobiology*. New York: Oxford Univ. Press.

Sherman, Gordon, Albert Galaburda, and Norman Geschwind. 1982. "Neuroanatomical Asymmetries in Non-Human Species." *Trends in Neurosciences* 5: 429–31.

Shipman, Pat. 1986. "Scavenging or Hunting in Early Hominids: Theoretical Framework and Tests." *American Anthropologist* 88: 27–43.

Shipman, Pat, and Alan Walker. 1989. "The Costs of Becoming a Predator." *Journal of Human Evolution* 18: 373–92.

Sibley, Charles G., and Jon E. Ahlquist. 1987. "DNA Hybridization Evidence of Hominoid Phylogeny: Results from an Expanded Data Set." *Journal of Molecular Evolution* 26: 99–121.

Sibley, Charles G., John A. Comstock, and Jon E. Ahlquist. 1990. "DNA Hybridization Evidence of Hominoid Phylogeny. A Reanalysis of the Data." *Journal of Molecular Evolution* 30: 202–36.

Simmel, Georg. [1902] 1950. "The Metropolis and Mental Life." In K. Wolff, ed. and trans., *The Sociology of Georg Simmel*. New York: Free Press.

———. [1907] 1978. *The Philosophy of Money*. Trans. T. Bottomore and D. Frisby. Boston: Routledge and Kegan Paul.

Simmons, R. M. T. 1988. "Comparative Morphology of the Primate Diencephalon." In Steklis and Erwin 1988.

Simons, Elwyn L. 1984. "Dawn Ape of the Fayum." *Natural History* 93: 18–20.

———. 1987. "New Faces of Aegyptopithecus from the Oligocene of Egypt." *Journal of Human Evolution* 16: 273–90.

———. 1990. "Discovery of the Oldest Known Anthropoidean Skull from the Paleogene of Egypt." *Science* 247: 1567–69.

Simons, Elwyn, and D. Tab Tasmussen. 1991. "The Generic Classification of Fayum Anthropoidea." *International Journal of Primatology* 12: 163–77.

Singer, Charles. 1954–56. *A History of Technology*. 2 vols. Oxford: Clarendon Press.

Sjoberg, Gideon. 1960. *The Preindustrial City*. New York: Free Press.

Skocpol, Theda. 1979. *States and Social Revaluations*. New York: Cambridge Univ. Press.

Smuts, Barbara, Dorothy Cheney, Robert Seyfarth, Richard Wrangham, and Thomas Struhsaker. 1987. *Primate Societies*. Chicago: Univ. of Chicago Press.

Snowdon, Charles. 1990. "Language Capacities of Non-Human Animals." *Yearbook of Physical Anthropology* 33: 215–43.

Somjen, George. 1983. *Neurophysiology: The Essentials*. London: Williams and Wilkins.

Southwick, C., and M. Farooq Siddiqi. 1974. "Contrasts in Primate Social Behavior." *Bioscience* 24: 398–406.

Spencer, Baldwin, and F. J. Gillen. 1899. *The Native Tribes of Central Australia*. London: Macmillan.

———. 1914. *The Northern Tribes of Central Australia*. London: Macmillan.

———. 1927. *The Arunta: A Study of a Stone Age People*. London: Macmillan.

Spencer, Herbert. [1852] 1888. *Social Statics*. New York: D. Appleton.

———. 1874–96, 1898. *The Principles of Sociology*. 3 vols. New York: D. Appleton.

Spencer, Robert. 1968. "Spouse-Exchange Among the North Alaskan Eskimo." In P. Bohannan and J. Middleton, eds., *Marriage, Family, and Residence*. New York: The Natural History Press.

Speth, John. 1989. "Early Hominid Hunting and Scavenging: The Role of Meat as an Energy Source." *Journal of Human Evolution* 18: 329–43.

Stebbins, G. Ledyard. 1969. *The Basis of Progressive Evolution*. Chapel Hill: Univ. of North Carolina Press.

Stebbins, William. 1965. "Hearing." In Allan Schrier, Harry Harlow, and Fred Stollnitz, eds. *Behavior of Non-Human Primates*. New York: Academic Press.

Steklis, Horst. 1985. "Primate Communication, Comparative Neurology, and the Origin of Language Re-Examined." *Journal of Human Evolution* 14: 157–73.

Steklis, Horst, and J. Erwin, eds. 1988. *Neurosciences*. Vol. 4. New York: Alan Liss.

Stephan, Heinz, and Orlando Andy. 1970. "The Allocortex in Primates." In Noback and Montagna 1970.

Stephan, Heinz, George Baron, and Heiko Frahm. 1988. "Comparative Size of Brains and Brain Components." In Steklis and Erwin 1988.

Stern, J. T., Jr., and R. L. Susman. 1983. "The Locomotor Anatomy of Australopithecus Afarensis." *American Journal of Physical Anthropology* 60: 279–317.

Steward, Julian H. 1930. "The Economic and Social Basis of Primitive Bands." In R. Lowie, ed., *Essays on Anthropology in Honor of Alfred Louis Kroeber*. Berkeley: Univ. of California Press.

———. 1955. *Theory of Culture Change: The Methodology of Multilinear Evolution*. Urbana: Univ. of Illinois Press.

Stewart, K. 1981. "Social Development of Wild Mountain Gorillas." Ph.D. diss., Univ. of Cambridge.

Stewart, K., and A. Harcourt. 1987. "Gorillas: Variation in Female Relationships." In Smuts et al. 1987.

Straus, Lawrence. 1989. "On Early Hominid Use of Fire." *Current Anthropology* 30: 488–91.

Stringer, Chris B. 1984. "Human Evolution and Biological Adaptation in the Pleistocene." In Foley 1984.

———. 1989. "Homo sapiens: Single or Multiple Origin." In John Durant, ed., *Human Origins*. Oxford: Clarendon.

Strominger, Norman. 1978. "The Anatomical Organization of the Primate Auditory Pathway." In Charles Noback, ed., *Sensory Systems of Primates*. New York: Plenum.

Strum, Shirley, and William Mitchell. 1987. "Baboon Models and Muddles." In Kinzey 1987.

Stryker, Sheldon. 1980. *Symbolic Interactionism*. Menlo Park, Calif.: Benjamin-Cummings.

Sturtevant, Alfred. 1965. *A History of Genetics*. New York: Harper and Row.

Sugardjito, J., I. J. A. te Boekhorst, and J. A. R. A. M. van Hooff. 1987. "Ecological Constraints on the Grouping of Wild Orang-utans (Pongo pygmaeus) in the Gunung Leuser National Park, Sumatra, Indonesia." *International Journal of Primatology* 8: 17–41.

Susman, Randall. 1989. "New Hominid Fossils from the Swartkrans Formation (1979–1986) Excavations: Postcranial Specimens." *American Journal of Physical Anthropology* 74: 451–74.

Sutherland, N. S. 1973. "Object Recognition." In Edward Carterette and Morton Friedman, eds., *Handbook of Perception*, vol. 3. New York: Academic Press.

Sutton, Dwight, and Uwe Jürgens. 1988. "Neural Control of Vocalization." In H. Steklis and J. Erwin, eds., *Neurosciences*, vol. 4. New York: Alan Liss.

Swanson, Guy E. 1960. *The Birth of the Gods*. Ann Arbor: Univ. of Michigan Press.

Swanson, L. W. 1983. "The Hippocampus and the Concept of the Limbic System." In W. Seifert, ed., *Neurobiology of the Hippocampus*. New York: Academic Press.

Swartz, Sharon. 1989. "Pendular Mechanics and Kinematics and Energetics of Brachiating Locomotion." *International Journal of Primatology* 10: 387–418.

Szalay, F. S., and E. Delson. 1979. *Evolutionary History of the Primates*. New York: Academic Press.

Takahata, Yukio. 1990a. "Adult Males' Social Relations with Adult Females." In T. Nishida, ed., *The Chimpanzees of the Mahale Mountains*. Tokyo: Univ. of Tokyo Press.

———. 1990b. "Social Relationships Among Adult Males." In T. Nishida, ed., *The Chimpanzees of the Mahale Mountains*. Tokyo: Univ. of Tokyo Press.

Tanner, Nancy. 1987. "The Chimpanzee Model Revisited and the Gathering Hypothesis." In Kinzey 1987.

Tattersall, Ian, Eric Delson, and John van Couvering. 1988. *Encyclopedia of Human Evolution and Prehistory.* New York: Garland.

Temerin, Alis, and John Cant. 1983. "The Evolutionary Divergence of Old World Monkeys and Apes." *The American Naturalist* 122: 335–51.

Terrace, H. S. 1979. "How Nim Chimpsky Changed My Mind." *Psychology Today* 13: 63–76.

———. 1985. "In the Beginning Was the Name." *American Psychologist* 40: 1011–28.

Terrace, H. S., L. A. Petitto, R. J. Sanders, and G. Bever. 1979. "Can an Ape Create a Sentence?" *Science* 206: 891–96.

Tiger, Lionel, and Robin Fox. 1971. *The Imperial Animal.* New York: Holt, Rinehart and Winston.

Tilly, Charles, ed. 1975. *The Formation of Nation States in Western Europe.* Princeton, N.J.: Princeton Univ. Press.

Tilson, R. L. 1981. "Family Formation Strategies of Kloss's Gibbons." *Folia Primatologica* 35: 259–87.

Tobias, Phillip. 1987. "The Brain of Homo habilis: A New Level of Organization in Cerebral Evolution." *Journal of Human Evolution* 16: 741–61.

Tonkinson, Robert. 1978. *The Marduojara Aborigines.* New York: Holt, Rinehart and Winston.

Touraine, Alan. 1988. *Return of the Actor: Social Theory in Preindustrial Society.* Minneapolis: Univ. of Minnesota Press.

Trivers, Robert L. 1971. "The Evolution of Reciprocal Altruism." *Quarterly Review of Biology* 46, no. 4: 35–57.

Turnbull, Colin. 1961. *The Forest People.* New York: Simon and Schuster.

Turner, Jonathan H. 1971. "A Cybernetic Model of Economic Development." *Sociological Quarterly* 12: 191–203.

———. 1972. *Patterns of Social Organization: A Survey of Social Institutions.* New York: McGraw-Hill.

———. 1974. "A Cybernetic Model of Legal Development." *Western Sociological Review* 5: 3–16.

———. 1984. *Societal Stratification: A Theoretical Analysis.* New York: Columbia Univ. Press.

———. 1985. *Herbert Spencer: A Renewed Appreciation.* Newbury Park, Calif.: Sage.

Turner, Jonathan H., and Alexandra Maryanski. 1979. *Functionalism.* Menlo Park, Calif.: Benjamin-Cummings.

Turner, Ralph H. 1978. "The Role of the Person." *American Journal of Sociology* 84 (July): 1–23.

Tutin, Caroline. 1979. "Mating Patterns and Reproductive Strategies in a Community of Wild Chimpanzees (Pan troglodytes schwein furthii)." *Behavioral Ecology and Sociobiology* 6: 29–38.

Tuttle, Russell. 1986. *Apes of the World: Their Social Behavior, Communication, Mentality, and Ecology.* Park Ridge, N.J.: Noyes.

———. 1988. "What's New in African Paleoanthropology?" *Annual Review of Anthropology* 17: 391–426.

Vaco, Steven. 1988. *Law and Society*. 2d ed. Englewood Cliffs, N.J.: Prentice Hall.

Valverde, F. 1985. "The Organizing Principles of the Primary Visual Cortex in the Monkey." In A. Peters and E. G. Jones, eds., *Cerebral Cortex*, vol. 3. New York: Plenum.

Van den Berghe, Pierre. 1973. *Age and Sex in Human Societies: A Biosocial Perspective*. Belmont, Calif.: Wadsworth.

———. 1974. "Bringing Beasts Back In: Toward a Biosocial Theory of Aggression." *American Sociological Reivew* 39: 777–88.

———. 1975. *Man and Society: A Biosocial View*. New York: Elsevier.

———. 1977–78. "Bridging the Paradigms." *Society* 15: 42–49.

———. 1981. *The Ethnic Phenomenon*. New York: Elsevier.

———. 1986. "Skin Color Preference, Sexual Dimorphism, and Sexual Selection." *Ethnic and Racial Studies* 9, no. 1: 87–113.

Van den Berghe, Pierre, and David Barash. 1977. "Inclusive Fitness and Human Family Structure." *American Anthropologist* 79: 809–23.

Van Essen, D. C. 1985. "Functional Organization of Primate Visual Cortex." In A. Peters and E. G. Jones, eds., *Cerebral Cortex*, vol. 3. New York: Plenum.

Vayda, A. P. 1974. "Warfare in an Ecological Perspective." *Annual Review of Ecology and Systematics* 5: 183–93.

Vehara, Shigeo. 1988. "Grouping Patterns of Wild Pygmy Chimpanzees (Pan paniseos) Observed at a Marsh Grassland Amidst the Tropical Rain Forest of Yalosidi, Republic of Zaire." *Primates* 29: 41–52.

Vilensky, Joel. 1989. "Primate Quadrupedalism: How and Why Does It Differ from That of Typical Quadrupeds?" *Brain Behavior and Evolution* 34: 357–64.

Von Bonin, Gerhardt. 1952. "Notes on Cortical Evolution." *American Medical Association Archives of Neurology and Psychiatry* 67: 135–44.

Von Hagen, Victor. 1961. *The Ancient Sun Kingdoms of the Americas*. Cleveland, Ohio: World.

Walker, Alan. 1974. "Locomotor Adaptations in Past and Present Prosimian Primates." In Farish Jenkins, Jr., ed., *Primate Locomotion*. New York: Academic Press.

Wallace, Anthony F. C. 1966. *Religion: An Anthropological View*. New York: Random House.

Wallerstein, Immanuel. 1974. *The Modern World-System*. New York: Academic Press.

Warren, Richard, and Roslyn Warren. 1976. "Auditory Illusions and Confusions." In Held and Richards 1976.

Washburn, Sherwood L., ed. 1961. *Social Life of Early Man*. Chicago: Aldine.

———. 1963. "Behavior and Human Evolution." In S. L. Washburn, ed., *Classification and Human Evolution*. Chicago: Aldine.

Washburn, Sherwood L., and Robert Harding. 1975. "Evolution and Human Nature." In D. A. Hamburg and K. H. Brodie, eds., *American Book of Psychiatry*, vol. 6. New York: Basic Books.

Watts, David. 1991. "Strategies of Habitat Use by Mountain Gorillas." *Folia Primatologica* 56: 1–16.

Weber, A. W., and A. Vedder. 1983. "Population Dynamics of the Gorillas: 1959–1978." *Biological Conservation* 26: 341–66.

Weber, Max. [1904–5] 1930. *The Protestant Ethic and the Spirit of Capitalism.* Trans. T. Parsons. New York: Scribner and Sons.

———. [1916] 1951. *The Religion of China.* Trans. H. Gerth. New York: Free Press.

———. [1922] 1968. *Economy and Society.* Trans. and ed. G. Roth and K. Wittich. New York: Bedminster Press.

Webster, D. 1975. "Warfare and the Evolution of the State." *American Antiquity* 40: 467–70.

Weiskrantz, L., and A. Cowey. 1975. "Cross-Modal Matching in the Rhesus Monkey Using a Single Pair of Stimuli." *Neuropsychologica* 13: 257–61.

Wellman, Barry, and S. D. Berkowitz. 1988. *Social Structures: A Network Approach.* Cambridge, Eng.: Cambridge Univ. Press.

Werblin, Frank. 1976. "The Control of Sensitivity in the Retina." In Held and Richards 1976.

White, Edward. 1989. *Cortical Circuits: Synaptic Organization of the Cerebral Cortex Structure, Function, and Theory.* Boston: Birkhauser.

White, F. J. 1989. "Ecological Correlates of Pygmy Chimpanzee Social Structure." In V. Standen and R. A. Foley, eds., *Comparative Socioecology.* Oxford: Blackwell.

White, Tim, and Gen Suwa. 1987. "Hominid Footprints at Laetoli: Facts and Interpretations." *American Journal of Physical Anthropology* 72: 485–514.

Williams, George C. 1966. *Adaptation and Natural Selection: A Critique of Some Current Evolutionary Thought.* Princeton, N.J.: Princeton Univ. Press.

Wilson, Donald, and Michael Leon. 1989. "Information Processing in the Olfactory System." In Jennifer Lund, ed., *Sensory Processing in the Mammalian Brain.* Oxford: Oxford Univ. Press.

Wilson, Edward O. 1975. *Sociobiology: The New Synthesis.* Cambridge, Mass.: Harvard Univ. Press.

———. 1978. *On Human Nature.* Cambridge, Mass.: Harvard Univ. Press.

Winterhalder, Bruce, and Eric Alden Smith, eds. 1981. *Hunter-Gatherer Foraging Strategies.* Chicago: Univ. of Chicago Press.

Wittenberger, J. F. 1981. *Animal Social Behaviour.* Boston: Duxbury.

Wolf, Eric. 1982. *Europe and the People Without History.* Berkeley: Univ. of California Press.

Wolin, Lee, and Leo Massopust, Jr. 1970. "Morphology of the Primate Retina." In Noback and Montagna 1970.

Wolpoff, Milford H. 1978. "Analogies and Interpretations in Paleoanthropology." In C. Jolly, ed., *Early Hominids of Africa.* London: Duckworth.

———. 1980. *Paleo-Anthropology.* New York: Knopf.

Woodburn, J. 1968. "An Introduction to Hadza Ecology." In Lee and DeVore 1968.

Woolley, Leonard. 1965. *The Beginnings of Civilization: UNESCO History of Mankind.* Vol. 1, Pt. 2. New York: Mentor.

Wrangham, Richard W. 1980. "An Ecological Model of Female-Bonded Primate Groups." *Behaviour* 74: 262–99.

———. 1987. "The Significance of African Apes for Reconstructing Human Social Evolution." In Kinzey 1987.

Wrangham, R. W., and B. Smuts. 1980. "Sex Differences in Behavioural Ecology of Chimpanzees in Gombe Natural Park, Tanzania." *Journal of Reproductive Fertilizaturr* (suppl.) 28: 13–31.

Wrong, Dennis. 1961. "The Overly Socialized Conception of Man in Modern Sociology." *American Sociological Review* 26: 183–93.

Wynn-Edwards, V. C. 1962. *Animal Dispersion in Relation to Social Behavior.* New York: Hafner.

———. 1986. *Evolution Through Group Selection.* Oxford: Blackwell.

Yamagiwa, J. 1983. "Diachronic Changes in Two Eastern Lowland Gorilla Groups (Gorilla gorilla graueri) in the Mt. Kahuzi Region, Zaire." *Primates* 25: 174–83.

Yeni-Komshian, G. H., and D. A. Benson. 1976. "Anatomical Study of Cerebral Asymmetry in the Temporal Lobe of Humans, Chimpanzees and Rhesus Monkeys." *Science* 192: 387–89.

Zeller, V. A. 1986. "The Systematic Relations of Tree Shrews: Evidence from Skull Morphogenesis." In James Else and Phyllis Lee, eds., *Primate Evolution,* vol. 1. London: Cambridge Univ. Press.

Zihlman, Adrienne, John Cronin, Douglas Cramer and Vincent Sarich. 1978. "Pygmy Chimpanzee as a Possible for the Common Ancestor of Humans, Chimpanzees, and Gorillas." *Nature* 276: 744–46.

Zihlman, A. L., and J. M. Lowenstein. 1983. "Ramapithecus and Pan paniscus: Significance for Human Origins." In Ciochon and Corruccini 1983.

# INDEX

# INDEX

In this index an "f" after a number indicates a separate reference on the next page, and an "ff" indicates separate references on the next two pages. A continuous discussion over two or more pages is indicated by a span of page numbers, e.g., "57–59." *Passim* is used for a cluster of references in close but not consecutive sequence.

*Adapis parisiensis*, 44
Advanced agrarian societies, 120–27 *passim. See also* Agrarian societies
Advanced horticultural societies, 96–102 *passim. See also* Horticultural societies
Aggression, *see* Human aggression
Agrarian societies: power-authority polity in, 113–19 *passim*; simple vs. advanced, 119–27 *passim*; social organization in, 119–38 *passim*; empire-building patterns, 131ff
Altruism (reciprocal), 111
American Sign Language, 32
Anthropoidea, 7f
Apes: evolution of, 15; gibbons, 16f; language research, 33f; Sylvian point, 52; social organization of, 66, 88; sociality among, 90. *See also* Great Apes
Ardrey, Robert, 1
Association cortex, 40
Attention theory, 54
Auditory cortex, 56f, 60
Auditory system: description, 47f; speech and, 60; human speech evolution and, 62f; vs. visual system, 64f
Australian aborigines, 88f
Australopithecus, 35, 69

Belief systems, 81, 97, 106f, 122, 141. *See also* Religions
Bellah, Robert, 134

Big Men societies, 83, 113–19 *passim*
Bilateral rule of descent, 81
Binocular vision, 48f
Bioprogrammers, 1f
Bipedalism: development of, 58, 60, 164; first hominid trait, 69; selection pressures for, 73ff
Bonobo chimpanzee, 22f
Brachiator adaptation, 10f, 30, 51. *See also* Locomotion
Brain, Lord, 36
Brains (evolution): mammalian, 36–40 *passim*; neomammalian, 37; paleomammalian, 37; protoreptilian, 37; non-human hominoid vs. monkey, 51f; Sylvian fissure, 51f; *H. habilis* size increase, 57; Broca's area, 62, 70; Wernicke's area, 62, 70; *H. sapiens sapiens* size of, 75; selection for increased size, 75. *See also* Evolution
Broca, Paul, 37
Broca's area, 62, 70
Buddhism, 133f
Bureaucratic structures, 145f

Cage of kinship, 95, 104, 110. *See also* Horticultural societies
Cage of power: creation of, 113–19 *passim*; inherent dialectic in, 129–38 *passim*; impact of industrialization on, 140f; biological bases for tearing down,

162; controlling the, 169. *See also* Agrarian societies

Calhoun, Craig, 160

Capitalism: positive impact, 138; exploitative nature of, 167; compatible with human nature, 169. *See also* Industrial societies

Carneiro, Robert, 93

Categoric dimensions: society, 77f; horticultural societies, 101, 109; agrarian societies, 126; industrial and post-industrial societies, 155, 159f

Catholicism, 133f

Ceboidea, *see* New World monkeys

Cercopithecoidea, *see* Old World monkeys

Chiefdom system, 114–19 *passim*

Chimpanzees (*Pan troglodytes*): recognized species, 8, 10, 22; social organization of, 21–29 *passim*; pygmy, 22, 34

Chomsky, Noam, 58

Christianity, 134, 136

Cladogram (hominoids), 16

Class formation: horticultural societies, 100; due to resource distribution, 109; agrarian societies, 125; industrial and post-industrial societies, 154f, 158f. *See also* Elite; Stratifying dimensions

Coevolution theory, 111

Cognatic rule of descent, 81

Cognitive functions, 35f

Collateral relatives, 81

Collins, Randall, 131

Color perception, 49

Communal cults, 105f

Communal religions, 105

Community organization, 22

Composite model, 82

Comte, Auguste, 2

*Conditions of the Working Class in England* (Engels), 139

Conservation of organization principle, 54. *See also* Evolution

Corporate dimensions: society, 77f; horticultural societies, 102; agrarian societies, 127, 136f; industrial and post-industrial societies, 156

Cortico-limbic associations, 41f

Cross-modal associations, 52, 55f

Cross-modal integration, 55f

Cross-modal sensory equivalence, 42

Cultivation, vs. domestication, 91

Cult structures: individualistic cults, 80, 105; shamanic cults, 80f; communal, 105f; horticultural system, 105f; professional clergy, 106f; agrarian societies,

123; religious, 134; industrial and post-industrial societies, 151, 160

Decision-making polity: horticultural societies, 98, 107f; agrarian societies, 123; industrial and post-industrial societies, 153. *See also* Power-authority polity

Delson, E., 45

Democratization, 145f

Demographic dimensions: society, 76; horticultural societies, 95f; abundant resources and, 113f; impact on power-authority polity, 115f; agrarian societies, 119f, 128f; industrial and post-industrial societies, 147f, 159

De-mythologization, 134

Depth perception, 48f

Descent rule, *see* Rule of descent

Dispersal patterns, *see* Transfer patterns

Division of labor: hunting and gathering societies, 79, 81f; horticultural societies, 97; displayed by cults, 105; agrarian societies, 121, 128; industrial and post-industrial societies, 149

Domestication, vs. cultivation, 91

Durkheim, Emile, 167f

Earle, Timothy, 93

Ecclesiastical religion, 106, 134f

Economic systems: horticulture, 101–7 *passim*; power centralization and, 117f; agrarian societies, 121, 127ff, 133; industrialization of, 141–44 *passim*, 156ff. *See also* Technology

Education: horticultural societies, 99, 102, 109; agrarian societies, 124–27 *passim*, 135; expansion of formal, 143f; industrial and post-industrial societies, 153–58 *passim*

Elite: development of, 117ff, 135f; impact of dissatisfaction, 129; development of religious, 134f. *See also* Class formation; Stratifying dimensions

Empire-building, 131ff

Endogamy rules, 81. *See also* Marriage

Engels, Friedrich, 139, 167

Entrance/exit rules, 145

Entrepreneurship: horticultural societies, 97; agrarian societies, 121; industrial and post-industrial societies, 150, 157; post-entrepreneurial corporation, 161

Ethnicity: horticultural societies, 101; agrarian societies, 126; industrial and post-industrial societies, 155, 159

*Ethnographical Atlas* (Murdock), 82

European Neanderthals, 53, 70
Evolution: of anthropoidea, 7f; of mammalian brain, 36–42 *passim*; of neocortex, 36; reptile-to-mammal, 37; of primate brain, 42–55 *passim*; visual predation theory of primate, 43; locomotion, 45, 49f; of prosimians, 45f; conservation of organization principle, 54; adaptive responses in, 57; of social organization, 65ff. *See also* Brains
External relations, 131f. *See also* War

Family-level societies, 94
Female-based exogamy, 82
Female-bonded societies, 25–30 *passim*
Fisher, R. A., 35, 57
Fission-fusion organization, 22
Fleagle, J. G., 43f
Foley, Robert, 27f
Fox, Robin, 1

Gabow, Stephen, 53
Geschwind, Norman, 62f
Gibbons (*Hylobates*), 8f, 16f
Gidley, J. W., 45
Goldstone, Jack, 129
Gorilla (*Gorilla*), 8, 10, 20f
Great Apes: description, 9ff; as modified brachiators, 10f; evolution of, 15; orangutans, 17–20 *passim*; gorillas, 20f; chimpanzees, 21–29 *passim*; cognitive function evolution, 35; crossmodal associations by, 52; use of visual-gestural language, 63

Habermas, Jurgen, 167
Hall, K. R. I., 61
Harem pattern, 12
Hermelin, B., 36
Hewes, Gordon, 63
Hiatt, B., 82
Hill, Jane, 63
Holly, B. Smith, 75
Hominidae, 8
Hominoidea (hominoids): described, 1, 8ff; predisposed social structure, 13; evolution of, 15, 164f; cladogram of, 16, 24f; vs. female monkey social ties, 26ff; Miocene, 30, 46, 50; origins of Pliocene, 69; trait of bipedalism, 69; female dispersal in early, 83
Homo (Human), 8, 10
*Homo erectus*: species recognized, 53; brain size increase, 67; cultural innovations of, 71ff; vocal sounds used, 71

*Homo habilis*: ascendance of, 53; brain size increase, 57, 67; origins of, 70ff
*Homo sapiens*, 53, 70
*Homo sapiens sapiens*, 73, 75
Horde pattern, 12
Horticultural societies: adoption of, 91–95 *passim*; social organization, 95–112 *passim*; declining status of women in, 103
Human aggression, 1, 110f. *See also* War
Human culture: evolutionary process of, 1–5 *passim*; origins of, 33–36 *passim*; basis of, 67f. *See also* Languages
Human nature: sociobiology basis of, 1, 4f; cultural codes vs. biological needs, 111f; presumption of social, 162f; individualistic tendency, 164–69 *passim*
Human societies, 76ff
Human speech, 55f, 60–65 *passim*
Hunting and gathering societies: social organization for, 75f; institutional structure, 77–87 *passim*; described, 78f; leisure-intensive lifestyle, 79; division of labor, 79, 81f; kinship structure, 81–89 *passim*; marriage in, 81f; composite band, 82; patrilocal-band model, 82; intraband obligations, 84f; legal codes of, 84; social organization of aborigines, 88f
Hylobates, 8f
Hylobatidae, 8f

Imagined communities, 160f
Incest, 87
Individualistic cults, 80
Industrial societies: rise of, 138; price of industrialization, 139, 162; dynamics in, 141–44 *passim*; bureaucratic structure, 145f; democratization impact, 145f; demographic dimensions, 148; institutional dimensions, 148–53 *passim*; spatial dimensions, 148; stratifying dimensions, 153f; categoric dimensions, 155; corporate dimensions, 156. *See also* Post-industrial societies; Technology
Institutional dimensions: society, 77, 86f; hunting and gathering societies, 78–85 *passim*; horticultural societies, 96ff; agrarian societies, 121ff; industrial and post-industrial societies, 148–53 *passim*, 160
Intermodal associations, 42
Intramodal associations, 42
Islam, 133f

Jerison, Harry, 43, 65
Johnson, Allen, 93
Judaism, 133

Kaas, Jon, 44
Kinship structure: collateral relatives, 81;
    hunting and gathering societies, 81–89
    *passim*; lineal relatives, 81; polygyny,
    81; Australian aborigines, 89; Yano-
    mamö, 94f; cage of kinship, 95, 104,
    110; horticultural societies, 97, 101f,
    109f; as organizing mechanism, 103;
    unilineal descent, 104, 113–17 *passim*,
    128; descent rules of, 107f; agrarian so-
    cieties, 122f, 126ff, 136; industrial and
    post-industrial societies, 150–60 *pas-
    sim. See also* Power-authority polity

Labor, *see* Division of labor
Languages: reconstructing parent speech
    forms, 14; research of ape, 33f; as sys-
    tem of symbols, 33; cognitive capacities
    underlining, 35; neocortical expansion
    and, 47–50 *passim*; Sylvian fissure and,
    52; sensory equivalence, 55f; primate
    vocalizations, 56f; bipedalism and, 58,
    60, 73ff; dependent on neural struc-
    tures, 62; disadvantages of visual-
    gestural, 63; evolution of, 66f; *H. erec-
    tus* use of crude, 71ff. *See also* Human
    culture
Last Common Ancestor, *see* LCA
Law: horticultural societies, 99, 108f;
    agrarian societies, 124, 135f; industrial
    and post-industrial societies, 145f, 152f,
    156
LCA: reconstructed social structure, 13ff,
    28–32 *passim*, 164f; cladogram due to,
    16, 24f; sociality of, 90
Leakey, M. G., 46
Lee, P. C., 27f
Lee, Richard, 82
Leisure-intensive lifestyle, 79
Lenin, Vladimir, 162
Limbic cortex, 37f
Lineal relatives, 81
Literacy, 143f
Locomotion: brachiator adaptation, 10f,
    30, 51; evolution of prosimian, 45, 49f;
    evolution of monkey, 49f; evolution of
    quadrupedal, 50; physical requirements
    for, 51f
Lorenz, Konrad, 1
Loss of community, 162, 167
Low-density networks, 13
Luhmann, Niklas, 145

MacLean, Paul, 36f
Mammals: evolution of, 36–40 *passim*;
    sensory system in, 41f; object recogni-
    tion, 55
Mann, Michael, 136
Marriage: hunting and gathering societies,
    81f, 85f; rules of endogamy, 81, 103;
    horticultural societies, 97; rules of ex-
    ogamy, 103; agrarian societies, 122; in-
    dustrial and post-industrial societies,
    151
Marx, Karl, 168
Mating patterns, 12. *See also* Transfer
    patterns
Matrilocal residence rule, 103
Medicine: horticultural societies, 99;
    agrarian societies, 124, 135; industrial
    and post-industrial societies, 153
Meggitt, M. J., 82
Menzel, E. W., 59
Miller, George, 61
Miocene hominoidea: decline of, 30; phe-
    netic link between Oligocene and, 46;
    early apes, 50
Mobility: demographic dimensions and,
    76; horticultural societies, 101; agrarian
    societies, 125; industrial and post-
    industrial societies, 154, 158f. *See also*
    Stratifying dimensions
Modified brachiators, 10
Monkeys: New World, 7f; Old World, 8f;
    neocortical expansion in, 47; vs. apes,
    50f; cross-modal associations, 52; patas
    (Erythrocebus), 61; sexual avoidance
    in, 87
Monogamous pattern, 12
Monotheism, 133f
Morris, Desmond, 1
Müller, Max, 34
Multimodal sensory processing, 40
Murdock, George, 82

Neanderthals, 53, 70
*Necrolemus antiquus*, 44
Neocortex: evolution of, 36; description,
    38f; operation of, 40ff; primate expand-
    ing, 43–55 *passim*
Neomammalian brain, 37
New World monkeys (Ceboidea), 7f, 41,
    51f
Nim Chimsky, 33f

Object recognition, 55
O'Connor, W., 36
Old World monkeys (Cercopithecoidea):
    species recognition, 8f; social organiza-

tion of, 11f, 25–29 *passim*; dispersal system, 23f; reproductive patterns, 23f; neocortical expansion in, 41, 51f
Olfactory system, 45
Oligocene hominoidea, 46
Orangutan (*Pongo*): species recognition, 8, 10; social organization, 17–20 *passim*
Outgroup population, 14, 25

Paleomammalian brain, 37
*Pan paniscus*, 22, 34
*Pan troglodytes, see* Chimpanzees
Parsonian functionalism, 163
Parsons, Talcott, 163, 168
Patas monkeys (Erythrocebus), 61
Patrilocal-band model, 82f
Patrilocal residence rule, 82f, 103
Philosophical Hinduism, 133
Pliocene hominids: origins of, 69; social organization of, 70–76 *passim*
Polity-authority dimensions: horticultural system, 101f, 108; agrarian societies, 123ff; industrial and post-industrial societies, 152–56 *passim*
Polygyny relatives, 81
Pongidea, 8f
*Pongo, see* Orangutan
Pons, 44
Population rates, *see* Demographic dimensions
Posner, Michael, 54
Post-entrepreneurial corporation, 161
Post-industrial societies: demographic dimensions, 148; institutional dimensions, 148–51 *passim*; spatial dimensions, 148; polity dimensions, 152f; stratifying dimensions, 153f; categoric dimensions, 155; post-modernity, 160ff. *See also* Industrial societies
Post-modernity, 160ff, 167–70 *passim*
Potlatch ceremonies, 113
Power-authority polity: horticultural societies, 98, 100f; political, 108; defining, 113; chiefdom system, 114ff; economic system and, 118f; agrarian societies, 122–25 *passim*; hereditary monarch, 128f; rational-legal authority, 138; industrial societies, 144f. *See also* Cage of power; Decision-making polity; Kinship structure
Prehensile hand evolution, 50
Primary cortex, 40
Primates: classification order, 7–11 *passim*; brachiator adaptation, 10f; movement patterns, 10; cortico-limbic associations in, 41f; evolution of brain, 42–55 *passim*, 166; visual predation evolution theory, 43; vocalizations, 56f; call system, 60ff; visual-visual associations, 63f; sociality among, 90. *See also* Savanna environment
Principle of reciprocity, 84, 89
Production, *see* Economic systems
Prosimians, 43–46
Prosimii, 7f. *See also* Primates
Protestantism, 134
Protestant Reformation, 141
Protoreptilian brain, 37
Proxy wars, 147, 157
Pygmy chimpanzees (*Pan paniscus*), 22, 34

Quadrupedal locomotion, 50

Radcliffe-Brown, A. R., 82
Radinsky, L. B., 43f, 46
Reciprocal altruism, 111
Religions: hunting and gathering societies, 79ff; cult structure, 80; belief system, 81; horticultural societies, 97f, 102, 105f; ecclesiastical, 106f; agrarian societies, 122–27 *passim*, 133ff; de-mythologization of, 134; ritual codes, 134; industrial and post-industrial societies, 151, 155f
Reproductive patterns: nonhuman hominoidea, 18f; Old World monkeys, 23–29 *passim*. *See also* Social relations
Reptiles (mammal-like), 37
Residence pattern, 103
Resource distribution: society, 77; class formation due to, 109; Big Man societies, 113; agrarian societies, 125, 135; industrial and post-industrial societies, 153f. *See also* Stratifying dimensions
Rhine, R. J., 61
Rituals: horticultural societies, 98; communal cults, 105; to reduce social tensions, 110; agrarian societies, 123; religious codes, 134; industrial and post-industrial societies, 151
Rock, Irvin, 53
*Rooneyia viejaenis*, 44
Rose, K. D., 43f
Rule of descent: bilateral, 81; cognatic, 81; unilineal, 103f, 113f, 128; hereditary succession, 107; horticultural, 107
Rumbaugh, Duane, 63

Sahlins, Marshall, 167
Sanides, Friedrich, 45
Sanskritic Hinduism, 133

Sapir, Edward, 33
Savage-Rumbaugh, E., 63
Savanna environment, 59–68 *passim*
Schultz, Adolph, 10
Science: horticultural societies, 99; agrarian societies, 125, 135; industrial and post-industrial societies, 153
Secularization, 141
Sensory equivalence, 55f
Sensory systems: perception and, 36; neocortex and, 38ff; multimodal processing, 40; supramodal processing, 40; cortico-limbic associations, 41f; cross-modal sensory equivalence, 42; intermodal associations, 42; intramodal associations, 42; olfactory system and, 45; auditory system, 47f; visual system, 47ff; cross-modal connections in, 53f; visual capture phenomenon, 53
Shamanic cults, 80f, 105
Siamang, 8
Simmel, Georg, 145f, 168
Simple agrarian societies: 119–27 *passim*. *See also* Agrarian societies
Simple horticultural societies, 96–102 *passim*. *See also* Horticultural societies
Simple shamanic religion, 80
Sister lineage, 14
*Smilodectes gracilis*, 43
Social cage: breakdown of, 139–46 *passim*, 162; social structure as, 166; living in a, 170. *See also* Industrial societies
Social organization: apes vs. monkeys patterns, 11f; Old World monkeys, 11f; reconstructing primordial hominoid, 12–16 *passim*; LCA reconstructed, 13ff, 28–32 *passim*; gibbons, 16f; orangutan, 17–20 *passim*; gorillas, 20f, 88; chimpanzees, 21–29 *passim*, 88; evolution of, 65ff; Pliocene hominids, 70–76 *passim*; evolution of cultural patterns, 73–76 *passim*, 165f; hunting and gathering societies, 75–89 *passim*; features of, 76ff; horticultural societies, 95–110 *passim*; agrarian societies, 119–38 *passim*; industrial and post-industrial, 146–160 *passim*
Social relations: identification of, 13f; cladogram of, 16; gibbons, 17; orangutans, 18ff; in reproductive units, 18f; gorillas, 20f; chimpanzees, 21–29 *passim*; LCA ties, 29; transfer patterns and, 31; genetic basis for sociality, 67; in unilineal systems, 103f
Sociobiology: development of, 2–5 *passim*; assumptions listed, 6; on cage of power, 162; errors in assumptions, 165f
Sociocultural cage, 110ff. *See also* Horticultural societies
Spatial dimensions: society, 76f; horticultural societies, 96; agrarian societies, 120; industrial and post-industrial societies, 148
Spatial information, 58
Spatial-temporal integration, 56
Spencer, Herbert, 115, 131, 168
State: centralized system creation, 128f; breakdown, 129–33 *passim*; legitimacy of, 131; dominant ecclesiastic cults and, 134f; education system funded by, 143f, 158; industrial society and growth of, 145; repressive, 157f
Stebbins, G. L., 54, 57, 64
Stebbins, William, 48
Stratifying dimensions: society, 77; horticultural societies, 100, 109f; elite development, 117ff; agrarian societies, 125, 135ff; industrial and post-industrial societies, 144, 153f, 158f. *See also* Elite; Resource distribution
Supramodal sensory processing, 40
Sylvian fissure, 51f
Symbolization, 60. *See also* Languages
Szalay, F. S., 45

Technology: horticultural societies, 96; agrarian societies, 121, 128; rise of industrialization, 138, 141; industrial and post-industrial societies, 147ff. *See also* Economic systems; Industrial societies
Terrace, H. S., 33f
*Territorial Imperative* (Ardrey), 1
*Tetonius hommunculus*, 43
Tiger, Lionel, 1
Transfer patterns: associated with mating pattern, 12; fission-fusion organization, 22, 83; Old World monkeys, 23f; apes, 28, 66; relational ties and, 31f; in early hominids, 83
Tree shrew (Tupaia), 42

Unilineal descent rule, 103f, 113f, 128
Urbanization, 144f, 167f

Van den Berghe, Pierre, 1
Vayda, A. F., 111
Visual capture phenomenon, 53
Visual-gestural languages, 63. *See also* Languages
Visual modality, 54f

Visual predation evolution theory, 43
Visual system: evolution of, 47ff; visual capture phenomenon, 53; attention theory, 54; visual modality domination, 54f; visual-auditory equivalence, 55f; spatial information through, 58ff; vs. auditory system, 64f

Wallace, F. C., 80
War: in horticultural societies, 110f; impact on chiefdom system, 117; population rates and, 119; impact on agrarian societies, 120, 129, 131f; industrial and post-industrial societies and, 147, 157f

Warren, Richard, 60
Warren, Roslyn, 60
Weber, Max: on external relations, 131; on industrialization abuses, 138; on worldly asceticism, 141; on iron cage of bureaucracy, 145f, 167f
Wernicke's area, 62, 70
Wilson, Edward O., 2
Wrangham, Richard, 28
Wrong, Dennis, 163

Yanomamö system, 94f

Zaire River study, 22f

Library of Congress Cataloging-in-Publication Data

Maryanski, Alexandra.
The social cage : human nature and the evolution of society /
Alexandra Maryanski, Jonathan H. Turner.
    p.    cm.
    Includes bibliographical references and index.
    ISBN 0-8047-2002-9 (cloth) — ISBN 0-8047-2003-7 (paper)
    1. Sociobiology.    2. Social evolution.    I. Turner, Jonathan H.
II. Title.
GN365.9.M4    1992
304.5—dc20                                              92-17311
                                                            CIP

∞    This book is printed on acid-free paper.